BERLITZ®

DISCOVER
FLORIDA

Edited and Designed by
D & N Publishing,
Lambourn, Berkshire.

Cartography by
Hardlines, Charlbury, Oxfordshire.

Although we have made every effort to ensure the accuracy of all the information in this book, changes occur incessantly. We cannot therefore take responsibility for facts, addresses and circumstances in general that are constantly subject to alteration.

 The Berlitz tick is used to indicate places or events of particular interest.

Phototypeset by Wyvern Typesetting Ltd., Bristol.

Printed by C.S. Graphics, Singapore.

Photographic Acknowledgements

Front cover: sailboats on Fort Lauderdale Beach; reproduced courtesy of the Greater Fort Lauderdale Convention and Visitor's Bureau.

Back cover photograph: the Everglades; copyright © Berlitz Publishing Company Ltd.

All photographs taken by the authors except for the following: copyright © Berlitz Publishing Company Ltd, 1, 6, 10, 17, 20/21, 24, 26, 28, 29, 31, 33, 36, 40, 44, 56, 66, 74, 76, 79, 80, 88, 96, 103, 104, 108, 115 (upper and lower), 120, 121, 122, 125, 130, 136, 142, 144, 146, 151, 154, 156, 158, 195, 198, 200, 204, 238, 243, 247, 258, 260, 262, 276, 298, 300; Florida Department of Commerce, Division of Tourism, 77, 78, 112, 135, 138, 140/141, 149, 163, 214/215, 254, 266/267, 268, 272/273, 274, 279, 280, 284, 287, 288/289, 290, 292/293, 294, 295, 304; Florida's Pinellas Suncoast, 234, 241, 246, 256; Greater Fort Lauderdale Convention and Visitors' Bureau, 116, 126/127, 129; Kennedy Space Center, 105; Lee County TDC, 218; Lee Island Coast, 218/219, 230/231; Second Unit Production, 64.

If you have any new information, suggestions or corrections to contribute to this guide, we would like to hear from you. Please write to Berlitz Publishing at the above address.

BERLITZ®

DISCOVER
FLORIDA

Eric and Ruth Bailey

Contents

"A Word to the Wise . . . "

How to organize your trip, from the practicalities of visas and customs regulations to advice on where to stay and what you may find to eat. Little needs to be said of the climate of Florida; the "Sunshine State", says it all. The best way to see it is to hire a car and follow your inclination and the road ahead. Keep your eyes open for the wonders, take it easy, and don't forget to enjoy yourself.

Visiting the "Sunshine State"

Many people who live in Florida will tell you that they wish Mickey Mouse had never been created. At the very

Mickey Mouse wanders around Disney World making friends, but when you are only a few months old meeting Orlando's most famous citizen can be a little overwhelming.

least, they would have preferred that he and his fellow cartoon creatures had stayed in California. To them, Mickey Mouse is "the Black Rat", an alien rodent who has stormed into the swamplands of central Florida, wrecking the area's peculiar environment forever. There is no denying, however, that Mickey and Minnie, Goofy and Cinderella—all the glitz and glamour, the schmultz and razzmatazz of *Fantasia*—have had a profound influence on the state's economic development, and on the world's holiday habits.

Without question, Florida is America's top leisure destination, attracting well over 41 million visitors in 1991. About half of the visitors who come to the United States each year head for Florida. The tourism statisticians claim

*M*ap of Florida's main towns, cities and roads.

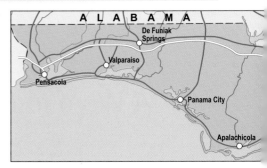

that 91 per cent of visitors go back again. The travel pattern is easy to trace. First-time visitors make for central Florida, which has the greatest concentration of attractions, not least of which is Walt Disney World. It has been estimated that to see everything Orlando has to offer takes at least 45 days—nearly a week for the Walt Disney offerings alone—so it is not surprising that many people restricted to two or even three weeks of holiday find it necessary to return to catch up on the things they missed the first time round.

Proudly dubbing itself "the Sunshine State", Florida wears its sub-tropical climate like a medal of honour. The city of St Petersburg, on the Gulf of Mexico, appears in the *Guinness Book of Records* for achieving 768 consecutive days of sunshine between 9 February 1967 and 17 March 1969. Indeed, the city is so cocky about its climate that the local evening newspaper is given away free to mark days when the sun fails to shine—so far the publishers have had to give the paper away on average fewer than four times a year.

Just off US Highway 27, more or less right in the middle of the state, the town of Frostproof makes another declaration of Florida's supreme

confidence in its weather. Yearly average temperatures in various parts of the state range from just below 20°C (68°F) to just over 25.5°C (78°F).

This means that there are times when the weather gets very hot, but not many occasions on which it gets very cold. But don't be fooled by the name of that centrally-based town. Florida is not entirely frostproof. Indeed, sub-freezing-point temperatures in recent years have severely damaged—and in some places all but wiped out—the state's traditional citrus-growing industry, and residents who can tell you anything you want to know about air-conditioning have been shattered and perplexed to find their pipes frozen.

Important though they are, however, such man-made attractions as Walt Disney World, Sea World and Universal Studios—to say nothing of the climate—are not the only things Florida has to offer. For a start, it has lots of space, covering an area of some 150,220 km^2 (58,000 square miles): about the size of England and Wales combined. It has 2,100 km (1,300 miles) of shoreline, 1,300 km (800 miles) of beaches, 30,000 lakes, and a comprehensive system of waterways for boating and fishing enthusiasts.

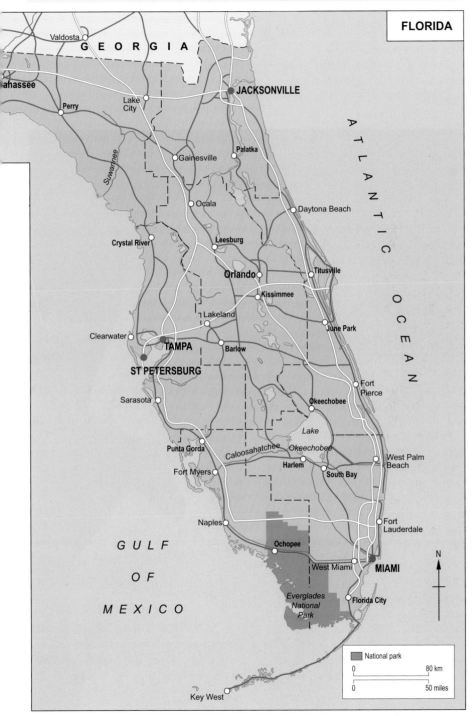

FLORIDA

*E*xotic wildlife can be seen throughout Florida, especially in state parks and recreation areas.

Part of its coastline is protected by continental America's only coral reef. The state maintains 113 wildlife, botanical and historical parks and recreation areas, covering a total of some 167,900 hectares (415,000 acres). Its history ranges over aeons—from

long before mankind's Ice Age migrations to the beginnings of space travel. Interestingly, the two oldest post-Columbian communities in what is now the United States are located within its borders. It has some of the most sophisticated cities in the world—surrounded by landscapes unchanged for thousands of years.

Holidaymakers can spend one day enjoying sophisticated electronic pleasure rides and the next paddling a canoe along a wilderness river. Their dinner may be a simple meal of freshly caught fish, cooked on a campsite barbecue, or a gourmet concoction from any national cuisine you care to think of, served in surroundings dignified, daring or downright spectacular. And the people they meet—the residents of Florida—may be anything from computer salesmen to killer-whale trainers, scuba-divers to balloon pilots. There are entertainers in their hundreds, and there are real cowboys and Indians.

Above all, Florida offers tremendous value for money in both goods and services. Car rental is the cheapest in the United States, and the price of petrol is much less than in other countries. Taking everything into account, Florida deserves its position as America's number one holiday destination.

Getting There

Few places in the world can be better served than Florida, so far as air travel is concerned. The state has three truly international gateway airports—Miami, Orlando and Tampa—with flights arriving daily from all over the world. A few other airports are described by enthusiastic authorities as "international", but overseas traffic in these cases is a restricted charter service from Canada. However, most places in Florida can easily be reached through connecting services from the three major gateways and from airports in many other parts of the United States.

Passports and Visas

Visitors to the United States from Europe must have a full ten-year passport valid for at least the duration of the intended stay. (The one-year Visitor's Passport—the kind you can obtain at a post office—is not acceptable.) For many other nationalities, passports must be valid for at least six months beyond their intended period of stay.

Most citizens of the United Kingdom, France, Germany, Italy, the Netherlands, Switzerland and Japan no longer need visas to enter the US. To be eligible for visa-free entry, travellers must hold an unexpired national or European Community passport and be travelling for business, pleasure or transit purposes only. Their stay in the US must not exceed 90 days, and they must hold a return or onward ticket issued by an air or sea carrier acceptable to the American immigration authorities.

Initial entry by land from Canada or Mexico without a visa is precluded, although travellers who have entered the United States visa-free may, within the 90-day admission period, make side trips to Mexico, Canada, the Caribbean islands and Bermuda, and return without a visa by any mode of transport. Canadian citizens and citizens of British Commonwealth countries and Ireland who have "landed immigrant" status in Canada or Bermuda do not need visas.

Travel for purposes other than short business or tourism trips often requires special documentation. Information can be obtained from the US Embassy or Consulate General. In London the American Embassy has special telephone numbers for visa enquiries. Recorded information about non-immigrant visas is available by dialling 071-499-3443. If you have questions to ask, dial 071-499-7010 to speak to a visa assistant.

Visa application forms—one for each traveller, including children and infants—can be obtained from, and after completion returned to: Visa Branch, United States Embassy, 5 Upper Grosvenor Street, London W1A 2JB. In Northern Ireland the address is: United States Consulate General, Queen House, 14 Queen Street, Belfast BT1 6EQ.

Visa applications—with passport-sized stamped addressed envelopes—should be mailed as early as possible—at least 14 days before departure. Personal applications are no longer possible, except in an emergency. Time can be saved with a postal application by personally delivering your application form and passport to the Embassy. If travel plans do not allow enough time for a postal application, travellers may use a travel agent or special courier service through whom an application can be completed in 24 hours, although a charge will be made in this instance.

If you do need a visa and are likely to make repeated visits to the United States, apply for a "multiple entry, indefinite period" visa. This will remain valid even when the passport in which it is stamped expires. Just make sure you have the old passport with you when you travel on the new one.

Visitors to the United States have to complete a landing card. It is not the world's best-designed questionnaire. Our tip: fill it in from the bottom, and all will fall neatly into place. Part of the card will be stapled into your passport by the immigration officer. Don't lose it—it should be collected as you leave the US.

Tourism information on the state's various regions, accommodation, attractions, etc. can be obtained in the United Kingdom from the Florida Division of Tourism, 18–24 Westbourne Grove, London W2 5RH; tel: 071-727-1661. In continental Europe the address is: Florida Division of Tourism, Schillerstrasse 10, 6000 Frankfurt/Main 1, Germany; tel: 69-13-10-731.

Customs Regulations

US Customs regulations allow travellers to import personal effects—clothing, personal jewellery, hunting, fishing and photographic equipment—a litre of alcoholic beverages (wine, beer or liquor—you know which to go for!), 200 cigarettes, or 100 cigars or 1.36 kg (3 lb) of smoking tobacco (great news for pipe-smokers or roll-your-own devotees). Non-residents may also take in articles worth up to $100 as gifts for other persons.

When to Go

All in all, it is fair to say that almost any time is the right time to visit Florida. Winter is the favourite season for North Americans, when "snowbirds" from Canada and the northern states flock there in their thousands. This is Florida's high season when accommodation is at its most expensive. Floridians love Europeans, who tend to visit the state during the summer months—July, August, September—keeping the cash flow rolling during the low season. This is the time when prices are at their lowest, and that's why you can so often find those wonderful bargain packages: flight, accommodation and car for next to nothing, it seems.

A word of warning, though. The high summer months are very, very hot and humid, and rainfall can be astonishingly heavy. The sky suddenly darkens and the heavens open. Thunder may crash and lightning sizzle. If you are caught outdoors you will be soaked to the skin within moments. It is true to say you could not get wetter if you jumped into the sea. We know. Lightning, by the way, can be extremely dangerous. Lifeguards clear beaches at the first hint. Wherever you are, it's prudent to seek cover when storm clouds gather.

June to October is also the hurricane season in the Gulf of Mexico, but Florida has rarely suffered a great deal of damage. The US National Hurricane Center keeps a close watch on weather patterns, and safety and evacuation procedures have been drawn up by local authorities. Do not take a hurricane warning lightly.

That said, however, you are much more likely to enjoy good weather than bad, even in those wet summer months. Rainfall tends to be predictable, occurring more or less at the same time each day, and storms, though violent, are short-lived. If you get soaked you'll be dry again in no time.

Clothing

Shorts, teeshirts and trainers are *de rigueur* for daytime wear, and dress tends to be informal at all times, though American men seem to prefer to wear a light jacket if they go out to dinner in the smarter restaurants, where women like to be seen in cocktail dresses. Ties are not usually worn, except by businessmen at work. Don't go overboard on the informality, though. Some shops and eating places display notices warning "No shirt, no shoes—no service". Women should note it is strictly forbidden to appear topless in any public place. Rangers or beach wardens may enjoy taking some time to explain this prohibition, but if it comes to the crunch they will arrest offenders.

Driving

Backpackers apart, few people are likely to get much out of a holiday in Florida without a car. Indeed, many tour operators offer a hired car as part of the package. Public transport is a bit thin on the ground, though some places—Daytona is one—are better off than others so far as local bus services are concerned. Without the use of a

car holidaymakers are handicapped, their choice of things to do and places to visit severely limited. Without a car, you may be forced to dine in the hotel restaurant every night of your stay while other holidaymakers are getting the best out of Florida's diverse cuisines. There are taxis, but they tend to be expensive.

Driving is cheap and easy. Petrol (gasoline, or more usually "gas") is cheap, and motorists generally are more courteous and tolerant than in Europe. The maximum speed limit on Florida roads is 104 kph (65 mph), and it is rigidly enforced. More people from Britain than anywhere else are fined for speeding in the state.

Storm clouds over Clearwater Beach harbour. The Sunshine State has high humidity and in summer sudden downpours can drench you in seconds, but drying out takes little time.

There really is no need to hurry. Roads are wide and well maintained and the traffic is usually very light. And after all, who wants to tear around on holiday?

Nothing could be easier than collecting a rented car at an airport in Florida—as long as you've remembered your driving licence. The best-

known car rental agencies will have reception desks in the arrivals terminals. Others, located close to the airport, will have a shuttle bus service for clients. After the briefest of formalities, the keys are handed over and you'll be waved off with a cheery "Have a nice day!" If you have any misgivings—if you want to know where the light switches are, for instance, or how the air-conditioning works, or even how to get to your hotel or holiday apartment—just ask. People want you to enjoy yourself, and they will be only too pleased to help.

After a flight that could well have lasted 12 hours or more and covered five time zones, some people may be too tired to face the ordeal of driving a strange car in a strange place, and on the opposite side of the road. In this case, it might be wiser to use an airport limousine ("limo") service, a kind of collective taxi, or a hotel courtesy bus, to get you to your accommodation and to arrange to collect a car when you've got over your jet lag. Most of the larger hotels have at least one car rental office on the premises.

Before setting out on a trip, it's a good idea to take a look at a map and

*D*riving is easy on Florida's highways, with no bends and little traffic.

get some idea of the general direction you'll be heading in, and to make a note of highway numbers. American highway signs always give both, e.g. "Interstate 4 East", "US Highway 19 South". Even numbers always indicate a highway that runs east to west, odd numbers north to south. Road numbers are usually abbreviated thus: I-4

E, US 19 S, SR 528 (State Road 528), CR 1234 (County Road 1234).

Eyes trained for driving on the left may find difficulty at first in readily spotting signs, traffic lights and street names. Traffic lights are often slung in the centre of intersections (crossroads), sometimes rather higher than drivers from the United Kingdom are used to, but the sequence is the same. A single flashing yellow light means proceed with caution. Unless there is a sign to the contrary, you can filter right on a red light, but take great care. Traffic coming from the left has right of way.

Street names at intersections always run in the direction of the street, so the name you see ahead of you refers to the street crossing at right angles, not the one you're on.

Under Florida law, the driver and front-seat passengers must wear seat belts, and the onus is on the driver to ensure that front-seat passengers up to the age of 15 are buckled up. Those unable to wear a belt for medical reasons are exempt from the law, but they must carry a certificate from a registered medical practitioner.

Tolls have to be paid on some roads and bridges throughout Florida, so it's a good idea to have some loose change at hand, and you'll also need a dollar note or two on the Florida Turnpike and the Beeline Expressway that runs from Orlando to the Space Coast.

Health

Sunburn is likely to be the greatest health hazard faced by most visitors to Florida. It takes no time at all for skin unused to intense exposure to

Enjoy the glorious Florida sunshine, but beware that your holiday isn't marred by miserable sunburn.

ultraviolet rays to become uncomfortably burned. Lack of care on the first day can ruin a whole holiday. Choose a suntan lotion with care—seek advice from a pharmacist if you are uncertain—and make sure you use it. Then sunbathe cautiously, gradually increasing the time of exposure. Remember, the ultraviolet rays are there even when you are strolling round the sights, or shopping in the street, and you can still end the day with badly burned arms, legs and face. A cotton hat or cap will be useful—men may be

surprised to find their parting, however narrow, can be uncomfortably affected.

Insects can be a problem, particularly mosquitoes and the minuscule, invisible sandflies known without affection as "No-see-ums". Mosquitoes are unlikely to cause discomfort in reasonably well-developed areas, where control measures are generally rigidly enforced, but they can make life difficult in rural areas. Skin irritation apart, mosquitoes are known to carry a number of diseases which can seriously affect human beings. No-see-ums can certainly be felt! Insect repellent is a wise addition to the holiday first-aid pack.

American catering is clinically hygienic, so visitors are unlikely to suffer complaints of the "Aztec Two-step" or "Montezuma's Revenge" type. Nevertheless, an unfamiliar diet, especially one rich in unaccustomed seafood, can cause stomach upsets, and it is well to be prepared for this eventuality.

Many supermarkets have well-stocked sections selling non-prescription medicines and preparations and offer advice on ailments and treatments.

Remember, there is no free health service in the United States. Medical attention can be a very costly matter. Make sure you carry adequate insurance. Adequate these days means at least £1 million cover for medical expenses. Some regular travellers to the United States wouldn't dream of going with less than £2 million in coverage.

If you wear spectacles ("eyeglasses"), make sure you take the prescription in case you lose them. US opticians can usually supply a new pair of glasses overnight—frequently within an hour—and at prices much cheaper then you'll find in western European countries. So it might be a good idea to treat yourself to a new pair, anyway.

Money Matters

You sometimes get the feeling in the United States that good old-fashioned cash has become obsolete, especially in hotels where the main ritual on checking in is taking an imprint of one's credit card. Many hotels issue guests with a house chargecard—more important then the room key, it seems—which can then be used to buy drinks, meals and goods from shops on the premises.

Personal cheques are anathema, and traveller's cheques are good only if they are in US dollars. Most North Americans, even in as sophisticated and cosmopolitan a place as Florida, are deeply suspicious of foreign currencies, and few banks have bureau de change facilities. The best solution we've found is to use an internationally accepted credit card in automatic teller machines. This enables you to obtain money as and when you need it—on a daily basis, if you like—and saves the expense of buying and cashing traveller's cheques. There is no commission to pay for the privilege of obtaining cash—you are simply charged at the exchange rate applicable on the day, plus a small transaction fee.

Security is improved because you only need to carry relatively small amounts of cash. The only problem we have found is that the list of places where you can use your card may not be up to date. We have found on some occasions that the card that did nicely in some banks' machines last year is politely but firmly rejected this year. If your card is rejected *do not* persist in trying to obtain money with it. After three attempts the hole in the wall will eat the card. Best to abandon the attempt and try another company's machine. Public supermarkets, of which there are many, have ATMs which accept a wide range of credit cards. Remember, though, that your card will have to be validated for ATM use before you leave home.

Bank notes come in denominations of $1, $5, $10, $20, $50 and $100. They are all the same size and the same shade of green. The only difference—

apart from the denomination itself, of course—is that each bears the portrait of a different US president. Coins are 1 cent (a penny), 5 cents (nickel), 10 cents (dime), 25 cents (quarter), 50 cents and, occasionally, $1.

Security

No one could pretend that Florida is crime-free, but not once, in trips covering nine years, have we ever felt at risk there. Thanks to television, Miami has an undeserved "vice" image. Most overseas visitors are surprised to find a most elegant city whose residents are proud of its position in the fields of international shipping and finance.

Miami—and for that matter, other Floridian cities—does have its shady side and there are districts which should be regarded as "no-go" zones for tourists. So let discretion dictate: don't go. If you do find you have strayed into a doubtful area, don't get out of your car, don't stop for anyone—except a cop, of course—and drive away as fast as you reasonably and legally can. The chance of being mugged, even in the sleaziest of districts, is not as high as newspaper headlines would have you believe, but it is better to be safe than sorry.

Accommodation

It is doubtful if anywhere else on earth can offer the wide range of accommodation found in Florida. There is everything from simple campsites for tents or motorhomes to the ultimate in luxury hotels—even one with a monorail station in its lobby—and the choice increases each year.

Those people who prefer to "do their own thing" on holiday will find a tremendous choice in self-catering properties, many offered as part of a flight/car/accommodation package put together by leading tour operators. These are at the top end of the range—elaborate modern bungalows and villas, often with their own swimming pools. Lower down the scale come the older-style frame houses and cottages, not quite so luxurious, perhaps, but comfortable and more than adequately provided with "efficiencies", the convenient short-form for refrigerators, microwave ovens, cookers, kitchen utensils and crockery. Such properties are often found on the outskirts of resorts, and what they may lack in facilities is often more than balanced by a superb location right on the beach.

Oddly enough, bed and breakfast in private homes and country inns does not seem to have caught on in Florida the way it has in many other parts of North America, although a few such enterprises have been established, mainly in the southern part of the state. Bed and breakfast in the United States is not necessarily the cheap option often expected in Britain. American standards tend to be exceptionally high and are reflected in the rates charged, but as with most things they do represent good value.

Two organizations that deal specifically with B & B are: Bed and Breakfast Company, PO Box 430262, Miami, Florida 33243 (tel: (305) 661-3270); and Florida Keys Bed and Breakfast Inc., 5 Man O' War Drive,

Camp out in the Everglades—but treat the unique ecosystem with the respect it deserves.

Marathon, Florida 33050 (tel: (303) 743-4118). If you write, a self-addressed envelope and International Reply coupons would be appreciated (stamped, addressed envelope if you write from within the US).

Another interesting option is home exchange, in which Britons can swap their home with an American family. Sometimes a car and a boat are thrown in at the Florida end of the deal. Prospective swappers pay a registration fee to have their home

areas. Furnishings here will be simple, to basic and the nearest thing to air-conditioning is likely to be an electric fan, but there is almost always the not inconsiderable compensation of a beautiful riverside setting with great opportunities for viewing wildlife. Anglers may well think they are in Valhalla.

Houseboats—motorized luxury floating bungalows with everything you could possibly need, right down to two-way radio and fishing gear—are found on the St Johns River in the Sanford area between Orlando and the Space Coast. This is a wonderfully relaxed way to stay put, or cruise, view wildlife and enjoy both the wilderness and the delights of such home comforts as air-conditioning and colour television.

Amazingly, the concept of holidays afloat does not seem to have caught on in other parts of Florida, a waterways state if ever there was one. Bareboat charters are available at popular marinas, especially in the Fort Lauderdale area, but there is no self-skippered cruising of the kind popular on the rivers, broads and canals of Britain and Europe, for example, and there are no hotel boats like those plying the Rhine, Danube or even the Thames.

included in a register. A company that deals exclusively in Florida exchanges is The Floridian Experience, 79 Ellerman Avenue, Whitton, Twickenham, Middlesex TW2 6AA (tel: 081-898-7902).

Adventurous travellers with an eye on the dollars and cents might like to consider the simple cabins often found on canoe rental locations, usually in rural, if not downright wilderness,

Hiking

At first glance you might think a place so lacking in hills and covered with so much water might be dull country for backpackers, but Florida is in the process of completing a 2,091-km (1,300-mile) trail through the centre of the state. The Florida Hiking Trail begins in the Ocala National Forest, in the northern part of central Florida and

Up to nine people can live in comfort on a St Johns River houseboat.

already covers a total of 1,287 twisting, winding kilometres (800 miles). Many state parks and recreation areas have hiking trails.

Camping

Bearing in mind the climate, it's hardly surprising that camping flourishes in Florida. In fact, the state has more campgrounds and pitches than any other in the Union—more than 1,200 licensed parks, 450 campgrounds and RV (Recreational Vehicle, or motor-home) sites and getting on for 800 other places with camping facilities. Altogether, there are more than 160,000 pitches.

Sites range from fairly primitive set-ups in out-of-the-way areas to highly sophisticated locations with full electrical, water supply and drainage hook-ups, restaurants, swimming pools, games and entertainment areas, and shops. At some places you don't even need a tent—they'll rent you one. Some campgrounds are available for nudists.

The best sites—i.e., the best locations at the most attractive rates—are to be found in the national, state and county parks and forests, but these tend to get booked up at peak holiday times. (Visitors from European countries should remember, their high season is Florida's low!)

22

The best of the state's private camp-grounds are the 200 or so listed in the annual directory published by the Florida Campground Association, whose members must meet strict criteria to qualify for inclusion. The directory is distributed free at Florida Welcome Centers, member camp-grounds, RV rental companies, Florida attractions, travel agencies and chambers of commerce. Copies can be obtained from overseas offices of the Florida Division of Tourism and by writing to the Florida Campground Association, 1638 N. Plaza Drive, Tallahassee, Fl 32308-5323.

Eating Out

Food and drink is another area offering a huge choice—and the emphasis here is very much on the word "huge", for the portions served are often gargantuan by European standards. City directories will list page after page of eating establishments—ranging from simple street corner sandwich bars to elegant food palaces and very entertaining themed restaurants—offering everything from hot dogs to *haute cuisine* and every imaginable type of ethnic cooking.

The local specialty, without question, is seafood—fish, lobster, jumbo shrimps, oysters—all fresh from the waters of the Atlantic Ocean or Gulf of Mexico, and often cooked according to the spicy, evocative recipes of the Deep South: Conch Chowder, Blackened Grouper, Shrimps Jumbalaya. One dish that will soon become very familiar is Key lime pie, a concoction prepared from a small, sweet native lime, meringue and pastry that truly deserves to be dubbed the state dessert if for no other reason than its ubiquitous appearance on menus high and low.

Visitors from European countries especially will be impressed by the standards of service in all types of American catering establishments—the cleanliness and, especially, the efficient, friendly waiters and waitresses—and will find that restaurant prices at all levels are unlikely to take the edge off anyone's appetite.

Beer, served frostily cold, is cheap and American, though there are places that serve British beer, Guinness, and Canadian and Mexican products. At Busch Gardens Zoo, near Tampa, and Sea World in Orlando, adults can drink free beer generously provided in a special sampling bar. As you might have guessed, both attractions are owned by a brewery.

In a number of states some very good wines are produced—even Florida now has at least one vineyard—but the majority of people in the United States are not great wine drinkers. Nevertheless, wine is generally available in most restaurants and is often sold by the glass. The price compares with what one might expect to pay in Europe. Spirits, especially those indigenous to the United States, are served in generous measures and are usually reasonably priced. It hardly needs to be said that beers, wines and spirits are much, much cheaper in supermarkets and liquor stores—so much so, in fact, that it is better to purchase liquor there to take back home than at a not-so-cheap airport duty-free shop.

One important point: it is illegal for anyone under the age of 21 to consume or purchase alcoholic beverages.

*T*he restaurants are as varied as the food—Florida caters to all pockets and palates.

Tips and Gratuities

You can expect to tip anyone who

performs any kind of personal service: waiters and waitresses, bellhops, airport baggage handlers and taxi drivers, especially. Give 15 to 20 per cent to waiters and taxi drivers, a dollar upwards to bellhops and baggage handlers, depending on the amount of luggage toted. It is also usual to tip a dollar or so to the person who returns your car from valet parking.

Post and Telephone Services

Stamps can be bought at hotel receptions, and for straightforward holiday correspondence—postcards and airmail letters—staff are usually familiar with the rates for most parts of the world. There is usually a mail "drop" (post box) somewhere in the lobby. Post offices are often located near other public buildings—the court room, mayor's office, sheriff's office and the like—though they can also be found in shopping malls. Public mail drops may be difficult to identify at first for eyes accustomed to Britain's crimson pillar boxes. US Post Office mail boxes are blue and are curved on top.

Telephone calls can be expensive if made from hotel bedrooms because hotels, as everywhere, can impose a hefty surcharge on top of the normal charge. However, there are usually plenty of public payphone cubicles in a hotel reception area.

The easiest way for visitors from the UK to make a phone call home is to dial 1-800-4455667. This connects you directly with a British Telecom operator in London through whom you can make a transfer charge call or use your British Telecom chargecard. Whether you go through an American or British operator, it might be cheaper to make a collect call (i.e., transfer the charge).

Sightseeing

Finally, a few tips to help you get the most out of sightseeing in Florida, especially the central region's theme parks, which can be heavy going for those not used to hot weather.

Dress comfortably—shorts and tee-shirts are perfectly acceptable—and wear footwear that gives firm support to ankles and the soles of your feet. Sandals or trainers will be fine; flip-flops will soon tire you out. Make sure you are well protected from the sun.

Sundays, Thursdays and Fridays are the least busy days for central Florida's attractions. There are plenty of eating places, but if you haven't booked a table at a sit-down restaurant try to eat a little earlier than normal. At the Epcot Center, visit the World Showcase in the morning then see Future World attractions in the afternoon. Most people do it the other way round.

Parades in Walt Disney World's Magic Kingdom begin in Town Square, go up Main Street, USA, then pass through Liberty Square and Frontierland. The least-crowded vantage points are in these last two locations.

Walt Disney World and the other major attractions publish guidebooks and daily timetables so that visitors know exactly what is going on each day. Without these you could easily miss a once-in-a-lifetime experience.

A Glimpse of Local Colour

Friendly and courteous, the people of Florida will welcome you to the Sunshine State and tell you to have a nice day. And you probably will. Whatever your idea of the perfect holiday, Florida can provide it. A wonderful family destination, Florida caters to all ages and tastes. State parks provide miles of wide open spaces; theme parks keep children amused; the beaches are perfect for lazing; the sea provides endless watersports and the cities cater to those who prefer a holiday with access to museums, art galleries, operas and gourmet dining.

Nowhere in the world can there be as many man-made attractions within easy driving distance as there are in Florida, and no people in the world are as good at providing spectacular entertainment with full back-up facilities as those in the United States.

They do have queues, yes, although the word "queue" isn't in the language. They have "lines", and they usually

Alligators are naturally shy of human company, but they should be regarded with the utmost respect. The golden rule is never, ever feed them.

move at an acceptable rate, so nobody gets too impatient. Visit the Epcot Center, in Orlando, at peak time and you may have to join a line that takes 45 minutes to reach the turnstile. It's gratifying to see a notice proclaiming, "45 minutes from this point", so you know what the situation is. It isn't often that you'd have to wait longer than that. Most of the people in the line with you will be from the United States—pleasant, chatty people happy to talk to strangers, especially foreigners, and the time passes quickly.

Public toilets are hygienically maintained, even in the most crowded venues. Car parking is more than adequate at attractions, and well planned, so that there is no stress in finding somewhere to leave your

27

*F*lorida's climate and casual lifestyle brings out the fun in everyone.

vehicle among several thousand others, or in locating it when it's time to leave.

If you're a visitor to the United States, you're unlikely to have a pet with you, unless you're on a house exchange, or staying with a family and have offered to take their dog out for the day. But if you do have an animal in your party, note that it is illegal to leave it in the vehicle. Kennels are provided—a facility that would be welcome at attractions on the other side of the Atlantic.

Also, pushchairs, or "strollers", are available for a small fee, or even free, so there's no need for toddlers to complain of aching legs.

People

The residents of Florida are easy to get to know. They like to chat to strangers. There are some 10 million Floridians and they come from a wide assortment of backgrounds. There must be some adults who were born and bred in Florida, but they're pretty thin on the ground compared with incomers. Your cab driver may be from Ohio, your waitress from Havana, the man who rents you a boat may have moved south from land-locked Kansas and the lifeguard on the beach may have fancied a change from California.

Maybe they're all nice guys by nature, or perhaps the climate and the casual approach to life bring out the best in everybody. There's rarely any hassle, even in that universal centre of stress, the airport immigration hall.

People from the United States should kindly avert their gaze for the next couple of paragraphs, while readers from anywhere else are warned about the blind spot that affects the nation generally and Florida in particular. This is it: they have no idea about distance. Ask how far it is to your hotel from Orlando Airport and you'll be told breezily: "Go out along here, make a left, drive to the toll booth and it's just along there on your right". "Just along there" can mean anything up to 50 km (30 miles). This is no exaggeration. Ask how many miles it is and how long the journey is likely to take. Add a bit to whatever the answer is to both questions, and with luck you'll find your hotel without too much trouble.

Another thing which soon becomes evident about Floridians is that, like many of their countrymen elsewhere, they are very hearty eaters. Unless you are ravenous, take a cautious approach to the menu card for a start. Portions served are extremely generous and offer great value for money.

Service is usually slick and efficient. If it isn't, it's probably because of some human error. We were once kept sipping our pre-prandial beer for 15 minutes before the waitress came for our order, full of apologies and admitting, frankly, that she'd forgotten us. The order included more beer, "Well, the drinks are on me. It's the least I can do," she insisted.

According to some—and you'll soon guess who they are—the only people who can claim to be real Floridians are those whose ancestors were settled there in the days when Florida attained statehood. These are the people

The Seminole Indians have been in the state longer than any other ethnic group.

who are proud to call themselves "Crackers", true, dyed-in-the-wool Southerners who speak with a y'all drawl and like nothing better than a rocking chair on the porch. Everyone else, they will tell you, is a Yankee.

Seminoles

However, if length of family roots is the measure, then the only section of today's resident population who can claim to be 22-carat Floridians are the Seminole Indians—and they've only been here since the early 17th century. The very few aboriginal natives of Florida who had not been wiped out by disease, slavery or warfare were taken to Cuba when the Spaniards ceded Florida to the British in 1763. By then the Seminoles, originally a branch of the Creek tribe living on the Oconee River in Georgia, were well established in the territory, their ranks having been swelled considerably by runaway slaves and refugees during their migration south. The name "Seminole" comes from the Creek Indian word for runaway.

Florida passed back into Spanish ownership, and the Seminoles began making cross-border raids into the neighbouring US state of Georgia. White settlers in Georgia were soon complaining to their government that the ineffectual Spaniards were doing nothing to keep the Indians in check. American army actions against the raiders led to the First Seminole War of 1817–18, which ended with the unauthorized invasion of Florida by General Andrew Jackson, who captured Pensacola.

As a US territory, Florida became a goal for land-hungry white settlers—and the land they hungered belonged, of course, to the Indians. The whites started a loud clamour to get the government to remove the Indians to reservations in the west. Guerrilla warfare continued, and treaties signed in 1832 and 1834 failed to end the bitter dispute.

The Second Seminole War began in 1835 when the young Chief Osceola killed a rival chief, who favoured removal to the west, then went on to massacre a US Army detachment from Fort Brooke on Tampa Bay. A 10,000-man force was sent to Florida to seek out Osceola and his 4,000 warriors. It was a long, hard battle, with the Seminoles running rings round the Americans in the swamps and marshes. Osceola became known as the "Snake of the Everglades", but he was captured deceitfully while riding into St Augustine under a white flag of truce in 1837. He died in prison a year later. When hostilities ceased in 1842 all but 300 of 4,230 Seminoles were rounded up and transported to Oklahoma.

The 300 who remained vanished into the Everglades and Big Cypress swamps, eluding capture under the leadership of Chief Billy Bowlegs. In 1855 the Third Seminole War was started when the Indians massacred a party of surveyors. This time the fighting went on sporadically for three years, with white troops and settlers hunting the Seminoles like wild animals among the sawgrass swamps. The government eventually lost interest and the search ended. Officially, however, the Third Seminole War went on until 1934 when a treaty was finally signed.

Today there are about 2,000 Seminoles living in Florida (and about 4,000 in Oklahoma), mainly settled on reservations straddling the Everglades Parkway (more popularly known as Alligator Alley) and at Brighton on the north-west shore of Lake Okeechobee. The headquarters of the Miccosukee Tribe, a Seminole subgroup, is about halfway across the Everglades, along the Tamiami Trail,

Many Cubans settled in the Miami area after the Castro revolution.

where there is a visitor centre with craft and cultural displays, a shop and demonstrations of alligator-wrestling and snake-handling. A similar centre is to be found on the outskirts of Tampa. The Seminoles based at Brighton are mainly occupied with cattle-raising.

Cubans

Although Spain never maintained more than a toe-hold in Florida, its culture and character have been stamped on the state, thanks to the Cubans, Puerto Ricans and other Latin Americans who have migrated in such numbers that Spanish is now the second language.

The major influences have come from the Cubans, who have fled to Florida in their thousands, since 1959, as refugees from the Fidel Castro regime. Many of them have settled in the Miami area, and some sections of the city reflect more of the ambience of Havana. One part of the city is actually known as Little Havana. Relaxed old men sit on straight cane-backed chairs, drinking tiny cups of thick black coffee and smoking cigars. Signs in shop windows are in Spanish, the language you hear all around you on the streets. The most popular fast-food dish is a Cuban sandwich—spicy meat trapped in a torpedo-shaped roll of flat-tasting bread. Exotic Latin rhythms pulsate from jukeboxes and ghetto-blasters.

A much older Cuban settlement is Ybor City on the north-east outskirts of Tampa, on the Gulf Coast. It was founded by Vincente Martinez Ybor, a cigar manufacturer. He brought

31

skilled workers over from Havana, and as his business grew other manufacturers moved in. Among cigar smokers Tampa became almost as big a name as Havana itself.

The Blacks

If the true Floridians were to be measured in terms of their population in the early days then those of African origin would probably take top marks. Thousands of Africans were shipped in to man the plantations and citrus groves. A Federal census of 1860 found nearly 62,000 Black slaves in a total Florida population of 140,000. There was also a substantial number of free Blacks, who owned almost $100,000 worth of property. In the 19th century, $100,000 would have been an unimaginably large sum of money by anybody's standards.

Before the abolition of slavery, Florida was a paradox for the Blacks. Politically and socially the northern part of the state was the deepest of the Deep South—the world of plantations and Uncle Tom's Cabin; a place where the plantation owners lived like dukes and the slaves like farmyard animals. More sparsely populated, southern Florida was quite different—wilder, but freer. Here runaway slaves from the north and beyond were able to find refuge and establish their own place in society.

Today, Black people represent only about 13 per cent of Florida's population, their numbers diminished proportionately by the huge influx of white migrants. In the old days they were an almost entirely rural group; now some 75 per cent of them live in urban environments. Many of them have had a tough time over the generations: first as slaves, then as low-status citizens segregated into second-rate schools and transportation systems; unable to eat in restaurants frequented by whites, and sometimes forbidden to use the beaches or swim in the sea. But the 1964 Civil Rights Act opened the way for a broader-based, true liberty, and there are encouraging signs that Florida's Black people are being given and are responding to the opportunities of a free society.

Senior Citizens

Seen from the viewpoint of Walt Disney World, Florida might seem to be a place of little people with ice cream smeared around their mouths, but in fact some 25 per cent of the state's residents are more than 60 years old. In some places every other person is a retiree. Florida's climate and relaxed lifestyle are obvious attractions after a lifetime of toil, to say nothing of a more generous official attitude towards taxation than you will find in many other parts of the world.

The preponderance of senior citizens means, of course, that they are generally well cared for in terms of facilities and amenities. They have their own clubs—their own communities, even—and the range of activities they undertake is astonishing: everything from flower arranging to hiking and deep-sea fishing.

Saga, the British tour operator that specializes in holidays for the over-60s, has recognized the long-stay potential in Florida's ready-made set-up for seniors, and has included in its brochures a programme offering independent travellers the chance to stay in Florida for up to four months at prices not much more than a more traditional winter holiday in southern Spain. The company has also forged links with local seniors' clubs whose members will happily involve visiting Britons in their social activities. Details can be obtained from Saga Holidays Ltd,

FREEPOST, Folkestone, Kent CT20 1BR (telephone free on 0800-300-400).

History

Florida has always been a destination for migrants. Strange aquatic creatures—primitive whales, turtles and a host of other shelled life-forms—made their home here during the age of the dinosaurs, and when ice covered other parts of the world the northern herds headed south in search of much the same things sought by modern mankind: sun, sea and sustenance. When humans arrived, probably some 10,000 years ago, the area was a warm paradise teeming with game, wildfowl and seafood. It still is.

*T*he oldest house in the state's oldest city, St Augustine. The building, occupied from the early 1600s, has a Spanish period ground floor and a wooden storey which was added by the British.

*P*once de Leon Inlet Lighthouse is the second tallest structure of its kind on the United States east coast.

Conventional theory has the North American Indian as a descendant of the Asians who poured across a land bridge between Siberia and Alaska some 20,000 years ago. The first Floridians, however, may have come from the south. Archaeologists have identified cultural similarities between Florida's early residents and the tribes of Central and South America.

In the beginning, the people survived by hunting and fishing, using flint-bladed spears to kill animals and fish. Conch shells were used as utensils, and other shells were used to carve trees into dugout canoes. Although life was easy compared with other parts of the world, the natives of Florida appear to have been an enterprising and innovative lot. Pottery was in use here some 800 years before it appeared in other parts of North America, and the cultivation of crops began about 1000 BC.

Archaeological digs throughout the state have uncovered evidence of a complex and relatively sophisticated culture. Irrigation ditches and horticultural plots have been found near Lake Okeechobee, and the positions of skeletons found in massive burial mounds hint at a strongly hierarchical society.

Early Explorers

The first Europeans known to set foot on Floridian soil were those in an expeditionary force led by the Spaniard, Don Juan Ponce de Leon, who had sailed to the New World with Christopher Columbus's second expedition. King Ferdinand V had commissioned

Ponce to seek a legendary island on which there was believed to be a fountain of youth. Ponce set sail from Puerto Rico on 3 March 1513, and, after sailing among the Bahamas, landed near the St Johns River. It was the Easter (Pascua Florida) of 1513, so Ponce named the land La Florida.

The Spanish explorer sailed south to the chain of islands now known as the Florida Keys, then travelled up the west coast, landing in a sheltered bay near Charlotte Harbour, north of the present city of Fort Myers. He was not welcomed by the natives, whose hostile reception has led historians to believe they may have had previous encounters with Europeans, possibly slave traders.

Ponce's second—and as it happened last—voyage to Florida came in 1521 when he returned with two ships, 200 men—including a number of priests—and 50 horses. His task this time was to establish a settlement and convert the Indians to Christianity. He landed again near Charlotte Harbor and his men had got no further than laying the foundations of the new settlement when they were attacked. In the battle Ponce was struck by an Indian arrow, and other Spaniards were badly injured. Survivors got their leader and other wounded back to one of the ships. They managed to sail to Cuba, where Ponce died.

During the next 40 years the Spaniards persisted with their efforts to conquer the Indians and settle Florida. They failed miserably, at a total cost of some 2,000 Spanish lives.

Panfilo de Narvaez was full of confidence when he led another Easter expedition in 1528. He and 400 men landed in Tampa Bay on Good Friday, warning the natives to knuckle under or face the wrath of the King of Spain. This time the Indians got rid of the Spaniards by telling them there was gold to the north, in a land called Apalachee.

Narvaez and a party of his men set off on foot for Apalachee, where they and the ships were to meet. The land party arrived on Florida's Panhandle coast, but the ships failed to turn up. Weakened by disease and Indian attacks, the group built six rough-and-ready boats and sailed off to find Mexico. The boats capsized in a storm and

Narvaez was among those who perished. Their fate came to light eight years later when four survivors turned up in Mexico.

Next came Hernando de Soto, who landed in Tampa Bay with a 1,000-strong army in May 1539. His force had no difficulty overcoming the

*T*he huge fortress of the old city of St Augustine, the Castillo de San Marcos, is a national monument.

Indians they encountered and pushed northwards in search of gold. It was a fruitless search that took them into Georgia, North Carolina, Alabama and beyond. After three years, de Soto died of fever on the banks of the Mississippi River.

A third attempt at conquest was made in 1559 in an expedition led by the wealthy nobleman, Tristan de Luna y Arellano, who had served with de Soto. De Luna had 1,500 men and tried to establish a settlement in the north, on Pensacola Bay. After a two-year struggle and a hurricane which left the party desperately short of food, the attempt was abandoned in 1561.

Spain was distracted in her efforts to colonize Florida by pirates from France, Holland and England who frequently raided with ease the fat, slow galleons that crossed the Atlantic, laden with gold, silver and gems, and with spices and rare cloths. A group of French Huguenots, led by Jean Ribaut, took advantage of the situation and in 1562 set up a fortified community on what is now called the Matanzas River, in the north-east of Florida. It lasted just three years.

Infuriated by the audacious French, the Spaniards mustered a huge force and set up a base on the coast, a few miles to the north. The day they landed was 28 August 1565, the Feast of St Augustine. They named the place St Augustine, and it is there to this day—the oldest, continuously occupied European settlement in the United States. The French were less durable: their ships grounded by a hurricane, the Matanzas settlement was attacked by the Spanish force. Ribaut and most of his men were put to death.

British Colonists

Spain continued her struggle to colonize Florida, but by the early part of the 18th century had established no more than St Augustine, on the Atlantic, and Pensacola, in the northwest. A small garrison had also been set up in the Panhandle, at San Marcos on Apalachee Bay. The British, who had extensive colonies elsewhere on the North American mainland and among the Caribbean islands, turned jealous eyes towards Florida; they made repeated attacks on St Augustine, but were repelled each time by the well-entrenched and heavily armed Spaniards. In 1763, however, Britain acquired Florida at the negotiating table. Havana, which had fallen into British hands during the Seven Years War, was handed back in exchange for Florida under the terms of the First Treaty of Paris.

Already reasonably friendly with the Indians in the neighbouring territories of Alabama and Georgia, some of whom had begun to migrate southwards in any case, the British were able to get on with the task of establishing settlements much more peaceably than the Spaniards had. Immigrants from Ireland and the British mainland were soon being settled in new communities; plantations were developed, the slave trade expanded, and commerce flourished.

For the first time Florida began to be identified with the rest of North America rather than Spain's Cuban-administered colonies, but its residents remained loyal to the Crown when rebels in the north made their unilateral declaration of independence in 1776. Effigies of American revolutionary leaders were burned in the streets of St Augustine.

US Territory

Spain took a leaf from Jean Ribaut's book of 1562: with the British distracted by the American Revolution, the Spaniards took Pensacola and occupied west Florida. In 1783 the whole of Florida was handed back to Spain in the Second Treaty of Paris. If anything, though, Spain's grip on Florida was even weaker than it had been during the first occupation and, after 38 troublesome years, the territory was acquired by the United States in an agreement which cancelled Spain's $5 million debt to the Americans.

The early years of the infant US territory of Florida were troubled by wars with the Seminole tribes (see PEOPLE on page 30)—wars which had begun while the region still belonged to Spain. In March 1845 Florida became an American state, but 16 years later, committed to the retention of slavery, it seceded from the Union and joined the Confederacy in the bitter civil war against the North.

The Seminole Wars had taken their toll on Florida, but the state had managed to make some modest strides since joining the Union. Agriculture had begun to flourish, particularly in the production of sugar, cotton, tobacco, rice and indigo. The world's first ice-making machine was made in the tiny community of Apalachicola in 1848, and in 1861 a rail link was opened between the state capital, Tallahassee, and Cedar Key, just south of the Suwannee River estuary on the Gulf coast. The Civil War brought everything to a halt, and in four years cost Florida 5,000 lives and $20 million in damage to homes, industry and commerce.

The Civil War was about slavery and race relations. Slavery ended with the South's surrender at Appomattox on 9 April 1865, but many of Florida's Blacks were kept down by segregation and wicked prejudice until the Civil Rights Act of 1964 put an end to such practices. There is no doubt that some prejudice persists in some places to this day, but tourists are unlikely to observe it. In general, Florida seems free of race relations tension, and among its citizens is a sizable Black middle class with a perceivable presence in professional and executive positions.

Encouraged by the prospect of snow-free winters and undeterred by such sub-tropical discomforts as malaria, cholera and yellow fever, settlers began to be drawn to the state in such numbers that between 1860 and 1880 its population almost doubled from 140,000 to 270,000. The new arrivals brought with them a wide range of skills, talent, imagination and energy. Towards the end of the 19th century two eager entrepreneurs developed extensive rail links—and luxury hotels—along both the Atlantic and Gulf coasts. Florida's tourism industry had begun

The Rail Barons

If any persons could claim to be Florida's pioneer dream builders they would surely be Henry Morrison Flagler and Henry B. Plant, whose railways and luxury hotels opened up routes along the east and west coasts in the closing years of the 19th century.

Plant's Atlantic Coast Railroad linked Richmond, Virginia, with Tampa, where he built the lavish Tampa Bay Hotel, still a landmark in the city. At Clearwater his Belleview Biltmore Hotel, opened in 1897, is said to be the largest wooden structure still in use in the United States.

Flagler, an associate of John D. Rockefeller, with whom he founded Standard Oil in Cleveland, Ohio, first visited Florida in 1883, and three years later bought several railway lines which he combined to form the Florida East Coast Railway. He built a chain of hotels which became resorts in their own right along the line of rail. These included the still famous Breakers at Palm Beach.

Flagler drove his railway further south to Miami, where he dredged the harbour and established steamship lines to Key West and Nassau in the Bahamas. Ever restless, he ploughed on southwards, extending his railway to the city of Homestead, then—his greatest triumph—taking it right down the Florida Keys, leaping audaciously from island to island in a series of bridges, many of which exist

A misty morning
breaks over the Everglades.

today, carrying tourists' cars on the road to Key West. Flagler's Overseas Railway was finished in 1912, the year before he died, and in 1935 it was destroyed in a terrible hurricane. It was quickly resurrected as the Overseas Highway in 1938.

Development of Florida

The sweet smell of success began to replace the cloying scent of swamp. Huge areas of damp lands were drained, mangroves cleared, channels dredged; new resorts and residential communities began to spring up. Then, once again, came the bugle call of battle. But the Spanish–American War of 1898 this time brought boom rather than doom. US troops who were held in transit camps in Florida, while they waited to sail to Cuba, later returned to their homes with tales of the wondrous land of beaches, sunshine and the good life. After demobilization, many of them stayed home no longer than it took to pack up, then headed back south. The remainder did an unpaid promotional job for Florida, persuading friends and relatives that they really ought to go there for a holiday visit at least.

Property development and speculation became a way of life between the two World Wars, when the state's population again doubled—this time to about two million. This was a daring time and a daring place. In New York and other northern cities they were building skyscrapers. In Florida they were building dreams—structures that looked good enough to eat; hotels like birthday cakes; pastel-shaded cities strewn along the shoreline like sweets dropped by a child. It was the age of innovation: of the world's first scheduled airline service—a flight across Tampa Bay in a wooden flying boat

with room for one passenger—of an audacious engineering feat that linked some 30 islands of the Florida Keys in a 185-km (115-mile) chain of road and bridges.

The innovations continue. In central Florida the fantasy worlds of leisure give tourists a taste of make-believe and a glimpse into the future. On the Atlantic coast, in an area which is largely a wildlife refuge, the Kennedy Space Center wrestles with unimaginable problems of mathematics, physics, chemistry and engineering to take mankind beyond the pull of Earth, to the outer reaches of the solar system and beyond. Florida looks to the stars in more senses than one.

Just the Essentials

On a first-time visit to Florida you may be overwhelmed by the wealth of choice you have wherever you start. The major landmarks and places to visit are proposed here to help you establish priorities.

Central Florida
Walt Disney World.
Sea World: leading marine-life park.
Universal Studios: largest working
studio outside Hollywood.
Wet 'N' Wild water park: centrally
situated, complex of rides and slides.
Winter Park: America's largest flea
market, Flea World—1,200 stalls.
Kissimmee: Old Town—reconstruction
of early 20th-century town.

Central East
Daytona Beach: giant seaside park.
Ponce de Leon Lighthouse: historic
monument, museum, spectacular views.
Titusville: "Space City USA".
Merritt Island National Wildlife
Reserve: wintering wildlife sanctuary.
Sebastian Inlet State Recreation:
premier salt-water fishing location.

The South-east
Palm Beach: view Ocean Boulevard
from a sightseeing cruise.
West Palm Beach: Lion Country
Safari—roaming animals and petting
zoo.
Boca Raton: Mizner Festival—historic
and cultural six weeks in April and May.

Greater Miami and the Everglades
Miami: tour on the Old Town Trolley.
Museum of Science and Space Transit.
Planetarium: "hands-on" exhibits.
Coconut Grove: fashionable "village".
Coral Gables: interesting attractions.
Metrozoo: animals live on islands
similar to their natural habitats.
Miccosukee Indian Village: native
crafts are made and sold here.
Everglades National Park.

The Keys
Key Largo: John Pennekamp Coral
Reef State Park.
Windley Key: Theater of the Sea.
Islamorada: Whale Harbor Marina.
Long Key: State Recreation Area.
Vaca Key: Crane Point Hammock—
botanical preserve, archaeological digs.
Marathon: Boot Key Harbor.

Lower Keys and Key West
Big Pine Key: Key Deer National
Wildlife Reserve.
Key West: Conch Train provides
informative journey through town.
—Mallory Square: daily sunset
celebration.
—maritime Heritage Museum: treasure
from Spanish galleons.
—Hemingway House: "Papa" lived
here for 30 years.

The South-west
Bonita Springs: a piece of old Florida.
Matanzas Pass Wilderness Preserve:
explore by elevated boardwalk.
Fort Myers: where Edison and Ford
lived next door to each other.
Sanibel: J.N. "Ding" Darling National
Wildlife Refuge—wilderness preserve
in memory of a pioneer conservationist.
Cabbage Key: popular with day trippers.

Central West
Tampa: Busch Gardens—family
entertainment centre and zoo.
St Petersburg: Salvador Dali Museum.
John's Pass Village: boardwalk
landing, fishing fraternity.
Homasassa Springs: State Wildlife
Park with floating underwater
observatory.
Indian Shores: Suncoast Seabird
Sanctuary for sick or injured birds.

The North-east
Jacksonville: Florida National
Pavillion and Metropolitan Park.
Kingsley Plantation State Historic
Site: Florida's oldest plantation.
St Augustine: tour by sightseeing train.
Marineland of Florida: opened in 1938.
White Springs: Stephen Foster State
Folk Culture Center.

The North-west
Cedar Key: lovely residential town.
Panama City: Gulf World—
underwater extravaganza in a tropical
garden.
Marianna: Florida's Caverns State
Park—guided tours of caves.

Going Places with Something Special in Mind

Travellers with special interests can supplement or scrap the standard itineraries, pursuing instead the angles that most appeal to them. Florida offers an incredible number of attractions and it could be quite a problem if you don't know where to start. For visitors with special interests, this selection may help you to choose your favourites from the large menu available.

Botanical Gardens

Many of the gardens provide entertainments or other activities.

1 CYPRESS GARDENS
32 km (20 miles) south-west of Kissimmee. A 19th-century-style garden, with costumed inhabitants, fairground rides, entertainment, nature trails and animal centre.

There is always something going on. This is a Medieval Fair at the Ringling Museum, Sarasota.

2 PRESTON B. BIRD AND MARY HEINLEIN FRUIT AND SPICE PARK
Greater Miami. Museum of living plants and botanical garden with 500 varieties of fruit, nuts and spices from around the world.

3 FAIRCHILD TROPICAL GARDENS
South of Coral Gables. A vine pergola and thousands of tropical plants from many parts of the world. 400 species of palm. Tram tours.

4 FLORIDA INSTITUTE OF TECHNOLOGY
Near Melbourne. The Dent Smith Trail and where 300 varieties of fern can be seen.

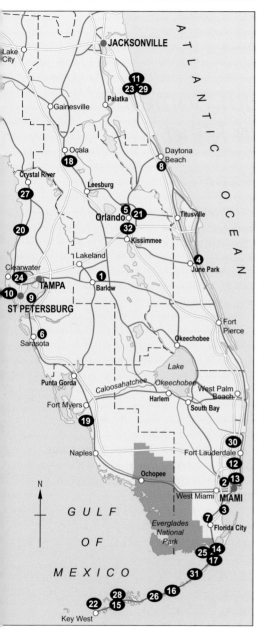

*B*otanical gardens
*(1–11), water attractions
(12–21) and places to see
marine life (22–32).*

5 LEU GARDENS
In downtown Orlando, the gardens feature orchids, camellias and roses.

6 MARIE SELBY BOTANICAL GARDENS
Sarasota. Plants from the tropics. Outstanding collection of orchids.

7 ORCHID JUNGLE
At Homestead, the southernmost part of Miami. Blossoms from almost every part of the world.

8 SUGAR MILL GARDENS
At Port Orange. Collections of flowering trees and other flora.

9 SUNKEN GARDENS
Tropical showplace at St Petersburg, with more than 5,000 flowers, plants and exotic birds and animals.

10 TIKI GARDENS
Indian Shores, St Petersburg. Polynesian gardens with adventure trail.

11 WASHINGTON OAKS STATE GARDENS
St Augustine. Ornamental gardens along the riverside.

Water Attractions

A range of unusual entertainments on a watery theme are offered in Florida.

12 ATLANTIS, THE WATER KINGDOM
Fort Lauderdale. There are 80 exciting water rides and chutes. Sample the Raging Rampage, if you dare!

13 BISCAYNE NATIONAL UNDERWATER PARK
Greater Miami. Canoe rentals, scuba diving and family snorkelling trips can be organized. Glass-bottomed boats to view the high coral reefs and exotic fish.

14 JULES' UNDERSEA LODGE
Key Largo. An underwater dining room and entertainment centre. Six guests at a time can explore the lagoon, day or night, using tethered breathing equipment.

15 LOOE KEY NATIONAL MARINE SANCTUARY
Lower Keys. Spectacular shallow-water diving. Annual underwater music festival.

16 SAN PEDRO UNDERWATER PARK
Near Indian Key. The remains of a Spanish galleon, wrecked in 1733, lie here. Submarine historic trail for divers through the vessel's wooden hull.

17 JOHN PENNEKAMP CORAL REEF STATE PARK
Key Largo. 300 species of fish and over 40 species of coral. Camping and watersports.

18 SILVER SPRINGS
Ocala. Awe-inspiring geological happening. Trips in glass-bottomed boats to see the springs.

19 WALTZING WATERS
South of Fort Myers. A novel entertainment with water, light and music. Fantastic colourful effects with lasers and fountains.

20 WEEKI WACHEE SPRING COMPLEX
South of Homasassa. Entertainment by mermaids.

21 WET 'N' WILD
Orlando. Water shute, mega slide and rapids. Water maze.

Marine Life

The marine attractions in Florida are in a class of their own.

22 AQUARIUM
Key West. Exhibits include a living coral reef, several tanks of sharks and a turtle pool.

23 ALLIGATOR FARM
St Augustine. Crocodiles and alligators appear in reptile shows. Other creatures include giant tortoises.

24 CLEARWATER MARINE SCIENCE CENTER
"Headstart" programme for baby turtles. Evening turtle walks.

25 DOLPHIN PLUS
Key Largo. Swimming with the dolphins and an informative programme on endangered marine life.

26 DOLPHIN RESEARCH CENTER
Grassy Key, near Marathon. Refuge for sick and injured dolphins. Swimming with the dolphins.

27 HOMASASSA SPRINGS STATE WILDLIFE PARK
Floating underwater observatory. Haven for manatees.

28 LOOE KEY NATIONAL MARINE SANCTUARY
Coral reef with a rich and diverse population of plant and animal life. Skin divers and scuba enthusiasts can arrange trips with dive centres. Fish can also be viewed from the surface as the water is very clear.

29 MARINELAND OF FLORIDA
St Augustine. The state's original marine life attraction, opened in 1938. Porpoises, manatees, turtles, dolphins, sharks, electric eels in oceanariums. Regular performances.

30 OCEAN WORLD
Fort Lauderdale. Performing sealions and porpoises; sharks and sea turtles on display.

31 THEATRE OF THE SEA
Islamorada. Visitors can join the dolphins in the water. Reservations are required.

32 SEA WORLD
Orlando. Leading marine life park, best known for the performing killer whales. At "Penguin Encounter" you can get a good view of the birds. Also sharks, dolphins, walruses, otters and manatees.

Bird Parks and Sanctuaries

Florida could be considered a haven for ornithologists as it is for overwintering birds.

1 BLUE HOLE
Big Pine Key. Freshwater man-made lake. Good variety of birdlife, which includes little blue herons, green-backed herons and gallinules.

2 GREAT WHITE HERON REFUGE
Big Pine Key. Offers protection to a number of rare and endangered species.

3 JUPITER ISLAND
Audubon Society bird preserve.

4 MERRITT ISLAND NATIONAL WILDLIFE REFUGE
Cape Canaveral. Home to more than 200 species of bird.

5 PARROT JUNGLE AND GARDENS
South Dade. Over 1,000 parrots, macaws and related species. Flamingoes.

6 PELICAN ISLAND
Indian River. First national wildlife refuge in the US. Important sanctuary for brown pelican.

7 SUNCOAST SEABIRD SANCTUARY
Indian Shores, St Petersburg. Refuge for injured and crippled birds. Attracts bird watchers, researchers, wildlife artists and photographers. More than 40 different species.

Zoos and Wildlife

Busch Gardens is one of the best US zoos and there is a splendid range of animal preserves. Many have petting zoos for small children.

8 BREVARD ZOO
Melbourne. More than 100 animal species, including the Florida panther.

9 BUSCH GARDENS
Tampa. One of America's top four zoos. More than 3,300 animals are displayed in eight distinctly themed African sections. Endangered species featured in natural habitat exhibits.

10 J.N. "DING" DARLING NATIONAL WILDLIFE REFUGE
Captiva and Sanibel. Just after dawn or before dusk wildlife emerges on the Wildlife Drive. Alligator habitat.

11 DREHER PARK ZOO
West Palm Beach. Nearly 100 animal species, nature trails and a picnic area.

12 EVERGLADES WONDER GARDENS
Bonita Springs. Bears, otters, deer, alligators, snakes, birds of prey and wading birds.

13 JUNGLE LARRY'S ZOOLOGICAL PARK
Naples. 30-minute tour by tram. Animal shows, a petting zoo and a conservation programme for endangered species.

14 KEY DEER NATIONAL WILDLIFE REFUGE
300 miniature deer are protected on the Keys by a hunting and overnight camping ban, strictly enforced speed limits and dog-leash regulations.

15 LION COUNTRY SAFARI
West Palm Beach. Roaming animals, a petting zoo, a dinosaur exhibit.

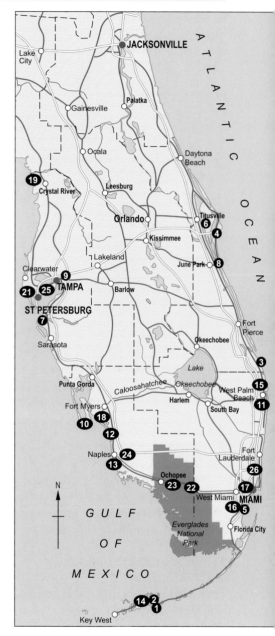

*B*ird parks and sanctuaries (1–7), zoos (8–18) and native American Indian sites (19–26) across Florida.

16 METROZOO
South Miami. Large collection of animals include koala bears and rare white Bengal tigers.

17 MONKEY JUNGLE
South Miami. Trained chimps and monkeys give daily talent shows.

18 TELEGRAPH CYPRESS SWAMP
Fort Myers. Wild turkeys and buffalo can be seen by swamp buggy.

Indian Country

There are a number of fascinating American Indian villages and sites in Florida.

19 CRYSTAL RIVER STATE ARCHAEOLOGICAL SITE
Inverness. Indian mound complex of pre-Columbian Indians from 200 BC to AD 1400.

20 INDIAN TEMPLE MOUND MUSEUM
Fort Walton. National historic landmark depicting more than 10,000 years of South-east Indians' life in the area (off map in north-west Florida).

21 MADIRA BICKEL MOUND HISTORIC MEMORIAL
Terra Ceia. Indian burial mound and temple site nearby. Artefacts found in the area are on display here.

22 MICCOSUKEE INDIAN VILLAGE
Everglades. Indian crafts of wood carving, basket weaving, doll-making and patchwork and beadwork. Native products sold to public. Indian museum showing films and displaying artefacts from different tribes.

23 OCHOPEE
Indian village 13 km (8 miles) from Monroe Station.

24 OSCEOLAS
Near Naples. Picturesque settlement where you can learn some authentic Indian history.

25 PHILIPPE PARK
Safety Harbor on Tampa Bay. Site of a settlement of Timucan Indians. A large Indian ceremonial mound is preserved in the park.

26 SEMINOLE NATIVE VILLAGE
Hollywood. Native animals. Museum of paintings of the Indian way of life. Gamble for high stakes in the federally protected bingo hall.

Art and Craft

1 APPLETON MUSEUM OF FINE ARTS
Ocala.

2 BASS MUSEUM OF FINE ART
Miami Beach. Permanent collection of European works, covering seven centuries. Sculptures, textiles, furniture and the decorative arts are all represented.

3 CENTER FOR FINE ARTS
Metro-Dade Cultural Center, Miami. Major exhibits from museums and art collections around the world.

4 CORNELL FINE ARTS MUSEUM
Rollins College in Winter Park, Greater Orlando. Collections of paintings by European old masters and 19th-century American artists.

5 EAST MARTELLO GALLERY AND MUSEUM
Folk art collections and exhibits of early Key West life are on display.

6 ECC GALLERY OF FINE ART
Fort Myers. Internationally known artists displayed.

7 JACKSONVILLE ART MUSEUM
Jacksonville. Contemporary paintings, sculptures, Oriental porcelain and pre-Columbian artefacts.

8 LEE COUNTY ARTS CENTER
Fort Myers. Features the work of local artists and craftsmen.

Offbeat Museums

Museums with a definite theme, or with a difference.

9 AMERICAN POLICE HALL OF FAME AND MUSEUM
Miami Beach. Items from the past and present and law enforcement memorabilia on display.

10 BREVARD ART CENTER AND MUSEUM
Melbourne. Touch gallery for the visually handicapped.

11 CARTOON MUSEUM
Orlando. Newspaper and magazine cartoons, with original artwork.

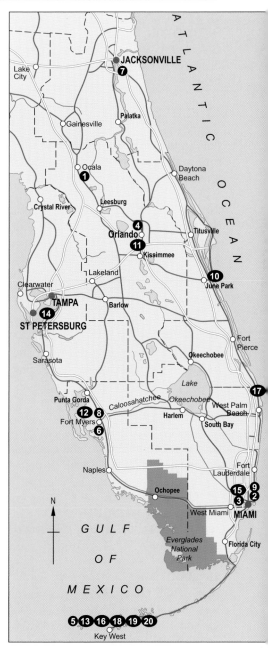

Art and craft centres (1–8) and offbeat museums (9–20) in Florida.

12 FORT MYERS HISTORICAL MUSEUM
Calusa and Seminole Indian civilizations from 1200 BC to 1913 depicted here.

13 FORT ZACHARY TAYLOR
Key West. One of four red-brick forts built in the latter part of the 19th century to protect America's strategically important southernmost shore.

14 GREAT EXPLORATIONS
St Petersburg. Six "hands on" areas in which visitors can pit their wits against a series of challenging exhibits.

15 HISTORICAL MUSEUM OF SOUTHERN FLORIDA
In the metro-Dade Cultural Center Miami. A fascinating insight into the region's past. Canoe trips at sunset and by moonlight, and walking and cycling tours.

16 LIGHTHOUSE AND MILITARY MUSEUM
Key West. Built in 1825 and contains maritime and navigational exhibits.

17 LOXAHATCHEE HISTORICAL MUSEUM
Jupiter. Built in the style of the pioneer days.

18 MARITIME HERITAGE MUSEUM
Key West. Large collection of gold, silver and other treasures recovered from Spanish galleons wrecked long ago along Florida's reef.

19 SLOPPY JOE'S BAR
Key West. The bar is plastered with old photographs of Hemingway and "Papa" bric-a-brac.

20 WRECKERS' MUSEUM
Key West. This is the oldest house in the area (1829). "Home" of a wrecker captain.

Open House

A number of historic houses and houses of the famous are open to the public.

1 AMSTERDAM CURRY MANSION
Classic Key West home open to visitors, dating from 1855. Beautifully furnished with valuable antiques.

2 AUDUBON HOUSE
Named after the ornithologist and painter John Audubon, who visited Key West for a few weeks in 1832. Numerous original engravings by John Audubon, including many from his famous Birds of America "double elephant" folio.

3 EDISON AND FORD HOUSES
Fort Myers. Thomas Edison and Henry Ford lived next door to one another in the 1920s. Both houses are restored to their original styles. The Edison home is now a museum and the tropical gardens contain some 6,000 tree and plant species.

4 HEMINGWAY HOUSE
Possibly Key West's major attraction. The house's contents are from Spain, Africa and Cuba. It has a large, restful garden.

5 LITTLE WHITE HOUSE
Key West. House of Harry S. Truman, the former President, in what was Truman Annex Navy base.

6 ROCKEFELLER HOME
Casements, Ormond Beach. Former winter home of the multi-millionaire John D. Rockefeller.

Children's Corner

More than most places, Florida seems to make a special effort to keep children informed and entertained. Here are just a few of them.

7 CHILDREN'S MUSEUM OF THE FLORIDA KEYS
Indoor and outdoor exhibition with 10 interactive exhibits demonstrating the Keys' unique ecology.

8 DISCOVERY CENTRE
Downtown Fort Lauderdale's museum for children.

9 LIONEL TRAIN AND SEASHELL MUSEUM
Sarasota. Operational toy trains and a collection of shells and coral from around the world.

10 LONDON WAX MUSEUM
St Petersburg. The noteworthy and the notorious from past and present are portrayed in wax.

11 MAGIC KINGDOM
Disney World, Orlando. Forty-five major shows and adventures, covering seven "lands"; Main Street, USA; Adventureland; Frontierland; Liberty

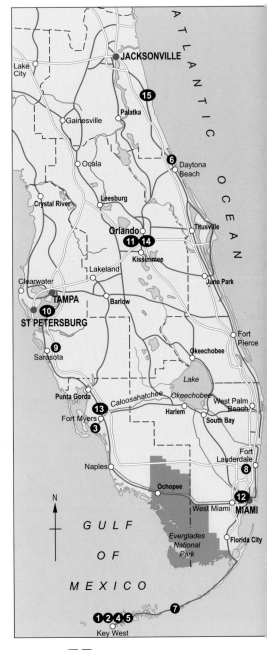

*H*istoric open houses *(1–6) and places to entertain and inform children (7–15).*

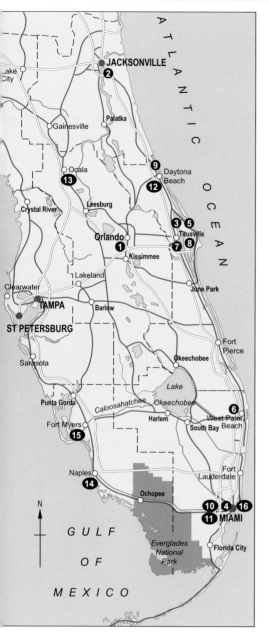

Space and science centres (1–8) and places of interest to the transport enthusiast (9–16).

Square; Fantasyland; Tomorrowland and Mickey's Starland.

12 MIAMI YOUTH MUSEUM
Guided tours by reservation only.

13 NATURE'S WONDERLAND CHILDREN'S MUSEUM
North Fort Myers. Hundreds of playthings from the past and present. A barrier reef reconstruction.

14 ORANGE COUNTY FIRE MUSEUM
Orlando. Fire station dating from 1926.

15 POTTERS WAX MUSEUM
St Augustine. Waxwork figures from history and waxworks theatre.

Space and Science

A Mecca for space enthusiasts at J.F. Kennedy Space Center, of course. Also, several of the science museums in Florida have splendid shows in their planetariums.

1 EPCOT CENTER
Disney World, Orlando. International exposition with two main areas: Future World, showing achievements of imagination and technology; World Showcase, presenting the culture, entertainment, crafts and architecture of various nations.

2 JACKSONVILLE MUSEUM OF SCIENCE AND HISTORY
Planetarium showing cosmic concerts. Displays on Florida history and wildlife.

54

3 SPACEPORT USA, KENNEDY SPACE CENTER

Near Titusville. Gallery of Space Flight, Rocket Garden, space-related exhibits at the Galaxy Centre, plus multi-media presentations.

4 MIAMI MUSEUM OF SCIENCE AND SPACE TRANSIT PLANETARIUM

Hands-on exhibits. State-of-the-art astronomy and laser shows daily at the planetarium. Observatory.

5 PATRICK AIR FORCE BASE

Near Titusville. Involved in guided missile and Space Shuttle programmes.

6 SOUTH FLORIDA SCIENCE MUSEUM

West Palm Beach. Hands-on exhibits, and aquarium and planetarium.

7 UNITED STATES ASTRONAUT HALL OF FAME

Near Titusville. Memorabilia from the early days of space flight and later missions.

8 US SPACE CAMP TRAINING CENTRE

Near Titusville. Five-day sessions of space orientation and astronaut training for youngsters. Visitors can watch.

History of Transport

Something of interest in the fields of aviation, railroads and motoring.

9 BIRTHPLACE OF SPEED MUSEUM

Ormond Beach. For motor-racing enthusiasts to trace the history of the sport.

10 CAULEY SQUARE

Greater Miami. Renovated railroad village where special events are staged.

11 GOLD COAST RAILROAD AND MUSEUM

Greater Miami. The train is pulled by a 1913 steam locomotive and the ride lasts half an hour. Steam and diesel engines and railroad cars.

12 HALIFAX HISTORICAL MUSEUM

Downtown Daytona. Replicas and memorabilia from the early days of beach racing.

13 MUSEUM OF DRAG RACING

Ocala.

14 NAPLES DEPOT

Naples. This is the old railroad station where restored storerooms and box cars make a quaint place to shop.

15 SEMINOLE GULF RAILWAY

The three-hour excursion train trip between Naples and Fort Myers includes an enjoyable meal.

16 WEEKS AIR MUSEUM

Greater Miami. The 35 aircraft on display have been restored to their former glory and preserved.

Mickey Mouse, Museums and Manatees

Take a trip to meet Florida's most famous inhabitant, Mickey Mouse (at Walt Disney World) and marvel at the performing killer whales at Sea World. Visit gracious Orlando for museums, art galleries and a gourmet's selection of restaurants. And if it all gets too much, hire a boat and a fishing line, or paddle on a canoe down river and take a look at the other inhabitants of central Florida— the indigenous wildlife.

The fact that central Florida has the world's greatest concentration of man-made attractions doesn't mean the area is all theme parks and urban sprawl. In a state the size of England and Wales—some 150,220 km² (58,000 square miles)—and a population of 10 million, a lot of territory is occupied by forests, water and wildlife. Central Florida has its share of accessible hiking trails and canoe routes through forest and jungle terrain, and there are great freshwater fishing opportunities.

Walt Disney World has come to epitomize central Florida, but the region has many other attractions.

Regard central Florida as extending from Ocala in the north to Sebring and Lake Placid in the south and, broadly speaking, from east to west to within about 32 km (20 miles) of each coastline. Tourism is by no means the only industry between these points. Cattle-rearing, racehorse breeding and training, citrus growing and some of the new high-tech industries are among other earners.

Orlando is on I-4, the road they call Fantasy Highway because it links the works of the area's "Imagineers" with the wondrous reality of the Kennedy Space Center to the east and the hedonist delights of the Gulf Coast to the west. The Atlantic is about an hour by car, and it will take about two hours to drive to the Gulf of Mexico.

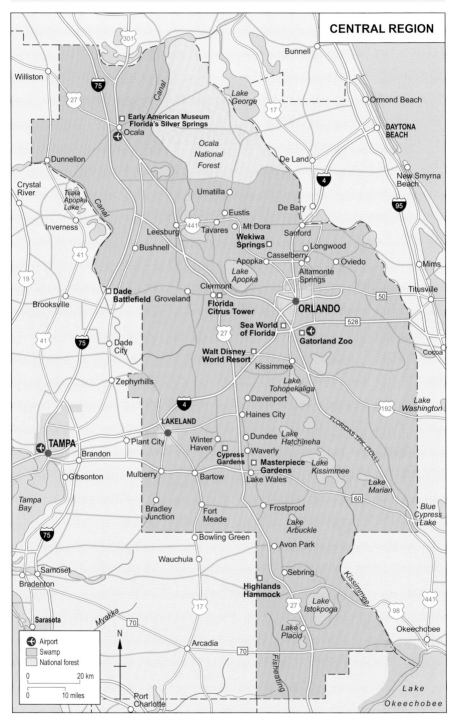

CENTRAL REGION

Williston
Bunnell
Ormond Beach
Lake George
DAYTONA BEACH
Early American Museum
Florida's Silver Springs
Ocala
Dunnellon
Ocala National Forest
De Land
New Smyrna Beach
Crystal River
Tsala Apopka Lake
Umatilla
De Bary
Inverness
Eustis
Mt Dora
Sanford
Leesburg
Tavares
Wekiwa Springs
Longwood
Bushnell
Apopka
Casselberry
Oviedo
Mims
Lake Apopka
Altamonte Springs
Brooksville
Dade Battlefield
Groveland
Clermont
ORLANDO
Titusville
Florida Citrus Tower
Sea World of Florida
Gatorland Zoo
Dade City
Walt Disney World Resort
Cocoa
Zephyrhills
Kissimmee
Lake Tohopekaliga
Davenport
Lake Washington
Haines City
LAKELAND
Plant City
Winter Haven
Dundee
Lake Hatchineha
TAMPA
Brandon
Cypress Gardens
Waverly
Masterpiece Gardens
Lake Kissimmee
Gibsonton
Mulberry
Bartow
Lake Wales
Lake Marian
Tampa Bay
Bradley Junction
Fort Meade
Frostproof
Blue Cypress Lake
Lake Arbuckle
Bowling Green
Avon Park
Wauchula
Samoset
Sebring
Bradenton
Highlands Hammock
Lake Istokpoga
Okeechobee
Sarasota
Lake Placid
Arcadia
N

Airport
Swamp
National forest

0   20 km
0   10 miles

Port Charlotte

Lake Okeechobee

Kissimmee
Myakka
Fisheating
FLORIDAS TPK (TOLL)

*M*ap of Central Florida, showing the main roads and towns.

Less than 30 years ago Orlando was just another sleepy city in America's Deep South, a marketing centre and railhead for the surrounding belt of orange and lemon groves that contributed to much of the state's wealth at that time. The city had an inauspicious start. It was originally named Jernigan, after one Aaron Jernigan who settled there in 1842, having moved from the neighbouring state of Georgia. Legend has it that the city's name was changed in 1857 to honour a soldier, Orlando Reeves, said to have died from an arrow wound while warning the infant community of an Indian attack. Today, Orlando is the seat of Orange County which until

*W*ho dares to stick his head in the jaws of Jaws? People love to be photographed doing the heroics at Universal Studios.

1845 was known, more ominously perhaps, as Mosquito County.

Metropolitan Orlando, straddling Orange, Osceola and Seminole Counties, has a population of just over one million, and statistics gathered by the Florida Department of Labor and Security leave little doubt about the impact of tourism on the area. Some 58,000 people are employed in the amusement/recreation industry, 27,000 work in hotels and lodgings, and about 40,000 in restaurants. Overall, tourism-related employment accounts for about one job in five. At the start of the 1990s, the area was attracting more than 11 million visitors a year, and in an average 12 months the tourists spent some $5.5 billion.What do they come to see, and what do they find to spend their money on?

The Orlando area is best known as the home of Walt Disney World, Sea World, Cypress Gardens, Disney-MGM Studios Theme Park, and Universal Studios Florida, but there are some 50 other attractions, with more constantly being developed. Here, it can truly be said, there is something for everyone.

Walt Disney World

Until 1967 few people would have imagined that a 11,330-hectare (28,000-acre) area of swampland and forest to the west of Orlando would have had much potential for anything more ambitious than an alligator. Today, it is a huge complex of resorts and attractions at Lake Buena Vista, some 20 minutes by car from Orlando. Officially, it is still known as the Reedy Creek Improvement District, the name it was given in 1967 when the state of Florida gave permission for development to go ahead, but it is known everywhere as Walt Disney World.

The Walt Disney World Vacation Kingdom—to give it its full title—has grown dramatically since October 1971 when the Magic Kingdom, first of the theme parks, opened. Featuring 45 "adventures", with attractions, restaurants and shops based on favourite Disney

A paddle steamer provides a leisurely cruise through the Magic Kingdom.

themes—everything from Mickey Mouse and Cinderella to a jungle cruise, pirates and Wild West gunmen—the Magic Kingdom was an instant success and set the pace for all that was to follow. Since then, the World's theme park adventures have quadrupled with the opening of the Epcot Center in 1982, and the Disney-MGM Studios and Pleasure Island in 1990. There are sporting and convention facilities, the world's fifth largest merchant fleet and more than 30,000 employees. Walt Disney World Village has some 30 shops, 10 restaurants, a jazz lounge and a riverboat landing stage.

There are about a dozen hotels within the Walt Disney World boundaries, as well as the Fort Wilderness campground with 1,200 pitches. The hotels represent an astonishing total of close on 13,000 bedrooms—Orlando as a whole has more than 70,000. Three new developments due to open before late1992 will add more than 4,000 additional rooms. In 1980, Walt Disney World offered fewer than 4,500 bedrooms in seven hotels. Properties

The monorail goes between the Magic Kingdom and Epcot Center— and a good view of the sights.

opened since then include the 900-room Disney's Grand Floridian Beach Resort and the Caribbean Beach Resort, both offering accommodation and facilities with a specific theme. The luxurious Grand Floridian presents the ambience of turn-of-the-century Florida, while the more modest Caribbean Beach, not surprisingly, has swaying palms and talc-white sands.

Four new hotels which opened in 1990 have easy access to the Epcot Center through an International Gateway which allows guests to travel by tram or walkway to a theme-park entrance near the French pavilion in World Showcase. Water taxis also link the hotels with the Disney-MGM Studios. Innovative transport links have always been a feature at Walt Disney World. Ever since the 1970s, for example, any guests staying at the Contemporary Resort Hotel have had the convenience of a monorail station situated right in the lobby. An advantage of booking into on-site accommodation is that guests get free shuttle bus transportation to attractions throughout Walt Disney World.

In general, the Magic Kingdom will appeal principally to families with young children, while Epcot—the Experimental Prototype Community of Tomorrow—has a more educational appeal. The emphasis in each case, though, is on entertainment, and it is unlikely that anyone—of any age or inclination—will be bored in either place.

The Magic Kingdom covers 40 hectares (100 acres). Its 45 major shows and adventures cover seven "lands": Main Street, USA; Adventureland; Frontierland; Liberty Square; Fantasyland; Tomorrowland; and Mickey's Starland, which opened in 1988 as Mickey's Birthdayland, to mark the 60th year of Mickey Mouse and the first new "land" since 1971. The Kingdom's many popular attractions include Mickey Mouse's House in Starland, Pirates of the Caribbean—lots of smoking pistols and clashing cutlasses—the crazy Big Thunder Mountain Railroad, Haunted Mansion and Space Mountain. Mickey Mouse and other Disney characters make frequent appearances, joining bands, singers, daily parades and street-corner performers.

Epcot Center is a 105-hectare (260-acre) international exposition with two main areas. Future World shows achievements of imagination and technology. This is where you will find that giant golf ball, the communications pavilion which has come to represent the whole of Florida, it seems, let alone the world of Disney. World Showcase presents the culture, entertainment, crafts and architecture of various nations set in pavilions surrounding a lagoon. Countries represented at present are: the United Kingdom, Canada, France, Morocco, Japan, Italy, Germany, China, Mexico and Norway, as well as the United States. Don't be fooled by that word "exposition". Epcot is no dry trade fair. Each pavilion, in both sections, is an exciting and entertaining experience, with mind-blowing technology and spectacular illusions.

Pleasure Island, a night-life complex where New Year's Eve is celebrated 365 days a year in themed bars, nightclubs and restaurants, is beautifully stage-managed—pure Disney hype that night after night builds up the once-a-year atmosphere of New Year's Eve. The 2-hectare (5-acre) complex offers "a new kind of night-life experience" in a waterfront setting inspired by the fabled sail-making magnate, Merriweather Adam Pleasure. The key word is "fabled", for Pleasure Island, it must be remembered, is a product of that amazing enterprise, Walt Disney Imagineering, which created the legend of Pleasure, an adventurous wag who built his sail-making business on the island during the Edwardian heyday of leisure yachting.

The millionaire sail-maker, the story goes, disappeared during a voyage round the world and his industrial complex fell into decay. Then along came the Imagineers and created the nightlife paradise from the island's abandoned lofts, warehouses and factories, turning them into a themed entertainment park featuring comedy and magic, live dance bands, high-tech video entertainment and a rockin' roller-skating rink. At the XZFR (pronounced "zephyr") Rockin' Roller Drome, guests can dance or roller-skate into the future in a wind tunnel and laboratory which you must believe was once used by Pleasure to develop a fantastic flying machine. A live band, the Time Pilots, play in a Starpod hovering beneath a giant "mother ship" above the main dance floor.

The Adventurers' Club, once a retreat for Pleasure's affluent yachting clientele, is Pall Mall gone totally mad, with wandering eccentrics chattering to themselves, walls covered with authentic African and Far Eastern masks, and the ghost of a headless explorer.

Mannequins Dance Palace has a strange, backstage atmosphere. Set in a cavernous warehouse once used to store Pleasure's canvas and sewing equipment, according to the story, the Palace now has a turntable dance floor which is surrounded by stage rigging, lights and catwalks.

HyperActive, an artificial intelligence, controls the giant video game that is Videopolis East, where teenage frolickers interact with 170 video screens to control flashing lights and other atmospheric effects.

The Neon Armadillo Bar tempts visitors with the flavour of the American South-west. There are toe-tappin' Country 'n' Western bands, a balcony lookout and a bathtub packed with ice to keep the beer cold. The Empress Lilly

Riverboat has a quartet of authentic New Orleans jazz performers, and roving the entire complex is the five-piece Pleasure Island Philharmonic, a raucous group of musicians who barge into the nightclubs and bars and take over whenever the spirit moves them.

Midnight comes at 11 p.m.—the island, of course, is on Disney Time—and as the amplified countdown begins everyone moves into the main street. Fireworks light up the night sky, cannon shoot out a blizzard of confetti, and things really start moving.

Disney-MGM Studios Theme Park was the Disney Corporation's response to Universal Studios' announcement that it was to open a combined working film studio and entertainment park in Orlando in 1990. The Disney enterprise opened first, but shows signs of a rather rushed development. In layout it is very similar to the

Magic Kingdom, and if you've been to one you'll have little trouble finding your way about the other. But it is still a fun place to visit, and those with a low inhibition factor will have a great time, joining in "audience participation" stunts and acting their hearts out in front of the cameras.

Close to the other major Disney World attractions, the Disney-MGM Studios Park is a whimsical reconstruction of Tinseltown in its Art-Deco heyday. The fun begins as visitors stroll down Hollywood Boulevard, meeting silver-screen hopefuls, autograph hunters, gossip columnists and occasionally the "stars" themselves. There's a backstreet speakeasy where bit players gather to chat wistfully about the big role they just failed to get.

You can watch the Muppets live, you can actually feel the heat when an ammunition dump blows up during the Indiana Jones Epic Stunt Spectacular. Star Tours is a thrilling adventure ride in a Star Wars spaceship captained by an inexperienced robot who soon gets lost among comets, whirling ice fragments, a black hole and an alien fleet. It's great stuff and a brilliant illusion for young and old.

Walt Disney World provides a passport to a number of different countries in the World Showcase. An entertainer attracts visitors to the Chinese Pavilion.

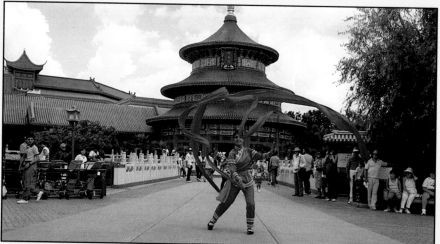

Universal Studios

On the outskirts of Orlando itself, near the junction of I-4 and the Florida Turnpike, Universal Studios Florida has more of the feel of a working film studio, and you can take tours of sets where production work is taking place—as, indeed, you can at Disney-MGM. Universal, though, is the largest working studio outside Hollywood, with more than 40 backlot locales, six state-of-the-art sound stages and a full range of technical and production services, including on-site stunt crews.

One of the exciting stunts performed daily at Universal Studios.

There are lots of exciting and interesting opportunities to take part in the make-believe at Universal Studios. Film stars like W.C. Fields, Humphrey Bogart and Marilyn Monroe roam the streets, cafés and restaurants. You can bump into the likes of Woody Woodpecker and Yogi Bear—or Dracula and Wolfman—around any corner. You can wander the streets of San Francisco, the New York waterfront or Amity Village, and in the Studio Commissary or Mel's Drive-In (from *American Graffiti*) you can rub shoulders with a host of stars. You can experience an earthquake, meet King Kong and watch spectacular stunts involving an exploding seaplane and a speedboat that crashes full throttle into a wall of flames.

Riding the Dolphin at Sea World, Orlando. Whales, walruses and other marine creatures with their trainers provide some amazing entertainment.

Sea World

Another of Orlando's best-known attractions, and said to be the world's leading marine life park, Sea World is a ten-minute drive south of the city, close to the junction of I-4 and the Beeline Expressway. You'll need to set aside eight hours to cover Sea World's 54 hectares (135 acres), seven major shows, and 23 educational exhibits. As with other Florida theme parks, a single admission fee covers everything, although there is a small additional charge to go up the 130-m (400-ft) rotating Sky Tower.

Sea World is probably best known for its performing killer whales, who do their tricks in a pool as deep as a three-storey building, containing 27,275 million litres (6 million gallons) of water and surrounded by a 5,200-seat stadium. There is also "Penguin Encounter" where hundreds of the delightful Antarctic creatures live in a carefully re-created environment in which man-made snow falls gently as the birds dive and swim. Visitors actually get a better view of the birds than they would in the natural state because the viewing area is below the surface of the water, set behind a tough acrylic screen.

Sharks, dolphins, walruses, otters, manatees—the gentle sea cows native to Florida waters—can all be studied at close quarters, as can Beluga and Pacific black whales.

Lots of people evidently fancy themselves as trainers at Sea World. More than 300 hopefuls write in each year to

Making a splash at Sea World. This whale plays to the crowd, and he isn't the only one to get wet.

ask if they can join the team that puts on the killer-whale show. Amazingly, many of them can't even swim.

"You have to be an excellent swimmer in this job, of course", says Chuck Tompkins, manager of Sea World's animal training department. "You also have to be a good public speaker, capable of standing comfortably and communicating effectively in front of 5,000 people. Most important of all, you have to be able to build a rapport with an animal. Not everyone has a knack for working with animals. You see some people who have a hard time petting the dog—they're just not comfortable around animals.

"Killer whales are much more intelligent than a dog, and you have to treat them with much more respect because of their intelligence and their size," Chuck adds. "The only problem is their size. We have a killer whale here that weighs 5,440 kg (12,000 lb). If you're in his way when he's swimming, or if he drops a pectoral flipper, you could be in trouble."

It's scarcely surprising that only one or two people in a hundred have the qualities to join Sea World's team of trainers—and they still have to survive a six-month trial.

"It's not a job you step into and there you are on stage, working with killer whales," Chuck emphasizes. "It could be a couple of years before you're actually in the water, performing with them. Everybody wants to do this job, but not many can."

Orlando

Theme parks and performing animals aside, the city of Orlando will come as a pleasant surprise to those visiting it for the first time. For a start, it is much bigger, much more pleasant, than might be imagined. And it does

66

not depend solely on tourism for its daily bread. Indeed, the city's computer-based industry is so strong that the area has been dubbed the "Silicon Swamp". In the ten years between 1980 and 1990 employment in the area's high technology industries increased by 114 per cent, compared with 40 per cent for the United States as a whole. Business support services— major financial institutions and international law specialists particularly— flourish, and the person who coined the phrase "Orlando—the city with no reason to be" must be kicking himself, if not actually turning in his grave.

Downtown Orlando, urbane as a pin-striped suit, spreads itself grandly around Lake Eola—by no means a swamp, with spectacular fountain and horse-drawn carriage rides. Oddly enough, this is not the area that most overseas visitors see, locked as they are into the theme parks and attractions outside the city. The nearest most tourists venture to the real heart of

Marching Ducks

Just around the corner from Sea World, the Peabody Hotel on International Drive has its own eccentric team of performing animals—a squad of carefully bred and well-pampered mallards who play the major role in a daily ceremony that means almost as much to Orlando as the Changing of the Guard does to London.

Every morning at eleven o'clock sharp the five mallards—four hens led by a drake—leave the Royal Duck Palace on the Peabody's recreation floor, descend in an exclusively reserved lift, and march along a red carpet to the strains of John Philip Sousa's *The King Cotton March*. That's the one with the words "Have a care for our web-footed friends..."The carpet leads them to a marble fountain, where they spend a happy splashy time until 5 p.m. when they march back to their palace.

The Peabody Ducks are no ordinary mallards. They belong to an exclusive blood line that goes back more than 50 years. Their palace is a $50,000 air-conditioned duck pen, furnished in Italian marble, and they have a specially qualified minder—Duck Master Keith Lauby, a graduate in wildlife biology.

The Peabody is so proud of its mallards that a duck logo graces the top of the 27-storey hotel, a landmark for miles. The story began in the 1930s when the then manager of the Peabody at Memphis, Tennessee, Frank Schutt, was a keen duck hunter. In those days they used live mallards as decoys, and one night the manager and his chums returned from a duck-hunting trip, and for a prank, placed their decoys in the hotel lobby fountain. The mallards and the hotel guests took to the notion like...well, you know. And a tradition was born. Soon afterwards the Peabody Memphis hired an animal trainer to look after the ducks.

Keith Lauby began his job as Duck Master when the Peabody Orlando opened in 1986. A graduate of Ohio State University, he had previously been working as an animal care specialist at Sea World.

"We have two teams of ducks," says Keith. "One here and another at the Peabody duck farm, just outside the city. They take turns. Part of my job is to oversee their breeding programme to make sure that future hotel guests will continue to enjoy the Peabody ducks."

Whatever you do, though, don't ask for roast duck in the Peabody restaurants. Even with all those Florida oranges, it never appears on the menu.

Orlando—a stately, tree-shaded centre of wide avenues, lazily extravagant architecture and a deceptively sleepy-eyed Deep South ambience—is **Church Street Station**, the traditional centre of the city. This is where it all began in the 1890s with a street of buildings associated with a curious railroad station, built of brick in the style of central Europe.

Church Street's original hotels, warehouses and shops have now been restored into a complex of themed saloons, restaurants and shopping arcades. Out on the street, the only cars to be found are such historic vehicles as a 1932 Rolls-Royce tourer, a 1933 Deusenberg limousine and a Packard of the same year. Inside the saloons and restaurants there is vintage music.

Rosie O'Grady's Good Time Emporium is locked in a time warp between the Gay Nineties and the Roaring Twenties. It's a rip-roaring saloon with brass chandeliers, etched mirrors, leaded glass, red velvet benches, cast-

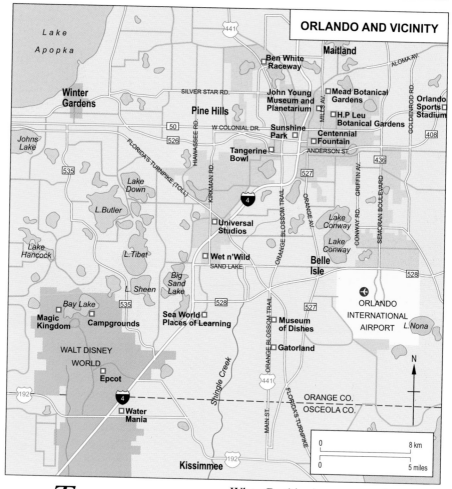

Town plan of Orlando.

Labels on the map:

Lake Apopka

ORLANDO AND VICINITY

Maitland

Ben White Raceway

Winter Gardens

SILVER STAR RD.

John Young Museum and Planetarium

Mead Botanical Gardens

Orlando Sports Stadium

Pine Hills

H.P Leu Botanical Gardens

Johns Lake

W COLONIAL DR.

Sunshine Park

Centennial Fountain

Tangerine Bowl

ANDERSON ST.

Lake Down

L. Butler

Universal Studios

Lake Conway

Lake Conway

Lake Hancock

L. Tibet

Wet n'Wild

SAND LAKE

Belle Isle

Big Sand Lake

L. Sheen

Bay Lake

Magic Kingdom

Campgrounds

Sea World

Places of Learning

Museum of Dishes

ORLANDO INTERNATIONAL AIRPORT

L. Nona

WALT DISNEY WORLD

Epcot

Gatorland

Water Mania

Shingle Creek

ORANGE CO.
OSCEOLA CO.

Kissimmee

N

0   8 km
0   5 miles

iron tables and bentwood chairs. Each piece of furniture is a genuine antique, from places as diverse as Chicago, Illinois, and Burnley, Lancashire.

At **Rosie's rocks** there are strumming banjos, bar-top can-can girls and Charleston dancers. In addition, there is Rosie O'Grady's Good-time Jazz Band, and Ruth Crews, described as the Last of the Red Hot Mamas.

When Ruthie sings a song, they say, it stays sung.

The **Cheyenne Saloon and Opera House** is the West at its wildest, with Country 'n' Western music in Grand Ole Opry style. When you are tired of "shaking a leg" on the dance floor you can play pool on a 19th-century rosewood table from Colorado. The Cheyenne has stained glass windows, chandeliers and a collection of antique handguns. It also has the Cheyenne Stampede Band, which soon has those chandeliers swaying.

*E*ntertainment while you eat and drink at Rosie O'Grady's, one of the attractions at Orlando's Church Street Station.

Apple Annie's Courtyard is the place to head for if you fancy some folk or bluegrass music. The courtyard is a garden of tropical plants and trees where you can drink daiquiris flavoured with banana, peach, strawberry, cherry or plum, and keep the elegant glass as a souvenir.

The latest in music is to be found in the unlikely surroundings of **Phineas Phogg's Balloon Works**, where the decor honours famous balloonists and their historic flights. You can order a hot-air balloon of your very own along with your food and drink, but you can expect a few thousand dollars to be added to your bill, of course.

"Those Magnificent Men" are honoured at **Lili Marlene's Aviators' Pub and Restaurant**, another entertainment and dining complex where guests dine in oak booths among stained glass transoms, burnished brass railings and copper gas lanterns.

Two newer attractions at Church Street Station are **Commander Ragtime's Midway of Fun, Food and Games**, with singing fudge-makers, arcade games and roller-skating waitresses, and **the Exchange**, a complex of more than 50 specialty shops and restaurants providing a range of cuisines, including Chinese, Italian and Mexican. Just along the street from there is **Mulvaney's**, a pub that is every bit as Irish as the pints of Guinness they pull.

Church Street Station provides a range of entertainment activities, with bars, places to eat, cabarets, shops and a balloon that gives dawn and evening trips over Orlando.

Water Parks

Central Florida has two theme parks where you can literally soak in the atmosphere.

Opened in 1977, **Wet 'n' Wild** is a 10-hectare (25-acre) complex of rides and slides, tubes and flumes, and it's very centrally placed—right on Orlando's International Drive. You can really let yourself go—from anything up to seven storeys high—at Wet 'n' Wild, and come up for more. Among the newer attractions here is the Black Hole, a mega-slide that defies the laws of aerodynamics as riders toboggan headlong down twin tunnels of darkness, dropping 167 m (500 ft), twisting and turning, before being deposited gently in the splashdown.

Blue Niagara takes riders through two intertwined translucent tubes looping from a height close on six storeys, and Bubble Up is a huge, colourful inflated bubble, 30 m (90 ft) in diameter and topped with a

71

cascading fountain. The Raging Rapids is Wet 'n' Wild's version of a Colorado whitewater adventure in which riders bump and bounce through whirlpools, waves and rapids before plunging over a waterfall. Kamikaze is a water chute as long as a football field and rising more than six storeys above pool level. Those who prefer taking it easy can float along the Lazy River on a raft or inner tube, moving along a stream 400 m (440 yds) long. Toddlers can splash about to their heart's content with pint-sized flumes and water cannon in water just a few inches deep.

Over at Kissimmee, a few miles west of Orlando, is the second water park. **Water Mania** offers a new 752 m^2 (8,100 ft^2) maze through which visitors must make their way, finding four different flags on the way and emerging in the fastest possible time. Water Mania also has two miniature golf-courses and a fairground with arcade games, as well as lots of splashy slides and rides.

It isn't all flippant make-believe in the Orlando area. There is a host of historic homes, gardens, museums and markets that give the region that lived-in feel. About 20 museums, art galleries and special interest centres are listed in the Orlando Visitors' Guide. These range from the Audubon House and Bird of Prey Center at Maitland, where there is a gallery of wildlife art and an aviary of owls, hawks and eagles, to the Elvis Presley Museum, on Orlando's American Way, which has some 300 items of Pelvis memorabilia. Clothing, jewellery, guitars, a gun collection, and his Mercedes limousine are on show.

Dining Out

Orlando's Official Visitors' Guide lists 30 pages of restaurants and cafés, representing every kind of cuisine from American fast food to French, Indian, Chinese, Japanese, Greek—even Polynesian. At many places dining out can be combined with a lavish touch of show business.

King Henry's Feast is easy to spot. It is a fortified Tudor mansion, incongruously placed among the palm trees of International Drive, and a "medieval" banquet is served nightly with much swigging of beer and mead among the wives and wenches, jester, jugglers and knights of the Court of Good King Hal. **Medieval Times**, on Highway 192 in Kissimmee, takes the "Knights of Old" theme even further, with jousting, sword play and wonderful demonstrations of horsemanship taking place in a huge arena as you eat with your fingers.

King Henry's Feast was opened in 1985 by Robert Earl, a British entrepreneur who has been the brains behind a number of Orlando's attractions. Now living permanently in the city, he was head of the company that launched one of its latest dining extravaganzas, Hard Rock Café Orlando.

The **Hard Rock Café** adjoins Universal Studios Florida. Shaped like an electric guitar, the huge building has two entrances. Guests from Universal can enter through the back door via an outdoor record-shaped plaza. Visitors entering from the front cross from the free car park on a 100-m (300-ft) bridge which forms the neck of the guitar. Within the main body of the guitar three stained-glass windows depict the rock stars Elvis Presley, Jerry Lee Lewis and Chuck Berry, and as, in Hard Rock Cafés in other parts of the world, there are lots of rock 'n' roll memorabilia in the 500-seat two-storey building. Visitors who like rock 'n' roll won't be too concerned about the food, which is the kind of Deep South fare—conch chowder, hickory-smoked barbecue chicken, pig sandwich, etc.—you might expect to be served in Liverpool.

The four-course Southern Hospitality dinner served at the **Mardis Gras Dinner Theater** at the Mercado Mediterranean Shopping Village, on International Drive, is rather more authentic, and the entertainment—a two-hour song and dance vaudeville show—is also more traditionally American.

There are lots of places where you can simply dine and chat in quiet, dignified surroundings. Of these, the top two are almost certainly the **Ming Court**, which specializes exclusively in Chinese dishes, and **Caruso's Palace**, as Italian as Naples itself. Both restaurants are on International Drive.

Cultural Attractions

Not far from downtown Orlando are the **Leu Gardens** and **Leu House Museum**. The botanical gardens feature orchids, camellias and roses on 20 hectares (50 acres) on the edge of Lake Rowena, and the house preserves the furnishings and appointments of turn-of-the-century Florida. Another magnificent garden is to be found at Lake Wales, about an hour's drive south-west of Orlando. The park features the Bok Tower, containing a carillon of bells, and was designed by Frederick Law Olmstead, who created New York City's Central Park.

If you want to find out something of the area's history, the **Orange County Historical Museum** traces its development from the days when it was known as Mosquito County. Adjoining it is a fire museum in an authentic 1926 fire station.

On South Semoran Boulevard, Orlando, you will find the **Cartoon Museum**—thousands of newspaper and magazine cartoons, with original artwork, comics, books and other printed material.

Art lovers will doubtless want to head for **Winter Park**, an elegant area of northern Greater Orlando, about 20 minutes from most of the tourist hotels. Winter Park was founded as a winter resort at the turn of the century, and its main street, Park Avenue, is filled with European-style boutiques, exclusive fashion stores, restaurants, hidden gardens, antique shops and art galleries.

The **Cornell Fine Arts Museum**, on the lovely campus at Rollins College in Winter Park, features collections of paintings by European Old Masters and the works of 19th-century American artists. It is open throughout the year and there is no admission charge. Just off Park Avenue is the **Charles Hosmer Morse Museum** of American Art, which contains an impressive collection of Art Nouveau—paintings, jewellery, and, of course, stained glass windows and lamps—from the estate of Louis Comfort Tiffany. The Morse Museum often features works by such distinguished artists as John LaFarge, Frank Lloyd Wright and

Cowboy Country

The Singing Tower at Lake Wales has a 53-bell carillon. The tower was presented to the state more than 60 years ago by Edward Bok, a Dutch immigrant.

Kissimmee is in cowboy country. Florida is a major beef-producing state and the area around Kissimmee supports many ranches. There are weekly cattle auctions, and a big annual rodeo takes place in July. Demonstrations of cowboy craft—such skills as horse-riding and cattle-roping—take place at weekends in Lake Kissimmee State Park, south of Kissimmee itself and actually closer to the city of Lake Wales.

René Lalique. There is a modest entrance fee. Albin Polasek, internationally known realistic sculptor and painter, spent the last 16 years of his life in Winter Park. His home, designed and built as a museum-cum-studio, is now a private foundation open to the public. The home, galleries and grounds are filled with the artist's most prized pieces. Admission is free.

Out at Kissimmee, half an hour's drive from Orlando, west on I-4, is the **Tupperware World Headquarters**, where there is a museum of food containers—from ancient Egyptian times to the present day—and there are also beautiful lakes and gardens surrounding the buildings.

Tourists can enjoy Western-style entertainment every day of the week at Kissimmee's **Fort Liberty Wild West Dinner Show and Trading Post**, replica of an early 19th-century US Cavalry stockade with a 600-seater mess hall and 25 shops with a Western theme. Dinner at Fort Liberty is honest-to-goodness family entertainment, with cowboys and Indians, comedians and dancers and singing waiters in cavalry uniform. The waiters bring out pans of beef soup, fried chicken, roast pork, corn on the cob and baked beans, followed by apple pie and ice cream. The pans are dumped on each table and an army-style "volunteer" Mess Sergeant—it could be you—dishes it out.

Old Town, just along the highway from Fort Liberty, is a reconstruction of traffic-free streets with raised wooden sidewalks and a leisurely turn-of-the-century ambience. There are more than 70 specialty shops. Here, also, is **Little Darlin's Rock 'n' Roll Palace** where the music of the fifties and sixties throbs from 8 a.m. to 2 a.m. seven days a week. Some of the most famous names in rock appear in person at Little Darlin's, and you

---

Flea World

If you are in the area of Winter Park over the weekend you should call in at Flea World, where there is always the chance that you might pick up a bargain masterpiece for your own collection. Located on Highway 17-92, just 15 minutes north of Orlando, Flea World is said to be America's largest flea market. It covers 42 hectares (104 acres), and some 1,200 stallholders sell everything from garage junk to authentic antique Americana. There is free live entertainment by bands, singers, jugglers and conjurers.

dance or listen, eat or drink, served by waitresses in poodle skirts, sweaters and saddle shoes.

At **Bartow**, 18 km (11 miles) south of Winter Haven on US 17, you could imagine you have landed on the moon. This is the world's biggest phosphate mining area, known as Bone Valley

Cypress Gardens hold a host of attractions for all the family, from water-ski shows and fairground rides to nature trails and an animal centre.

Cypress Gardens

Some 32 km (20 miles) south-west of Kissimmee, near the town of Winter Haven, is Cypress Gardens, which was a major tourist attraction in the days when Mickey Mouse was still making a name for himself. Not to be confused with Grand Cypress Resort near Orlando, Cypress Gardens opened in the 1930s. Elegantly costumed Southern belles stroll through its landscaped grounds along paths which meander between flower beds, pools, grottoes, and cypress trees draped with Spanish moss. There are fairground rides, entertainment, nature trails, and an animal centre. Water-ski shows are held daily, as they have been since just after World War II.

because of the many fossils and skeletons of prehistoric creatures that have been unearthed here. Some are displayed in the **Bone Valley Phosphate Museum**.

One of the highest parts of Florida is at **Lake Wales**. It's 76 m (250 ft) above sea level, so there's no risk of altitude sickness. The 61-m (200-ft) Bok Tower there has a carillon of 53 bells, which provide a 45-minute concert every day, as well as shorter recitals. Fifth Avenue in Lake Wales has a "magnetic" hill, a phenomenon caused by optical illusion. Drivers who release their brakes from a standstill at the bottom of Spook Hill, as the locals call it, will find their car apparently rolling uphill.

Sebring, at the southernmost end of Central Florida, is known to motor racing fans for its twisting racetrack. Nearby **Hammock Highlands State Park**, opened in 1931, was one of Florida's first public parks. Its 1,538 hectares (3,800 acres) host many types of wildlife, with white-tailed deer and alligator viewed every day. Activities include hiking and nature study, horse-riding and guided tours into the park's remoter areas.

The Great Outdoors

Northwards now—and first to Ocala, where there are many thoroughbred horse farms. Some are open to the public, who can watch early morning training gallops. **Ocala**, which has a variety of good accommodation, is an ideal base for those keen to penetrate the wild and rural aspect of Central Florida. Also in the area are such

*O*cala, in Central Florida, is renowned for its racehorse breeding and training. Some stables are open to the public and early morning gallops can be watched.

attractions as the **Appleton Museum of Fine Arts** and a **Museum of Drag Racing**.

The **Ocala National Forest** is the only national park in Central Florida. It has springs, streams and 600 lakes where fishing from boats is a popular activity. A fishing licence is necessary except for children under 15 and Florida residents over 65. A five-day or 14-day licence can be bought at good sports stores or at a tax collector's office.

The springs and streams can be explored by canoe. Canoes can be hired at Juniper Springs, Alexander Springs and Salt Springs. The water at the springs is very clear and pleasantly warm—a constant 22°C (72°F). According to state law, canoeists have to be equipped with flotation aids. The chances of capsizing along these

North-east of Ocala is Silver Springs, a world class natural wonder where early Tarzan films were made. Indigenous and African creatures roam the "jungle".

twisting waterways are fairly high, with shallows and submerged logs to impede progress and fallen palm trees under which you have to duck.

Falling in is something which has to be accepted with pragmatism. You can rely on any alligator that happens to be basking close by to put some distance between you and it. The water is warm and clear and you may well be glad of a refreshing ducking, though the mud and gunge on the riverbed is a bit of a hazard. The embarrassing part is returning to the august lobby of the Ocala Hilton drenched, mucky and with one sandal missing. Take spare shorts, teeshirt and flip-flops in your car if you feel you'd like a quick change before returning to civilization.

There's no need to rush things in a canoe.

Camping is a year-round pursuit in the forest. The three grades of campground range from primitive, with few facilities, to more modern areas with parking place, fireplace and picnic table, garbage disposal point and toilets. The essence of camping for many is pitching the tent in any suitable place when evening approaches, and this is permitted except during the hunting season, which is from mid-November to early January.

The **Florida National Scenic Trail** is a hiking trail which extends more than

Silver Springs visitors can view birds and animals from a river boat (previous page).

1,300 km (800 miles) through the state, and will eventually be more than 1,931 km (1,200 miles) long. A 106-km (66-mile) stretch of it goes through Ocala National Forest. Self-guided walks along interpretative tracks can be found at the recreation areas at Alexander Springs, Juniper Springs and Clearwater Lake. There are three horse-riding trails totalling 60 km (100 miles).

Ocala itself is one of the fastest-growing cities in the USA. The Metropolitan area includes all of Marion County, an important thoroughbred breeding and training area with more than three-quarters of the 600 establishments in Florida. The land is rich in calcium and phosphorus, the grass is lush, and Ocala is bracketed with three other locations as the top horse-breeding centres in the world. (The others are Newmarket, England; Chantilly, France; and Lexington, Kentucky.)

Marion County was a major citrus-growing area until a series of frosts in the 1980s took their toll. Many acres of water melon fields have also disappeared.

Tourism is no new pursuit for Ocala. It has played an important role in the economy since steamboats cruised up the Oklawaha River to Silver Springs a century ago. Silver Springs is where swimming champion Johnny Weismuller took to the trees and made six Tarzan films between 1932 and 1942. Jane Russell, Rock Hudson, Claudia Cardinale, Esther

Spacious houseboats can be rented on the St Johns River.

Williams, Gary Cooper, Spencer Tracy and William Holden are just a few of a long line of world-class stars who have worked on location at Silver Springs. Countless TV programmes and commercials have been shot there.

But watching the screen is nothing like experiencing the real thing. **Silver Springs** is an awe-inspiring geological happening, with underground springs pushing some 2,500 million litres (550 million gallons) of water a day into the Oklawaha River via the 11-km (7-mile) Silver River.

And what water! It is 97.76 per cent pure, and its extraordinary clarity is attributed to the limestone that has filtered the waters over the centuries. At one of the springs, known as the Bridal Chamber, you can see a crevice with water churning from it as clearly as you can see your face in a mirror. Yet it is 25 m (83 ft) down.

Take a trip by glass-bottomed boat. There's a wealth of fascinating geological and historical study to grip the mind, and to draw the visitor back to Silver Springs again and again.

Apart from the Springs, there's plenty to intrigue day-trippers. Particularly popular with children is the deerpark, with white-tail, sika, muntjac and fallow deer and various other creatures which the public can feed with appropriate foodstuffs available from coin-operated dispensers. Residents include llamas, sheep, goats, cattle, peacocks, turkeys and other poultry. Educational reptile shows in three arenas take place at set times each day. The first theatre has a cast of rattlesnakes, the second stars boa constrictors—spectators are invited to be photographed wearing one around the neck—and the third presents the Alligator Bowl Show.

Your visit can also include a Jungle Cruise, during which animals and birds from outside the USA can be seen on the river banks—ostrich, llama, barbary sheep, giraffe, spider monkeys, gibbon, zebra and, on an island, rhesus monkeys—the numerous descendants of two pairs left behind after the filming of the Tarzan movies.

Sixty free-roaming species of native and foreign creatures can be seen from the Jeep Safari, introduced in 1990.

Silver Springs, 1.6 km (1 mile) east of Ocala, is open every day of the year. It has restaurants, cafés and souvenir shops.

Fishing and Boating

North American nationals who enjoy fishing visit Florida in their recreational vehicles (RVs) or cars, with all their fishing equipment, and find a suitable lakeside or riverside camping site. It isn't so easy for overseas visitors, who may fancy a day or two's inland fishing among other holiday pursuits and don't want to cart their rods and reels around with them.

Fortunately for them, there are companies like Captain Tom's, PO Box 1836, Silver Springs, Florida 32688. He and his wife operate 8-m (24-ft) pontoon boats which can be hired, with skipper, for half a day, a day or longer, with rods and bait, refreshments, local knowledge and instruction on techniques for catching the various species of fish all provided.

The boats take up to six people. Trips on the Silver River and Oklawaha River can concentrate on other pursuits as well as fishing. Bird-watching, photography and moonlight cruises are among the options.

Nearly half of Florida's 30,000 lakes, holding stocks of bass, bream and other species, are in the Central region. Here, too, the wide St Johns River flows placidly northwards to Jacksonville and into the Atlantic. Boats can be rented by the week at Sanford and De Land, for a cruise to Jacksonville, and perhaps some fishing, stopping now and again to explore the small communities which have grown up on or near the river banks.

From your boat you can observe ospreys and many wading birds and waterfowl. There's the chance of a glimpse of a manatee, the gentle giant related to the elephant family, which grazes under the water. It is an endangered and protected species. Boat is perhaps the wrong word for the craft you hire. Although it may not appeal to the traditionalist, it will bring a sparkle to the eye of those who appreciate home comforts. The craft are virtually rectangular pontoons, with luxurious and spacious accommodation for up to ten people, including a full-size bathroom. You don't sleep in cabins, but in bedrooms. The roof is used as a sundeck. Houseboat holidays on the St Johns River can be arranged in Britain through Blakes Holidays, Wroxham, Norwich NR12 8DH (tel. 0603-784131).

The St Johns River is not a long one—slightly over 150 km (93 miles)—but it is up to 3 km (2 miles) wide for much of its length, allowing plenty of room for private cruisers, sailing boats, small open boats used by anglers, and speedboats which sometimes make more wash than they should.

Every evening there's a dinner cruise, with live entertainment, aboard the *Grand Romance*, a wonderful new 41.5-m (135-ft) replica of a sidewheeler steamboat. Daytime trips also depart daily from Sanford. The whole ship, or separate decks, can be chartered for weddings and special functions, and group excursions. Buffet-style parties for up to 600 people, and full dinner events for 350, can be arranged. Contact Grand Romance of Florida, 433 N. Palmetto Avenue, Sanford, Florida 32771.

Hontoon Island State Park, 10 km (6 miles) west of De Land, off SR 44, has had a chequered history. Bordered by the St Johns River and the Hontoon Dead River, the island was first inhabited by Timucuan Indians whose mounds can be viewed on the park's nature trail. It has also served as a boat yard, a cattle ranch and a pioneer homestead. Today, the 668-hectare (1,650-acre) island is accessible only by private boat or by a passenger ferry which operates daily from 9 a.m. until an hour before sunset. Activities include camping, nature study, boating, picnicking and fishing. Six rustic cabins are available, but reservations must be made with the Florida Division of Recreation and Parks.

Katie's Landing

This is one of those wonderful places with log-cabin accommodation and fully equipped sites for RVs (recreational vehicles or motorhomes). Katie Moncrieff and her husband Russ also offer canoe rentals and have a programme of downstream "runs" along the Wekiva River system. The runs range from a 10-km (6-mile) trip lasting two to three hours to a 30-km (19-mile) voyage involving six to eight hours paddling and, probably, an overnight camping stop.

Because the runs are downstream—Russ and Katie either drive canoeists upstream to a setting-off point or pick them up downstream at a pre-arranged time—there is no really strenuous paddling to do and no chance of getting lost since you have only to follow the current. After close on 20 years in the business, the couple have lots of expertise and local knowledge and they will give instruction to those with no canoeing experience. Sensibly handled, the Canadian-style craft are very stable. There really is no need to charge along the river like an Olympic slalom contestant. The best way to get maximum enjoyment out of the trip is to let the current do the work and your paddles do the steering. That way you will be able to observe undisturbed wildlife above, on, below and on either side of the waterway.

A tributary of the St Johns, the **Wekiva River** is protected by the state as an Outstanding Florida Water and parts of it are officially designated as "scenic and wild"—parts that have remained unchanged over the centuries. Even within a few miles of Sanford, you can experience Florida as encountered by the earliest explorers, and it well worthwhile spending a day—or even half a day—paddling a rented canoe. Katie's Wekiva River Landing, 1.6 km (1 mile) off SR 46, on Wekiva Park Drive, is a good starting point.

Flowing through 8,000 hectares (20,000 acres) of state-owned land—much of it a densely forested wilderness—the waters of the Wekiva are remarkably clear and in most places shallow, so it is easy to spot the shoals of mullet, the sunfish, speckled perch, largemouth bass, catfish, pickerel and gar that frequent the river. There's a good chance of seeing an alligator or two, and you will certainly see lots of red-bellied and cooter turtles basking on logs. Colourful dragonflies and butterflies flit above the surface, and among the many birds to be seen are the brown and white speckled limpkin with its down-curved bill, the red-billed white ibis, great blue heron, snowy egret, osprey, turkey vulture, pileated woodpecker and the belted kingfisher.

Village of Psychics
Two kilometres (just over a mile) east of I-4, about halfway between Sanford and De Land, is one of the strangest places in Florida. **Cassadaga**, a village of not much more than three or four sleepy streets, is a community of spiritualists. Signs on the sides of houses identify the residents: "Clairvoyant", says one. Another, "Psychic Reader". Others are "Mediums" or "Spiritualists". The **Cassadaga Hotel**, in the centre of the village, is a venue for many psychic and paranormal conventions, and just along the street, looking much the same as any community's tourist information centre, is a small office building where you can find out all about the place and get guidance on who to see if you want a consultation.

Cassadaga owes its existence to a man named George Colby, from Pike County, New York, who first visited the area in 1875. According to legend, Colby was a boy of twelve in 1869 when he was visited by the spirit of a dead uncle who said the boy would become a medium and establish a spiritualist community in the South. Six years later Colby travelled to Florida and took the traditional tourism route—by steamboat up the St Johns River to Blue Springs, near Orange City. From there he walked into the wilderness until spirit guides told him to stop. This was the site of Cassadaga, in a setting of tall pines, gentle hills, lakes and springs.

Colby built a crude log cabin, claimed homesteader's rights on a 14-hectare (35-acre) plot, and spent the next few years establishing a reputation as a medium and getting neighbouring communities interested in forming an assembly of spiritualists. He became famous in Florida for locating buried treasure and for helping the police to solve crimes and find missing persons. In 1883 Cassadaga became a spiritualist campground, and from 1895, when Colby donated the 14 hectares (35 acres) to what had become known as the Southern Cassadaga Spiritualist Campmeeting Association, the place began to attract permanent residents.

The river basin is the habitat of some large mammals, such as the threatened Florida black bear, white-tailed deer, otter and bobcat, but these are very shy creatures and are rarely seen. Other animals frequenting the banks are grey squirrels, raccoons, grey foxes and opossums. Trees common to the Wekiva include bay, ash, bald cypress, oak, southern magnolia, pine and palm trees. Plants that thrive in the running water or on the swampy banks include spatterdock, the Florida water lily, the crinkly-leaved water lettuce, spider lily and sawgrass. Beware of poison ivy which climbs up trees and has leaves in formations of three. Touching it causes a painful rash.

With some 1,300 lakes, forests of pine and hardwoods, rich pasturelands, and delightful freshwater springs, Central Florida has much to gee up souls jaundiced by "attraction-fatigue". Taking a few days out of the holiday to explore the countryside, abandoning the freeways in favour of lesser roads, will introduce travellers to the heart of "real" Florida, and bring the reward of rich experiences.

Cassadaga, a village near DeLand, is devoted to astrology and psychic matters.

Sun, Sports, Symphonies and the Space Center

A playground for all those who love water, here you can fish, windsurf, or just mess about on and along the river. Dining out in one of the local restaurants will convince you why the local seafood has such an excellent reputation. Take a cultural breather at the Museum of Cuban Art or spend the evening listening to a world-famous Orchestra at the Peabody Center. Those who prefer dry land can wander contentedly around one of the many parks and wildlife areas. For a glimpse of life a long way beyond the Sunshine State—and the rest of the earth—a visit to the Kennedy Space Center is a must.

In more ways than one, Florida's Central East Region is pioneer country. This is where the first settlers began to arrive after the American Civil War, following the St Johns River inland to establish plantations and farmsteads, then making their way to the coast where sporadic fishing villages and citrus-growing communities were set up. There was also a certain amount of primitive tourism as adventurers took steamboat trips into the interior just for fun, but the industry did not get a real toe-hold until the 1880s, when Henry Flagler's East Coast Railroad began to push south. A series of resort towns, often built by Flagler himself, began to dot the coast. In those days, the gateway would have been Jacksonville, to the north. Today, it is more likely to be Orlando, which has the nearest of Florida's three truly international airports.

From Orlando to Daytona Beach, by way of Interstate 4, is a distance of 85 km (53 miles), barely an hour's run. The journey to the Space Coast—where you will find NASA's launch pads, the Astronaut Hall of Fame and the US Space Camp Florida—covers less than 80 km (50 miles) via the Beeline Expressway toll road. Charges are

A crop of hardware in the Rocket Garden at the NASA Kennedy Space Center.

89

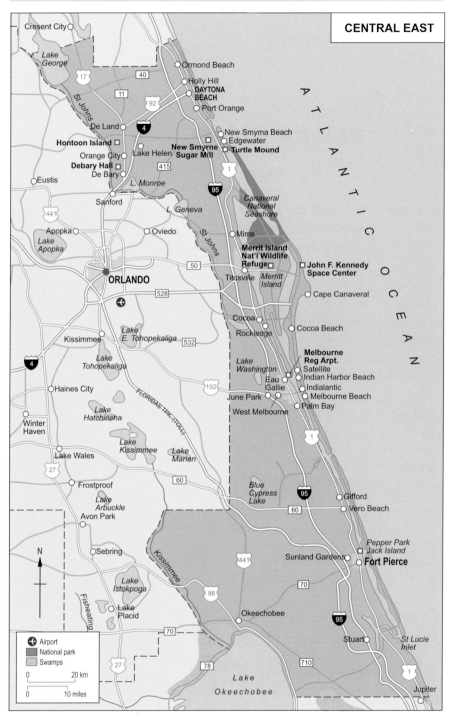

CENTRAL EAST

Cresent City
Lake George
Ormond Beach
Holly Hill
DAYTONA BEACH
Port Orange
17
40
11
92
De Land
4
New Smyma Beach
Edgewater
Hontoon Island
New Smyrne
Turtle Mound
Orange City
Lake Helen
Sugar Mill
Debary Hall
415
De Bary
Eustis
L. Monroe
Sanford
441
L. Geneva
Apopka
Oviedo
Mims
Lake Apopka
Canaveral National Seashore
St Johns
Merrit Island Nat'l Wildlife Refuge
John F. Kennedy Space Center
50
ORLANDO
Titusville
Merritt Island
Cape Canaveral
528
Cocoa
Rockledge
Cocoa Beach
Lake E. Tohopekaliga
532
Kissimmee
Lake Tohopekaliga
Melbourne Reg Arpt.
Satellite
Lake Washington
Indian Harbor Beach
4
Eau Gallie
Indialantic
Haines City
June Park
Melbourne Beach
192
Palm Bay
West Melbourne
Lake Hatchineha
Winter Haven
1
Lake Kissimmee
Lake Wales
Lake Marian
27
Frostproof
60
Blue Cypress Lake
Lake Arbuckle
95
Gifford
Avon Park
60
Vero Beach
N
Sebring
Pepper Park
Jack Island
441
Sunland Gardens
Fort Pierce
70
Lake Istokpoga
98
Lake Placid
Okeechobee
95
Stuart
St Lucie Inlet
70
710
27
78
Lake Okeechobee
1
Jupiter

ATLANTIC OCEAN

FLORIDAS TPK (TOLL)
Kissimmee
Fisheating
St Johns

Airport
National park
Swamps
0   20 km
0   10 miles

*M*ap of the Central East Region.

reasonable and the route is much shorter than the toll-free alternatives. From north to south, between the Daytona Beach area and Stuart, on the St Lucie River estuary, is about 225 km (140 miles), and there is a choice of highways to take: I-95 is the most direct; US 1 follows the coast and meanders a bit to miss one or two of the smaller places, and SR A1A leaps and snakes along a chain of barrier islands. For the sake of continuity, we'll travel first to Daytona.

A quiet day at Daytona International Speedway, one of the finest motor racing-facilities in the US.

Speed Record at Daytona Beach
Daytona Beach, dubbed "the world's most famous beach" at the turn of the 20th century, leapt into the British headlines in 1935 when Sir Malcolm Campbell drove his rocket-powered car along the resort's firm white sand at the then astonishing and record-breaking speed of 448.17 kph (276 mph). Sir Malcolm's achievement was the fastest ever in a tradition of speed which had begun with motor races on the beach in 1902, when the record was set at 91.73 kph (57 mph). A stone clock-tower on the beach near the Marriott Hotel is dedicated to the memory of Sir Malcolm.

Daytona Beach Resort Area

Ormond Beach, the northernmost community in the Daytona Beach area, is known as the "Birthplace of Speed". Such motoring pioneers as Henry Ford, Ransom Olds and Louis

Chevrolet were attracted here by the 37 km (23 miles) of hard-packed sand, which is up to 154 m (500 ft) wide at low tide, and was considered ideal for speed trials and engine tests. Later, stock-car racers began to compete on an oval track along the beach near Ponce Inlet, and fans from around the world gathered on the shores to watch. To this day, anyone can drive along the beach—but no faster than a sedate 16 kph (10 mph). Rangers ensure that the limit is observed, and that drivers keep to the correct lanes and park properly. They also make sure that no alcohol is taken on to the beach. Volusia County charges a modest fee for vehicles entering the beach. Entering on foot or bicycle is free.

Daytona Beach, of course, is still famous for speed, but those shrill, high-performance cars now scream around a high-banked 4-km (2½-mile) oval track—the **Daytona International Speedway**—rather than on sand. One of America's finest motor-racing facilities, the track is the scene each February of the world-famous Daytona 500, but other spectacular events take place there throughout the year. Major motor-cycle races are staged in March and October, and the stock-car season starts in July. Go-karts zoom round the track just after Christmas. Antique and classic car shows are staged in the area throughout the year.

At times, car manufacturers, tyre companies and racing teams use the track for research, development and training purposes, and visitors get the chance to glimpse some of the sport's big names and fastest machines. The grandstands are then often thrown open to the public free of charge.

Minibus tours of the track are available to the public on days when it is not in use.

Race enthusiasts can trace the rich history of the sport and the area's role in the development of the motor industry at the **Birthplace of Speed Museum** at 160 East Granada Boulevard in Ormond Beach. The **Halifax Historical Museum** at 252 South Beach Street in downtown Daytona Beach features a replica of the Stanley Steamer, a 1922 Model-T and a 1929 Model-A as well as memorabilia from the early years of beach racing.

But we must not lose sight of the fact that the Daytona Beach Resort Area—to give it its official title—is, above all, a region for leisurely holiday-making—and in that respect, it has lots to offer. Daytona Beach is the largest municipality in the area. The others are Ormond Beach, Holly Hill, Daytona Beach Shores, South Daytona, Port Orange and Ponce Inlet.

Student Holiday-makers

Daytona is known throughout the United States as a major holiday destination for college students, and there are times—especially during the spring break—when the area is rather crowded. However, Destination Daytona, the area's visitor and convention bureau, has been working hard to change the focus, if not the picture, in this respect. The spring break brings in something like $125 million a year from students—not the kind of business anyone wants to turn away—so the bureau points out that the area is a year-round destination with plenty of room and attractions for all, including families and senior citizens, with whom it is becoming increasingly popular during the winter months.

Getting around

A major advantage Daytona has over many other cities in Florida—if not the United States as a whole—is an efficient and comprehensive local transport system. VOTRAN, the Volusia County Transit Authority, provides a bus service throughout the area, and the bright red Jolly Trolley, replica of a turn-of-the-century vehicle, runs a regular service parallel to the Atlantic Ocean on SR A1A. Taxi and limousine services are plentiful, both at Daytona Beach Regional Airport and in town, and DOTS, the Daytona–Orlando Transit service, runs coaches to and from Orlando International Airport and to Walt Disney World and the other major attractions in central Florida.

Rivers and Beaches

The area has three rivers—the north flowing St Johns, the Tomoka River, which reaches the resorts by way of the Tomoka State Park, just north of Ormond Beach, and the Halifax River, part of the US Intracoastal Waterway. It also has that famous beach. It's a bit unsettling at first to see those cars on it, but don't be fooled into thinking it's as hard as a motorway surface. The sand becomes softer as you move further from the water-line, and in places there are sand dunes up to 8 m (25 ft) high.

Daytona Beach is managed as a giant seaside park by the Volusia County Beach Department. Beach rangers patrol the area on little three-wheeled motor vehicles, and the most popular mode of transportation for visitors is the beach cruiser, a wide-tyred bicycle.

Floats, umbrellas and motor bikes can be rented, and sea-front vendors sell everything from hotdogs to beach towels and teeshirts. An alpine-style chair-lift carries visitors high above the **Main Street Pier**, giving a bird's-eye view of the famous **Boardwalk** area, where an amusement park features rides, miniature golf, arcades and snack bars. With the annual temperature averaging nearly 21°C (71°F), it's not surprising that the beach is open throughout the year, but it can be decidedly cool at times during the winter when only the hardiest of Canadian "snowbirds" are to be seen in the water.

The area is rich in watersports. Championship competitions in sailing, surfing and jet-skiing are held throughout the year, but you don't have to be a champion to enjoy these sports yourself. On the Halifax River and Intracoastal Waterway sailboats, jet skis, sailboards and powerboats can be rented by the hour. The *Dixie Queen Riverboat*, modelled after a turn-of-the-century paddle-wheeler and accommodating up to 500 people, sets out daily on sunset and dinner cruises along the river.

If you fancy going out into the Atlantic after red snapper, grouper or other fish, deep-sea charter boats depart daily from several marinas. The cost for a half-day trip, with bait and gear included, is surprisingly reasonable.

Other Entertainments

There is always something going on to interest sports fans. In Daytona Beach the **Ocean Center**, a $40-million convention complex which opened in

A chair-lift carries holiday-makers high above Daytona Beach's Main Street Pier.

1985, regularly offers professional and college basketball, karate, boxing and wrestling championships and ice-skating events. The centre is also capable of handling groups of 50 to 10,000 delegates, and is one of Florida's leading convention facilities.

Just across the street from the Ocean Center is the new 402-room **Marriott Hotel**. Built at a cost of $51 million, the ocean-front property has a variety of restaurants and lounges and a festive shopping marketplace. There is also an outdoor bandstand and an 800-seat beachfront amphitheatre

as the London Symphony Orchestra appearing at the **Peabody Auditorium**. In summer months concerts spill from the auditoriums to the beachside Bandshell, beside the Marriott Hotel, where free performances are presented under the stars. The **Daytona Playhouse** at 100 Jessamine Boulevard presents a troupe of talented local actors in a variety of plays, and a series of Seaside Music Theater productions is held from June to August.

One of America's largest collections of Cuban art is to be found at the **Museum of Arts and Science**. Much of the collection was taken to Daytona Beach by the former Cuban president, Fulgencio Batista, who maintained a holiday home in the area. Batista was ousted in the Cuban Revolution of 1959. The museum, at 1040 Museum Drive, also features the skeleton of a

used for concerts and shows. The resort area already has nearly 440 hotels and motels with more than 16,000 rooms, suites and apartments, many directly on the ocean. Condominium rentals are also available and there are campgrounds and motorhome parks throughout the region.

Cultural activities feature strongly. Orchestral concerts are performed regularly, with such prominent orchestras

Rockerfeller Home

Overlooking the Halifax River at Ormond Beach is Casements, the beautiful former winter home of the almost legendary multi-millionaire John D. Rockefeller. Local people will tell you that Rockefeller had the place built when he discovered he was being overcharged at the Ormond Hotel on the opposite side of the street. Today, Casements is used as a cultural centre and museum, and there are guided tours daily. The nearby Rockefeller Gardens along the Halifax River have also been restored close to their original design, and feature a patio, fountain and pond. The Ormond Hotel, said to be the largest wooden structure in the United States, is closed and in a sad state of repair. The building is considered a fire hazard by the local fire brigade, and its days may well be numbered.

Beach, was once home to the Timucua Indians, and today visitors can walk beneath the same ancient oaks that once shaded the Timucuas' huts some 400 years ago. The marshes and tidal creeks may be explored by canoe, and the scenic state park is a perfect location for fishing, camping, hiking and boating. Escorted boat trips along the Tomoka River are available at a modest fee, but swimming is not allowed in rivers within the park.

The ruins of an old sugar mill once owned by English settlers form a backdrop for the **Sugar Mill Gardens**, a 5-hectare (12-acre) botanical park at Herbert Street, Port Orange. There are collections of flowering trees and other flora and statues of dinosaurs erected some 40 years ago when the gardens were used as a kind of early theme park. The gardens are open daily and admission is free. The ruins are all that is left of one of more than a hundred plantations established by the British administration which took over Florida from the Spanish in 1763. The plantations, which grew sugar cane, cotton, rice and indigo, were intended to attract dependable settlers, but fell into disuse when the settlers fled or were killed in the bloody Indian wars that followed Britain's handing back of the state in 1783. **Bulow Plantation Ruins State Historic Site**, about 13 km (8 miles) north of Ormond Beach, has a scenic walking trail and an interpretive centre which gives the plantation's history. There are picnic facilities, and canoeing and fishing are also available.

Another scenic area is **Ponce Inlet**, the southernmost point of the Daytona Beach Resort Area. **Lighthouse Point State Park** has a beach and a walkway

Cars are permitted to drive slowly on Daytona Beach, formerly the scene of international motor racing and speed trials.

4-m (13-ft) prehistoric ground sloth found near the museum grounds and considered to be the finest specimen of its kind in North America.

State Parks
The area has many parks and wildlife areas for nature lovers to enjoy. **Tomoka State Park**, north of Ormond

that winds over the natural sand dunes. A popular attraction is the **Ponce de Leon Inlet Lighthouse**, the second tallest of its kind on the US east coast. First put into service in 1887, the lighthouse is still in use. It also acts as an historic monument and museum and offers a spectacular view of the neighbouring countryside. Ponce Inlet has an intriguing boardwalk waterfront area, where the deep-sea charter fishing boats are moored. This is also a good place for restaurants, many of which are right on the water.

Eating Out

Seafood straight from the Atlantic Ocean is the region's culinary specialty, and there are more than 400 restaurants serving everything from fast food to colourful buffets and elegant gourmet dinners. Sophie Kay's **Top of Daytona Restaurant** has the finest view in the area. There's no shortage of night-life, either. Top names appear regularly at the Ocean Center, and there are numerous nightclubs along the beach and on the mainland.

Shopping

Malls and shopping centres offer a diverse selection, and two European-style open-air markets take place each weekend. The Farmers' Market, held in downtown Daytona Beach on City Island, features fresh produce, citrus fruit and seafood—a boon for self-caterers. Bargain hunters will have the time of their lives at the Daytona Flea Market where everything—from food and clothing to antiques—is sold on a 16-hectare (40-acre) site where US 92 joins I-95.

Things do not stand still in the Daytona Beach Resort Area. The local authority and private interests have invested $165 million in projects in the downtown and Main Street areas. Among recent developments is the **Halifax Harbour Marina**, opened during the summer of 1989 and developed as a village-style commercial area with retail and specialty shops, offices and restaurants at a cost of $16 million. The complex includes a 440-slip marina and a 16-hectare (10-acre) park and river garden.

At the Daytona Beach Regional Airport plans have been drawn up to replace the existing terminal with a more modern facility costing $35 million. The project is expected to be completed by late 1992 or early 1993, and authorities are hoping to achieve international status for the airport.

Day Trips

The Daytona Beach Resort Area is an ideal launching pad for day-trips by car. The attractions of Orlando—Walt Disney World, Sea World, Universal Studios, etc.—historic St Augustine, Spaceport USA and the United States Astronaut Hall of Fame are all within an hour's drive.

On the south side of Ponce de Leon Inlet lies the community of **New Smyrna Beach** where there are another 13 km (8 miles) of beach with sand so firm and smooth that again motorists can—and do—drive on it, though not fast. It is claimed to be the world's safest beach because there are no currents—rock ledges out in the Atlantic act as a barrier—and there are beach patrols and lifeguards on duty throughout the year.

Mediterranean Colony
New Smyrna's first residents were some 1,500 Greeks, Italians and Spaniards from the Balearic Islands who arrived in 1767, under the leadership of a Scotsman, Dr Andrew Turnbull. He named the settlement in honour of his wife's birthplace, Smyrna, then in Greece but now the Turkish city of Izmir. The colonists raised citrus fruit, sugar cane, cotton, rice, maize and indigo, and built a system of irrigation channels and drainage canals which is still in use. In 1777, however, the colony was disbanded as a result of political chicanery and lack of funds. Plantations and sugar mills were developed later, but these were destroyed during the Seminole Indian wars. Evidence of the 18th-century colony and the mills built later is to be found in the Old Fort, on Riverside Drive, New Smyrna Beach, and at the Turnbull Ruins and New Smyrna Sugar Mill Ruins. In the early 1800s the sugar mill, on Mission Drive, was the nucleus of a large plantation owned by two New York merchants and managed with slave labour and draught animals.

A traffic island in the centre of Canova Street, New Smyrna Beach, is the site of the grave of a 16-year-old boy who was accidentally killed during a hunting trip in 1860. The road was built around the youth's last resting place as the city developed.

Indian shell mounds surrounding the city indicate that New Smyrna Beach is one of the oldest settlements in North America. Ponce de Leon is believed to have landed here after sailing through a storm in the area in 1513. He and his men managed to take on supplies of fresh water before being driven off by Indians. Right on the southern boundary of Volusia

*H*alifax Harbor Marina is a new village-style development in the Daytona Beach Resort Area.

98

County—and on the edge of the Canaveral National Seashore—is the highest point in the area: Turtle Mound, a 10-m (35-ft) high pile of ancient oyster shells deposited over a period of six centuries by Indians. The mound is approached via SR A1A and is finally reached by way of a boardwalk which helps to protect the many plant species which have established themselves on and around it.

Space Coast

US 1 crosses the boundary into Brevard County—and into the world of tomorrow. This is the start of the Space Coast, the area which has seen some of mankind's greatest exploration achievements since the 1960s when the launch facilities and support base of the John F. Kennedy Space Center were carved out of miles of virgin savannah and marshland.

The story of America's space exploration programme actually begins soon after World War II. With rockets outgrowing the desert ranges used in the west, the US War Department chose Florida's Cape Canaveral as the testing area for long-range guided missiles. The Atlantic Missile Range came into existence in 1947, and a year later the National Aeronautics and Space Administration (NASA) was founded to carry out the peaceful exploration and use of space. NASA's early launch operations were centred on Cape Canaveral, where the manned launches of the Mercury and Gemini projects took place. Unmanned spacecraft were sent on one-way journeys—some were burned up on re-entering the earth's atmosphere, others will continue through the outer reaches of space for years to come. In 1964 the NASA Kennedy Space Center was moved to nearby Merritt Island, which had been selected as the site from which to launch Apollo—the Moon Mission. From 1976 the Merritt Island facilities were modified and expanded to accommodate the launch and landing of the re-usable space shuttle.

Amazingly, all but the operational areas of the Spaceport's 34,000 hectares (84,000 acres) are designated as a National Wildlife Refuge, much of it open to the public. Since 1975 16,600 hectares (41,000 acres) have been designated as part of the Canaveral National Seashore. "Space" in every sense is the key word for the area's holidaymakers, with 116 km (72 miles) of unspoiled beaches, some superb places for wildlife viewing and nature trails, and, of course, the wide Atlantic Ocean.

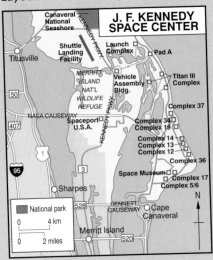

Layout of the Kennedy Space Coast.

Titusville

Straddling US 1 and standing on the Indian River, the city of Titusville is the gateway to NASA's world of tomorrow and proudly tags itself "Space City USA". It is undoubtedly one of the best places in the world from which to view a launch from the Space Center. Not surprisingly, the city is a major centre for space-related manufacturing industries. Concerns located here include the McDonnell Douglas Corporation's Satellite Division, the Hughes Satellite Division and Lockheed Space Operations Company. Titusville is also a growing residential city (present population over 40,000), with fine riverfront homes, about twenty hotels and

100

The United States Astronaut Hall of Fame commemorates international achievements in the development of space travel.

motels, extensive shopping facilities, and three public golf-courses, although the major recreational emphasis is on water sports.

Titusville's Main Street has many fine buildings from the late 1800s and early 1900s and has been designated a National Historic District. The city was founded in 1867 when it grew as an off-shoot of LaGrange, a former commercial centre, with a steamboat landing stage, a post office and some three hundred residents. In 1879 it was named in honour of Colonel Henry Titus, a local entrepreneur and philanthropist who had donated land for the Brevard County Courthouse.

Just outside the city, on part of the Space Coast Executive Airport, is the headquarters of the Valiant Air Command, which is dedicated to preserving World War II and post-war military aircraft. There are static aircraft displays and memorabilia, and visitors may watch aircraft restorations taking place in a huge operations hangar. In March each year the VAC presents an air show in which the veteran flying machines can be seen in action.

Astronaut Hall of Fame
One of Florida's newest attractions is the United States Astronaut Hall of Fame. It is located on NASA Parkway (SR 405), Titusville, close to the Executive Airport and 16 km (10 miles) or so from the launch pads where those space pioneers, the *Mercury Seven*, started their historic journeys. One of the seven, former astronaut L. Gordon Cooper Jr, took part in the hall's opening ceremony in March 1990. The six

surviving crew members of *Mercury Seven*, along with Betty Grissom, the widow of Gus Grissom who was killed in a launch pad fire in 1967, were honoured guests when the hall was officially dedicated a few weeks later.

The Hall of Fame takes visitors back to those early days of space exploration. Strolling through a "Time Tunnel", visitors are able to relive the 1957 launch of the Soviet *Sputnik* that ushered in the Space Age and America's response with Explorer 1. Displays focus on the personal stories of the *Mercury Seven* astronauts, each of whom is featured in his own special section, with personal memorabilia on display.

Film and photographs show Alan B. Shepard Jr's brief vault across the threshold of space as America's first space traveller. Gus Grissom is seen swimming for his life as his spacecraft sinks, and the emotion on John H. Glenn's face as he becomes the first astronaut to orbit Earth is seen in close-up.

Other sections show the increasingly longer orbital flights of Malcolm Scott Carpenter, Walter M. Schirra Jr and L. Gordon Cooper and the *Gemini* and *Apollo* missions flown by Grissom, Cooper and Schirra, as well as Shepard's walk on the moon and Donald K. Slayton's meeting with Soviet cosmonauts during a joint US–Russian flight.

Memorabilia on display from those historic days include Schirra's *Sigma 7* Mercury spacecraft, the spacesuit worn by Grissom during his "swim for life", the hand controller Shepard used to guide his lunar ship to the moon's surface, medals, flight jackets and rare photographs.

The US Astronaut Hall of Fame also features a roll of honour of all astronauts who have flown, and devotes a section to flights that followed the *Mercury* missions. Another section highlights future space programmes, such as *Space Station Freedom* and possible return trips to the moon and manned voyages to Mars in the next century.

The tour of the hall, which visitors can take at their own pace, concludes with a film featuring actual footage of the early space flights. Visitors then have an opportunity to watch student activities in the adjoining US Space Camp training centre, where youngsters experience a mission in a space shuttle simulator and mock mission control centre on various devices that simulate space flight.

The US Astronaut Hall of Fame is a joint venture between the Mercury Seven Foundation and the US Space Camp Foundation. Both are non-profit organizations, and there is a nominal charge for admission to the hall.

The Mercury Seven Foundation was founded by the six surviving astronauts and Mrs Grissom. Its main task is to raise money for scholarships for students specializing in science or technology fields leading to an aerospace career. The scholarships are awarded annually to students entering their senior year or going on to earn their masters or doctorate degrees.

Funds for the scholarships have been raised mainly through public appearances by the astronauts. Money from admission fees also goes into the scholarship fund.

The US Space Camp, part of the 3,437 m² (37,000 ft²) Hall of Fame facility, expanded into Florida when its headquarters in Alabama reached capacity in 1988. Florida's prominence in the space programme made it a natural choice. The camp enables youngsters to take part in five-day sessions of space orientation and astronaut training, including simulated weightlessness and a mock space walk. There is even a full-scale mock-up of a space shuttle orbiter.

The camp's proximity to the Kennedy Space Center means students can learn on the spot about NASA's launch, landing and payload operations, while the Astronaut Hall of Fame enables them to learn something of the history of space travel. In its first season in 1988, the Florida Space Camp had a total attendance of 3,700 students. A year later the figure had grown to 5,200, and by the end of 1990 close on 6,000 youngsters had received training.

British children between the ages of nine and 14 will be pleased to learn that they are eligible to attend Space Camp. Parents will be interested to know that fees for the five-day programme include tuition, accommodation—in a private wing of the Howard Johnson Lodge in Titusville—training and supervision 24 hours a day, and all course material. British children can be booked into the Space Camp through the Leisure Corporation Ltd., Maiden Lane Centre, Kilnsea Drive, Lower Earley, Reading, Berkshire RG6 3HD (tel: 0734-351994).

Spaceport USA

Five miles from the US Astronaut Hall of Fame and Space Camp is the Kennedy Space Center's Spaceport USA, said to be Florida's fourth most popular attraction. It is certainly the best bargain. Open from 9 a.m. to dusk every day of the year except Christmas and certain launch dates, the Spaceport offers free admission and parking, although visitors must pay a modest fee to see the spectacular IMAX Theater presentation, *The Dream is Alive*, or

A Kennedy Space Center jeep is dwarfed by a Saturn rocket.

take a two-hour bus tour of the Kennedy Space Center. Make sure you buy tickets for these as soon as you arrive at the Spaceport.

To take everything in, you'll need to set aside six hours, but the tour is worth every minute. Stop first at Spaceport Central, the main entrance building, where information on all activities is available and you can get yourself orientated. The local Chamber of Commerce also has a booth here with information on restaurants and accommodation.

The Gallery of Space Flight displays a combination of actual space hardware and some models portraying many of the significant programmes and events that have occurred in space exploration. Visitors follow a path through displays of historic events, spanning both manned and unmanned efforts to conquer, understand and utilize outer space.

In the Gallery you'll find the *Gemini 9* spacecraft flown by astronauts Stafford and Cernan in 1966, the *Apollo* craft that docked with the Russian *Soyuz* vessel in 1975, and models of a *Lunar Rover* and the *Viking Mars Lander*. A one-tenth scale model of the *Saturn V Moon Rocket* and *Apollo* spacecraft is cut away to show its inner workings.

Outside, in the Rocket Garden, you can stroll among a bed of authentic rockets and pose for photographs with a fully suited "Spaceman".

Space-related exhibits and space art can be viewed in the huge Galaxy Center, which houses the IMAX and Gallery Theaters. The 500-seat Galaxy Theater shows free multi-media

"Fly me to the moon ..." and these engines did just that.

Launch viewing areas are set aside along the coast between Titusville and Sebastian Inlet State Park.

presentations on a number of space topics. One of the newest of these is a full-production quality film, *The Boy from Mars*, a 20-minute story of a 10-year-old boy born and raised on the planet Mars, son of the first Earthlings to bear a child away from Earth. The film follows him on his first visit to the "foreign" planet, Earth.

Another new presentation at Spaceport is Satellites and You, an entertaining 55-minute walk through a simulated future space station. Lifelike electronic characters who move, talk and even blink their eyes, tell visitors how satellites affect everyday life on Earth.

Don't miss *The Dream is Alive*, a special 37-minute film shown on a 21-m (70-ft) wide screen as tall as a six-storey building. It contains footage shot by astronauts on several space shuttle missions.

You should certainly leave time for the tour of the Kennedy Space Center in a luxury air-conditioned double-decker bus. Tours leave every 15 minutes from 9.05 a.m. with the last one departing two hours before dusk, and leave most visitors stunned by the sheer enormity and complexity of the organization behind space research, development and exploration.

If you're lucky, your visit to Spaceport USA might coincide with a live space shuttle or unmanned rocket launch. Launch dates are posted at entrances to the Space Center and there is media build-up before the event, so you would be unlikely to be unaware of it. Launch viewing areas are set aside at numerous locations along the coast between Titusville and Sebastian Inlet State Park.

Merritt Island

Most of the Kennedy Space Center is a national wildlife refuge where nature lives in harmony with the very latest in human technology. Man, however, is no newcomer to the island. Burial and shell mounds provide evidence of aboriginal settlement around Mosquito Lagoon, and later there were groups of Spanish explorers, British colonists and American pioneers who took up citrus fruit growing. In the early 1960s the Kennedy Space Center was established, but not all the island was required for the space programme so the US Fish and Wildlife Service, working closely with NASA, founded the **Merritt Island National Wildlife Refuge** as a sanctuary for wintering wildlife. The National Park Service came on to the scene in 1975 when the Canaveral National Seashore was created and took on the job of preserving the primitive barrier beach and of providing the public with an opportunity to enjoy its resources.

For 40 km (25 miles) Merritt Island protects Florida's east coast, acting as a barrier against the actions of wind and waves. On its western side, the waters of Mosquito Lagoon and the Indian River have helped to create a year-round sub-tropical environment in which many temperate and sub-tropical plants intermingle and provide habitat for a tremendous variety of wildlife, including some of America's rarest and most unusual species.

The 37,000-hectare (92,000-acre) refuge is home to more than 300 species of birds, 25 types of mammal, 117 fish species, and 65 different amphibians and reptiles. Twenty-two of the island's species are shown on Federal or State lists as either endangered or threatened—more than in any other single refuge in the United States. Among the endangered mammals flourishing in the area is the manatee, the gentle sea cow once plentiful in Florida waters, but now reduced to an estimated 1,200 in the entire United States. Patient birdwatchers may catch sight of the southern bald eagle, another rare creature, in graceful flight.

Three walking trails and one you can follow in the car give visitors the chance to obtain close-up views of Merritt Island's natural inhabitants. Leaflets showing maps of the trails, and a wealth of information about the area generally, can be obtained at the visitor information centre.

Two beaches—**Apollo** and **Playalinda**—fringe the wildlife refuge. Both have parking areas and crosswalks to provide access without trampling the native dune vegetation. Both beaches are great places for picnics, but swimmers should beware of rough surf conditions, strong ocean currents and stinging jellyfish.

A limited amount of unsophisticated camping is allowed in the refuge, but permits are required. Information about these and other matters can be obtained from The Manager, Merritt Island National Wildlife Refuge, PO Box 6504, Titusville, FL 32782. There are many privately operated camping and RV grounds in nearby communities. Picnic tables are available at the Apollo Beach information centre and picnicking is allowed on the beaches themselves, but open fires are prohibited. Portable barbecue grills are allowed, but coals must be removed from the beach. Drinking water is available only at the Apollo Beach information centre and the refuge visitor centre. There is no running water anywhere else, and there are no beach showers. Mosquito Lagoon, by the way, means exactly what it says, so visitors should be well armed with repellent.

Although much of Merritt Island is wilderness, there is a permanent human community with a population of around 40,000, and there are a number of attractive residential areas. Permanent settlements began springing up in the 1840s and 1850s, but new homes and farms mainly came after the Civil War. Until the Space Age dawned, Merritt Island's economy depended largely on citrus fruit, sugar cane, pineapple plantations and cattle. The newer residential developments are in the central and southern parts of the island—well away from the wildlife refuge—and the Merritt Square Mall is one of the largest shopping centres in the region, with more than 100 shops, and several cinemas and enticing restaurants.

Old River Road

Back on the mainland, you can take an interesting side trip by leaving US 1 at Williams Point, Sharpes, and following SR 515 to Bonaventure, south of Rockledge. This is part of the original US Highway 1, and before that it was an unpaved track trodden for hundreds of years, first by Indians and later by pioneers and settlers. It is known as the Old River Road, following the course of the Indian River

and changing its name as it progresses: Indian River Drive, Riversedge Boulevard, Riverside Drive and Rockledge Drive. There are many fine old buildings along the River Road, including some which have been abandoned and are crumbling into ruin. The Indian River—which is actually a lagoon—is part of the Intracoastal Waterway, along which luxury yachts and power cruisers sail on their way to the fleshpot marinas of Palm Beach, Fort Lauderdale and Miami—a far cry from the days when smoke-belching steamboats navigated the river, bringing supplies to isolated communities.

Both the Old River Road and US 1 pass through the riverside downtown areas of the city of Cocoa and the adjoining town, Rockledge. **Cocoa** is a picturesque city whose downtown area has been tastefully renovated from an area that was rapidly decaying as shops and offices were deserted in favour of new business locations on the outskirts and on Merritt Island. Luckily, a group of citizens launched a civic improvement campaign and transformed the district into a quaint shopping village with a New England ambience. There are florists, boutiques, antique shops and art and craft workshops, including a pottery and a hardware store more than a century old.

Founded in 1882, Cocoa was originally named Indian River City, but the US Post Office felt it was too long to go into a postmark and insisted it should be changed. According to legend, the locals got together to discuss the matter on the dockside where someone saw the word "cocoa" on the side of a crate which had arrived with the latest batch of freight. Another

Merrit Island National Wildlife Refuge surrounds much of the Kennedy Space Center and is home to many endangered species (previous page).

story is that the city was named after the secret ingredient used by a certain Mrs James, renowned for her baking in the 1880s—though, on reflection it couldn't have been much of a secret if the whole city knew about it.

Rockledge, first settled in 1837, is Brevard County's oldest city. Settlement was sparse at first, but the place grew and prospered as river traffic increased and the railway service developed. It gets its name, as one might expect, from rock formations still to be seen along the western shore of the Indian River. The city's economy was once dependent almost entirely on citrus fruit. Now, it has an 323-hectare (800-acre) industrial park which houses many major industrial and manufacturing businesses.

The Beach Resorts

Causeways lead traffic across Merritt Island to reach the city of **Cape Canaveral** and a number of small beach resorts strung to the south along the Atlantic Ocean shore. Cape Canaveral, the city, is often confused with the Cape Canaveral Air Force Station to the north. In fact, the city developed as a result of the station's missile launch programme in the early

1960s when a number of contractors involved in the projects opened local offices, workshops and warehouses. Today, internationally known electronics and computer companies are among the city's major employers. Cape Canaveral has many sandy beaches and is a growing community of ocean-front properties.

Port Canaveral, at the northern end of the city, is the third largest cruise passenger port in the United States. You can take a "Cruise to Nowhere" for a day with Europa Cruise Line or slip over to the Bahamas for three or four days with Premier Cruise Lines. The port is said to have more recreational facilities—boat launching ramps, camping grounds, parks, fishing areas and the like—than all other ports in Florida combined. Party boats and private charters are available for deep-sea fishing, and there are special charters for shark fishing at night.

Cocoa Beach, a favourite with discriminating British holidaymakers, is the home of **Ron Jon's**, "the world's largest surf shop", which opened in the 1950s as a small surfboard rental and now covers 2,880 m² (31,000 ft²) on two floors, with shopping for everything anyone is likely to need for a holiday in the sun and surf.

Once a sleepy little seaside community, Cocoa Beach today is a bustling place with tall buildings, including hotels and condominiums, and many excellent restaurants and nightspots. Nevertheless, it manages to retain its small-town ambience, and there is ready access to more than 20 km (12 miles) of sandy beach. Beachside parking and changing facilities are to be found at Lori Wilson and Fisher

Patrick Air Force Base
South of Cocoa Beach, Patrick Air Force Base occupies a narrow isthmus between the ocean and the Banana River. Much of the early work in space technology was undertaken here, long before the Kennedy Space Center was built, and the base is still closely involved in both guided missile and space shuttle programmes. It has also had a profound influence on the make-up of the local population, which now includes more than 16,000 retired military personnel. Beyond the base lie the mainly residential oceanside communities of Satellite Beach, Indian Harbor Beach, Indialantic and Melbourne Beach.

Parks, and the city has a recreational complex which features an 18-hole championship golf-course and outstanding tennis courts. Shopping is plentiful.

Causeways and bridges connect these South Brevard beach communities with the city of Melbourne on the mainland. The city and its surroundings form the high-tech centre of the Space Coast, with many manufacturing and light industries. It is also an outstanding residential area, with a population of about 50,000. The present city is the result of a merger between "old" Melbourne and Eau Gallie, its adjoining neighbour to the north. Eau Gallie, the older of the two communities dating from the 1870s, was named from the French word for "water" and an Indian word meaning "rocky" because of the rock ledges alongside the Indian River. The character of an old Southern river landing community is still very strong, especially in the area of the Eau Gallie Yacht Basin.

Despite its workaday nature, **Melbourne** has much to offer the holiday-maker. **Brevard Zoo** houses more than a hundred animal species, including the now rare Florida panther. The **Brevard Art Center and Museum** has one gallery designed especially for the visually handicapped, who are encouraged to touch the exhibits. In the grounds of the Florida Institute of Technology, the **Dent Smith Trail** displays more than 300 varieties of ferns, palms and other tropical foliage.

Palm Bay, south of Melbourne, has become the fastest-growing city in Brevard County and one of the fastest growing in the entire United States. Only a few years ago, it was no more than a sleepy little town; now it enjoys a dynamic and diverse economic base, with extensive cultural and recreational amenities, thanks largely to the multinational electronics companies which have moved into the area.

Beyond Palm Bay, US 1 passes through a rural area with small communities like Malabar, Valkaria, Grant and Micco providing a taste of life in the old Florida. **Sebastian Inlet State Recreation Area**, right on the southern boundary of Brevard County, is reached from Melbourne Beach by

Giant Sea Turtles
During July and August beaches to the south of Melbourne attract giant sea turtles, some weighing as much as 317 kg (700 lb), which lay their eggs in the sand at night. The turtles and their eggs are protected by law, but visitors are allowed to view the nests, sizable mounds of sand covering up to 100 eggs. Bulldozer-like tracks betray the route taken from sea to nest and back by the parent turtles.

Careful visitors are permitted to take part in turtle-watching when eggs are laid in the sand at night.

way of SR A1A. Described as the premier salt-water fishing location on Florida's east coast, the park has two Atlantic jetties and one of the most popular beach areas along the 40 km (25 miles) of coast between Melbourne Beach and Vero Beach. Fishing is also available in the Indian River. Other water activities are swimming, surfing, boating and scuba-diving. Campsites with electricity and water overlook the inlet. Countless shore and wading birds

nest and feed in the park's varied aquatic habitats, and the McLarty Visitor Center tells the story of a Spanish fleet laden with gold and silver that was wrecked 1 km (½ mile) offshore during a hurricane in 1715. Treasure is still being retrieved from the sunken vessels.

Indian River Country

The quiet fishing community of Sebastian, on US 1 on the mainland, marks the start of Indian River County which, together with the counties of St Lucie and the northern edge of Martin, constitutes the area known as Indian River Country. There is some sophistication along this stretch of coast—Vero Beach is one of the wealthiest small towns in the state, and nearby Windsor (where else?) has a polo field on which Prince Charles has played more than once—but in the main this is traditional Florida, still largely dependent on citrus, and a great place for fishing, both commercial and recreational. It is also the land of the clam ranch, where the delectable shellfish is raised commercially on leased areas of the bed of the Indian River. As in the Wild West, where you get ranches you also get rustlers, and clam rustlers have been very active in this area, with some growers losing shellfish worth thousands of dollars in a single night. Unlike cattle, however, clams cannot be branded, so detection is very difficult.

Vero Beach is a posh oceanside resort that is proud of its cultural amenities. These are the professional **Riverside Theatre** (spelt the British way) and the (US spelling, this time) **Center for the Arts**, where national and international exhibitions are featured throughout the year. The city has up-market boutiques and shopping galleries, restaurants and hotels, and its beaches are firm, sandy and uncrowded. Opportunities abound for sailing, fishing and diving, and on shore there are golf and tennis facilities of championship standards. But a visitor's most enduring memory of Vero Beach is likely to be the bizarre **Driftwood Inn**, a rickety-looking construction of beach driftwood, ships' timbers, and planks and window frames salvaged from an abandoned bar. Antique bric-a-brac recovered from ancient Spanish wrecks include cannon, lengths of chain and ships' bells.

The St Lucie County line is crossed some 10 km (6 miles) south of Vero Beach, and the first place worth visiting, right on the outskirts of the city of Fort Pierce, is the **St Lucie Museum and Fort Pierce Inlet State Recreation Area**. The museum displays a collection of treasures recovered from the deep. The 138-hectare (340-acre) park has a good beach and dunes and is a birdwatcher's delight. Recreational activities include swimming, surfing and hiking, and there is a youth camping area.

Pelican Island
Just south of Sebastian is Pelican Island, established in 1903 as the first national wildlife refuge in the United States. The 1.2-hectare (3-acre) island has always been an important breeding ground for pelicans and other birds, which at the turn of the century were being slaughtered by plume hunters. Lobbied by the Florida Audubon Society and the American Ornithologists' Union, President Theodore Roosevelt signed an Executive Order which permanently set the island aside as a wildlife sanctuary.

Today, the sanctuary that was the first of nearly 350 units comprising the National Wildlife Refuge System has expanded to cover more than 1,740 hectares (4,300 acres) along the eastern shore of the Indian River and on a number of neighbouring mangrove islands. It continues as an outstanding nesting site for the endangered brown pelican and for wood ibis, white ibis, common egret, double-crested cormorant and the Louisiana heron. Public use of Pelican Island itself is restricted to avoid disturbance of nesting birds, but there are opportunities for bird-watching and photography from a reasonable distance offshore.

Workaday Fort Pierce, the sea port for Indian River Country, is very much a home for blue-collar industry, and as such is dismissed by some of its more genteel neighbours as Port Fierce. The city and its environs have a community of some 15,000 refugees from the island of Haiti, most of them employed in the citrus industry which is still the area's economic mainstay.

SR A1A leads from Fort Pierce to **Hutchinson Island**, which has a nuclear power station and lots of high-rise condominiums. The island houses the **Elliott Museum**, opened in 1961 to commemorate the work of the American inventor, Sterling Elliott. On show here are the prototype addressing machine, a knot-tying machine and the original quadracycle, a forerunner of the motor car. One wing of the museum displays 14 reconstructed shops dating from the turn of the century, and other sections display collections of shells and contemporary art. One building contains a collection of vintage and veteran cars and motor cycles and horse-drawn vehicles.

Also on the island is **Gilbert's Bar House of Refuge**, a lifeboat station built in 1875 and the last survivor of six such buildings put up along the coast at about the same time. The House of Refuge was restored in 1975 and designated as a National Historic Site. There is a boathouse with early lifesaving equipment and a Victorian house with an upstairs dormitory with room for up to ten shipwreck survivors.

Hutchinson Island is another area where giant turtles come ashore each May to lay their eggs in the sand.

As a change from US 1, County Road 707, also known as Indian River Drive, runs south from Fort Pierce on a 32-km (20-mile) scenic route to Jensen Beach and Stuart. The hilly road meanders along the high bank of the Indian River and skirts Edenlawn, a former pineapple plantation. **Jensen Beach** is a quiet, charming community with good, undeveloped beaches. It has, however, been discovered by the yuppie set who have used their influence as residents to get a series of what the long-term locals call "cuteness laws" passed to make the place twee. Clothes lines on front lawns and boats parked in driveways are forbidden, as are exposed brick and concrete exterior walls on new buildings.

Stuart, at the confluence of the St Lucie and the Indian Rivers—each more than 1.6 km (1 mile) wide at that point—is a highly popular boating, fishing and water-skiing area. Surrounding the city, and worth a day out, are cattle ranches, citrus groves, fishing villages and flower farms with massed chrysanthemums and lilies. Golf and tennis facilities, nightspots with live entertainment, waterside family restaurants and a choice of places for gourmet eating make Stuart a pleasant and relaxed holiday destination.

Sport and recreation continue throughout the year along Florida's Central East coast. Some of the best fishing anywhere is to be found in both the sea and fresh waters. Inland cruises

Indian River Country is renowned for its citrus fruits.

The fishing is good in both salt and fresh water along the Central East coast.

and fishing charters are available on the Intracoastal Waterway.

Along the St Johns River and in various lakes, you can try airboating, and on the sea you can surf, boardsail, jet ski. There's golf, tennis, racquetball and shuffleboard—or you can just lie around and get a tan.

The area has more than 8,300 resort, hotel and motel rooms, some great shopping areas and nearly 1,500 restaurants. The specialty is seafood caught in local waters or the world-renowned Indian River citrus fruits grown locally.

Palm Beach and the
"Venice of America"

Named the Gold Coast for its beautiful beaches, this area is famous for its resorts. Here you can try every sport associated with the sea, or just lie back on your lounger and watch other people showing off their skills. If you're feeling starved of culture, Palm Beach has a wide selection which should keep you happy. There are good facilities for playing tennis and golf, and you may be lucky enough to catch a glimpse of Prince Charles playing polo.

Much of south-east Florida is known as the Gold Coast, perhaps because of the long stretches of sand or the opulence of many of its residents. West Palm Beach, Fort Lauderdale and Miami are the main resorts, with superb, wide beaches along the Atlantic shoreline. The Florida Keys, linked by causeways, form a long, slim tail curving below the main body of the state.

The Intracoastal Waterway follows the coastline, making a navigable highway between the mainland and offshore islands, sometimes plying a course near the edge of the mainland, like blue braid along the hem of a dress.

A few miles inland from Stuart, boat crews can go through a lock into the St Lucie Canal. About 40 km (25 miles) later, cruising through wild countryside, they can enter Lake Okeechobee—at 1,890 km^2 (730 square miles) the fourth biggest lake in the USA. If they have the time, they can emerge into the Caloosahatchee River and cross the state, reaching the Gulf of Mexico at Fort Myers Beach.

Most visitors, of course, are seeking the attractions along or close to the glorious coastline. Water-skiing, windsurfing and other watersports provide

The Intracoastal Waterway is an important highway along the Gold Coast.

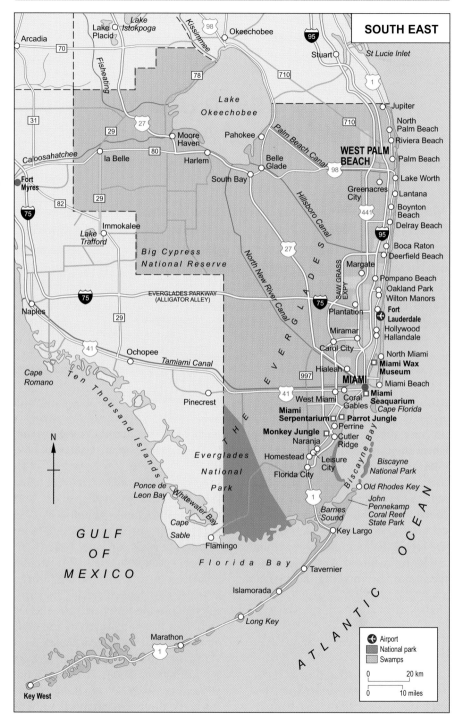

SOUTH EAST

Lake Istokpoga
Lake Placid
Lake Okeechobee
Arcadia
70
Okeechobee
95
Stuart
St Lucie Inlet
Kissimmee
Fisheating
78
710
Lake Okeechobee
31
29
27
Moore Haven
Pahokee
Palm Beach Canal
710
WEST PALM BEACH
98
Jupiter
North Palm Beach
Riviera Beach
Palm Beach
la Belle
80
Harlem
Belle Glade
Caloosahatchee
Fort Myres
South Bay
Lake Worth
Greenacres City
Lantana
82
29
441
Boynton Beach
Delray Beach
75
Immokalee
Lake Trafford
Big Cypress National Reserve
Hillsboro Canal
27
95
Boca Raton
Deerfield Beach
SAW GRASS
Margate
Pompano Beach
Oakland Park
Wilton Manors
75
75
EVERGLADES PARKWAY (ALLIGATOR ALLEY)
North New River Canal
SAW GRASS EXPY
Plantation
Fort Lauderdale
Naples
29
Miramar
Hollywood
Hallandale
41
Ochopee
Tamiami Canal
Carol City
North Miami
Cape Romano
Ten Thousand Islands
Pinecrest
997
Hialeah
MIAMI
Miami Wax Museum
Miami Beach
41
West Miami
Coral Gables
Miami Seaquarium
Cape Florida
Miami Serpentarium
Parrot Jungle
Monkey Jungle
Perrine
Cutler Ridge
Naranja
Everglades National Park
Homestead
Leisure City
Florida City
THE EVERGLADES
Biscayne Bay
Biscayne National Park
Old Rhodes Key
Ponce de Leon Bay
Whitewater Bay
John Pennekamp Coral Reef State Park
Barnes Sound
Cape Sable
Flamingo
Key Largo
GULF OF MEXICO
Florida Bay
Tavernier
ATLANTIC OCEAN
Islamorada
Long Key
Airport
National park
Swamps
Marathon
1
0   20 km
0   10 miles
Key West

N

118

a colourful spectacle for beach loungers and some excitement for the participants. Golf and tennis are played throughout the year. Prince Charles has played polo in Palm Beach County. There are fields from which the public can watch.

Jupiter is the first main place of interest at the northern end of the Gold Coast. You may see a familiar face there—that of the actor Burt Reynolds. He grew up in Jupiter, where his father was once the sheriff, and left home to make his fortune as a star of the silver screen. Years later he returned and, in 1979, opened a dinner theatre, where he appears in the occasional play himself.

Tourists are not encouraged to go rubbernecking at Jupiter Inlet Colony on Jupiter Island, where people who are rich or famous or both have magnificent residences. They live between the Intracoastal Waterway and the mainland. There is an **Audubon Society bird preserve** on the island—48 hectares (120 acres) of ocean front where there are also shell mounds 4 m (14 ft) high, on the site of an old Indian campground. Jupiter has a new museum, the **Loxahatchee Historical Museum**, built in the style of the pioneer days.

A few miles north of Jupiter is the **Dickinson State Park**. A large area of tall sand dunes forms an unusual landscape. There are campsites and hiking trails, and activities include canoeing, fishing, horse-riding, cycling and wildlife watching. A 30-passenger boat gives jungle cruises on the upper reaches of the Loxahatchee River.

Palm Beach County

Follow the shoreline southward to the Palm Beaches. Hedonists may feel the odd twinge of envy here as most of the residents seem to spend their time sunbathing, cruising in splendid motor yachts, skimming along in powerboats, playing golf and generally enjoying an up-market lifestyle. They seem pretty content with their lot.

Palm Beach County stretches from Jupiter to Boca Raton and has 75 km (47 miles) of sandy beaches. There are more than 130 golf-courses in the county, and the Professional Golfers' Association of America is based here. Tennis, too, is a major sport year round, with more than 1,000 courts in Palm Beach County, and the big names of international tennis playing there. Polo matches take place on Sunday afternoons in the season. Spectator stands are usually packed, and celebrity spotters have a field-day. Dog racing is America's sixth-largest spectator sport, and the track at West Palm Beach has attracted crowds for 60 seasons. Eighty per cent of the revenue from bets goes back to the punters.

Visitors wanting to fish have a choice of inshore waters—the Intracoastal Waterway with its system of canals and tidal flats—and rivers, as well as the Atlantic Ocean, through which the Gulf Stream flows. Boats can be chartered by the half-day or full

M ap of South-east Florida—"The Gold Coast".

119

*P*olo is a popular
spectator sport in Palm Beach
County on Sundays.

day, with an experienced captain to
advise, and tackle provided. Drift fishing boats offer morning, afternoon and
evening trips.

Shell collecting, snorkelling and
nature study can be enjoyed at the
John D. MacArthur Beach State Park,
a barrier island at North Palm Beach.
Mr MacArthur, who died in 1976, developed much of the town which has
a population of 13,000 people. One of
its golf-courses, the exclusive Seminole,
is considered by many to be among the
finest in the county.

Imagine planning a small town,
starting with an undeveloped beachside
site. That's how **Lake Park** began. The
developer was Harry Seymour Kelsey,
and the original name in 1920 was
Kelsey City. Lake Park has two golf-
courses and a 40-hectare (100-acre)
sports complex with bandstand. **Riviera Beach** is another of Kelsey's developments, in association with Paris
Singer, the sewing machine magnate. It
comprises Singer Island, Mangonia
Park and Palm Beach Shores.

*F*ashionable Worth
Avenue is where everyone likes
to shop in Palm Beach.

The Celestial Railroad

A railroad only a few miles long gave the small community of Juno Beach considerable importance after it opened in 1888, and the following year the hamlet became the county town of Dade, which at that time encompassed the present three-county area of Dade, Broward and Palm Beach. The line went northward from Juno to Jupiter, with two stations in between, Mars and Venus. Predictably, it was known as the Celestial Railroad. Within eight years it was obsolete. Magnate Henry Flagler wanted to buy it to extend his Florida East Coast Railroad, but he considered the price too high. So he built his own, which by-passed Juno, knocking it back to village status, while Miami took over as county seat. However, Juno Beach, with a population below 2,000, still has its heavenly aspect and is a relaxing place to spend a holiday.

Palm Beach

A few miles farther south is **Palm Beach**, so called because of the coconut palms growing there as a result of an unexpected delivery of coconuts one day in 1870. They had been in the hold of a ship from Trinidad which foundered, spilling its cargo, and settlers planted them.

Palm Beach's tourism began more than 120 years ago, when an enterprising homesteader extended his home, met the steamers which brought northern visitors from Titusville down the Indian River to Jupiter, and transported them by covered wagon to Lake Worth. They sailed across the lake to the jetty at Coconut Grove House.

Today there are many beautiful hotels, including **The Breakers**, which has a resident historian, a croquet lawn

and a 36-hole golf-course. Originally opened by Flagler and called the Palm Beach Inn, it was extended and given its present name. It caught fire twice and was rebuilt. The present building was opened in 1926.

The house that Flagler built in 1901 for his third wife is now the **Flagler Museum**. As well as antiques and fine arts, there are exhibits of railroad memorabilia.

Worth Avenue is the place to go for fashionable shops. Close by is the elegant **Colony Hotel**, where the well-heeled locals meet for cocktails. Strong

Lion Country Safari is a drive-through wildlife preserve with animals roaming freely.

on culture, Palm Beach offers opera, theatre (including a children's theatre), and, under one roof, the **Society of the Four Arts**, dedicated to painting, music, literature and drama.

Ocean Boulevard, with its splendid mansions, entices tourists anxious to see how the other half lives. One way to get a view of the multi-million dollar residences is to take a sightseeing cruise aboard a 150-passenger Mississippi sternwheeler or a Hudson River Steamboat replica which can carry 500 passengers. Lunch cruises and dinner-dance cruises are available.

West Palm Beach
On the western side of Lake Worth is **West Palm Beach**. The population of 70,000 makes it Palm Beach County's biggest city. Its mix of business, commerce and industry dilutes the

impression of a paradise top-heavy with wealthy senior citizens and early retirees. Computer and electronic manufacturing companies in the region have attracted people with young families. Eating out offers a wide choice of international cuisines, including Italian, Spanish, Mexican, Thai and Chinese.

Of special interest to children are four huge water slides in a park which also has a 19-hole minigolf-course, and the **Dreher Park Zoo**, with nearly 100 animal species, nature trails and a picnic area. The **South Florida Science Museum** close by has hands-on exhibits, an aquarium and a planetarium.

A drive-through wildlife preserve, the **Lion Country Safari**, is based 24 km (15 miles) west of West Palm Beach. As well as the roaming animals and a petting zoo, there are paddleboats and a Safari Queen cruise, miniature golf and a dinosaur exhibit.

West Palm Beach is justifiably proud of its **Norton Gallery of Art**. It has a permanent collection and a programme of exhibitions, concerts, films and lectures.

Field-study groups and individuals learn much about caring for the environment at the **Pine Jog Environmental Sciences Center**. Nature walks are organized, and there's a gift shop.

Go a little farther west for **Palm Beach Gardens**, headquarters of the Professional Golfers' Association of America and also the US Croquet Association.

Lake Worth is, in fact, a salt-water lagoon, and the town that grew up there, also called Lake Worth, with a population of about 28,000, is renowned for its fishing. The Gulf Stream, like a warm river in the ocean,

is only 8 km (5 miles) away, and there is excellent fishing from the long city pier at Lake Worth, or from the many other piers and bridges. Offshore, novices and experts alike may catch large sailfish from a chartered boat. These game fish are plentiful and are available all year round.

Several small communities have grown up near Lake Worth as recently as the 1950s. By far the biggest, with a population of 10,000, is Palm Springs.

The last Palm Beach to mention is **South Palm Beach**. These and other beach communities in south-east Florida tend to merge, but they all like to keep their own identities. This one, as its name suggests, is at the southernmost tip of Palm Beach. The town has about 400 people, and another 1,500 people—mainly retired—occupy the condominiums and residences of Manalapan, on the oceanside just north of South Palm Beach.

For a place with fewer than 9,000 people, **Lantana** offers some exciting pursuits. You can take a ride in a glider, a biplane or a helicopter, and you can learn barefoot and slalom water-skiing. Moreover, the fabled *National Enquirer* has its headquarters in Lantana. Browse through the newspaper's files if you enjoy being scandalized.

Boynton Beach was a small settlement until Flagler's Florida East Coast Railroad reached it in the 1890s. Flagler built a hotel, and many people who visited decided to set up home there. It's an ill wind that blows nobody any good, and the building boom went into full swing when a Norwegian ship sank offshore. Its cargo of timber was hauled in and used to build houses, some of which still exist. Today the living is easy for the 45,000 residents and the tourists, with golf, tennis, fishing, boating and a range of watersports to while away the time.

Palm Beach County's original polo centre was at Delray Beach, when fashionable figures of the forties and fifties, like Woolworth heiress Barbara Hutton and British-born film star Cary Grant graced the grandstand. Horses are still trained there.

The "Gold Coast", as the south-east coast of Florida is called, could just as aptly be called the "Golf Coast". There are more than 30 courses within a 40-km (25-mile) radius of Delray Beach, and nearly four dozen hard and soft courts at the international tennis resort of Delray.

For the non-sporting, there's a choice of two cruises along the Intracoastal Waterway to a restaurant lunch. One passenger boat, *The Patriot*, takes you to the Pal Captain's Table every day except Sunday. The other is a steamboat replica which goes to the Tropics Restaurant.

The **Morikami Museum** of Japanese Culture gives a glimpse of a lifestyle different from Florida's in the form of a 63-hectare (155-acre) park with Japanese gardens, a museum of furnished rooms and a fine display of bonsai trees.The Japanese connection dates from the early 1900s when Japanese farmers settled in the area, growing vegetables and other crops. A street festival, taking up seven blocks of Main Street, brings in the crowds for the weekend after Easter. It's called the **Delray Affair**, and home-cooked food is served.

Boca Raton

The town of **Boca Raton** lost its farming image long ago. There's a strong business community, and the leisure scene has a lot to offer. For a start, there's the beach—more than 3 km (2 miles) of it. And there's the 18.6-hectare (46-acre) **Spanish River Park** with nearly 615 m (2,000 ft) of ocean frontage. The beaches are connected to the rest of the park by tunnels which go under the highway. Nature trails lead through natural hammock and woodland, and there's a picnic area and observation tower.

Gumbo Limbo Nature Centre also has an observation tower within its 6 hectares (15 acres). Environmental education classes are held, research is carried out and there are seminars, workshops and field trips. Trips to see alligators and other wildlife in their natural habitat are available at Loxahatchee Recreation Area.

Professional theatres include the **Royal Palm Dinner Theater**, a museum of art and a children's museum, with computer games among its hands-on activities.

The highly regarded **Royal Palm Polo Sports Club**, set in 65 hectares (160 acres), has other equestrian facilities and tennis courts, and picnic areas. Polo matches are held on Sundays in the season (December to April), often with international stars taking part.

The city goes *en fête* several times a year. In spring there's a **Meet Me Downtown Festival**. The **Mizner Festival**, featuring cultural and historic events, lasts for nearly six weeks in April and May. The **Boca Festival Days** event takes place throughout

August. At Christmas there's the **Winter Fantasy Boat Parade**.

As you can imagine, in such a lively place there are some fine restaurants and cafés where excellent fresh seafood is on the menu. Night-life ranges from the informality of live reggae and rock 'n' roll at **Tugboat Annie's** to the splendidly upscale **Club Boca**. The **Good Times Comedy Café** is the place for plenty of laughs.

Broward County

Greater Fort Lauderdale

Just south of Boca Raton is the resort city of **Deerfield Beach**, like all resorts today geared to conference business as well as leisure in its sun-sea-and-sand setting. We have now left Palm Beach County, entered Broward County and are in the Greater Fort Lauderdale area. Broward County has 37 km (23 miles) of continuous beach and 260 km (160 miles) of wide, navigable canals and inland waterways which give it the predictable tag "Venice of America". Another 160-plus km (100-plus miles) are navigable by small craft. Many of the navigable waterways go through cities and suburbs. Water taxis provide a pleasant and convenient way of getting about, and some of the hotels have a waterways pick-up service. Lighthouse Point, at Hillsboro Inlet, is the site of a 40-m (130-ft) lighthouse which was built in 1907.

Travelling south from Deerfield Beach, the first sizeable place you reach is **Pompano Beach**, an agricultural centre as well as a resort. The place is said to have been given its

*T*here is a nautical flavour to Greater Fort Lauderdale, which has dozens of canals and inland waterways.

name by a surveyor, who wrote the name "pompano" on a map to mark the place where he had eaten a tasty local fish of that name.

The Intracoastal Waterway, running roughly parallel with the coast, is the place for motorway-style boating. It's slightly less hectic on weekdays than at weekends, but this is where the jet-set boaters like to see the speedometer needle hit the high spots. You can dine in fantastic restaurants overlooking the water where multi-millionaires' yachts are moored.

*I*t is worth getting up early to see the sunrise over Fort Lauderdale Beach.

Fort Lauderdale is a big, busy city and a lot goes on there. Adjacent **Lauderdale-by-the-Sea** is altogether more sedate. On either side of Fort Lauderdale the Atlantic Ocean tends to hide behind high-rise buildings. Since the mid-1980s there has been considerable development of hotels

and condominiums plus the infra-structure to add enormous tourism capacity to the area. But the surf and sand are there, and the facilities for fishing. The glamour catch from the ocean is the blue marlin. Deep-sea boats can be chartered—at a price—or you can fish from one of the long piers

that are a feature of the Gold Coast. Freshwater game fish can be found in Broward County's inland waterways and marinas.

Drift fishing is a popular sport, especially with novices. Four-hour excursions are offered daily, in the morning, afternoon and evening. The fee per person includes instruction, fishing tackle and bait and the crew's local knowledge about where the fish lie. The boats head for reefs within 3 km (2 miles) of the shore. Their engines are switched off and they drift with the tide, while the eager occupants hope to catch a tasty supper of snapper, grouper or tarpon.

Likely catches from a fishing pier include pompano, amberjack, bluefish, snapper, snook, mackerel and, maybe, a spiny Florida lobster. Pompano Beach's Fisherman's Wharf juts more than 300 m (1,000 ft) into the ocean. Another very popular fishing pier is the 265-m (875-ft) one at Lauderdale-by-the-Sea. There is a modest charge for fishing from these piers. Rods and reels can be rented cheaply.

Along the Gold Coast most of the population lives close to the shore, but between Pompano Beach and Miami there are quite large communities some 30 km (20 miles) into the interior, adjoining The Everglades. These areas are still growing.

One of them is **Davie**, where the Wild West makes an impact on the south-east. Earlier this century this was cattle-raising country, with cowboys to herd the cattle. Orange groves, sugar-cane fields and dairying are part of the agricultural scene. An annual **Orange Blossom Festival** is held during a weekend in March. Rodeos, horse shows and parades are held. Catchy music and out-of-doors food make it a great country celebration.

Horses are very much a year-round aspect of life in Davie, with twice-weekly rodeos. There are equestrian estates all around the town, which has a population of around 35,000. The local uniform is boots, stetson and Western-style shirt and jeans. The town hall and the local McDonald's have hitching posts outside.

Special Events

Downtown Fort Lauderdale's attractions include a museum for children called the **Discovery Centre**, opened in 1905, and a new **Museum of Art**. Special events take place throughout the year—more in winter than in summer. There's an international boat show in late October and early November, claimed to be the world's biggest on-water exhibition. In January there's the World Rowing Marathon, a six-day race in which teams from many countries row 122 km (76 miles) down the Intracoastal Waterway from Palm Beach to Miami.

Winterfest takes up most of December. Among the highlights are the Fort Lauderdale Boat Parade, with several million dollars' worth of decorated and illuminated boats parading for 11 km (7 miles) along the Intracoastal Waterway, and as a grand finale on New Year's Eve, the Light Up Lauderdale event—a fireworks and laser display. In addition an Arts and Crafts Festival, Christmas music performances, a children's theatre Christmas pageant, a triathlon and the Candy Cane Parade—floats, bands, skaters and all the razzmatazz you can think of—are some of the special activities.

Other Attractions

Permanent attractions, apart from the 11-km (6.5-mile) stretch of wide beach that is the city's pride and joy, include the **Swimming Hall of Fame**, with gold medals and trophies of the sport's celebrities and exhibits from more than 100 countries. At **Butterfly World** visitors can stroll through tropical gardens where there are hundreds of species of butterflies flitting about. Sea lions and porpoises entertain like true professionals at **Ocean World**, and sharks and sea turtles are on display.

For a city tour, take the Voyager Sightseeing Tram. It makes four 29-km (18-mile) trips a day. Passengers see magnificent waterside homes, the beach, residential avenues, shopping malls, marinas, and get a good general overall picture of the city. "Greater Fort Lauderdale, where the fun never sets" is the publicity claim made for the area, and there's certainly a sparkling lifestyle, especially after dark.

Fort Lauderdale has become a popular destination for families. For years students from all over North America arrived in such vast crowds as to cause a problem which the local authorities addressed. Today numbers have diminished to manageable proportions and there's elbow room in the bars and nightspots. The conference and exhibition markets are increasingly important, and the corporate and business traveller is being courted. The new Greater Fort Lauderdale/Broward County **Convention Center** has 34,400 m^2 (370,000 ft^2) of exhibition space. Also new is the $50 million

128

*B*utterfly World is a favourite attraction, with hundreds of species to be seen in the tropical gardens.

Broward Center for the Performing Arts in downtown Fort Lauderdale. Its multi-use facility includes a theatre seating 2,700 people.

Just south of Fort Lauderdale, and another important resort, is **Hollywood**, which has a wide range of accommodation. South Florida's largest water theme park is here—**Atlantis, the Water Kingdom**, is set in 26 hectares (65 acres) of park around an 4.5-hectare (11-acre) lake. It has more than 80 exciting rides and chutes. Sample the Raging Rampage if you dare. It has a 37-m (120-ft) slide at an angle of 45 degrees.

Seminole Village

Near Hollywood is a Seminole Native Village where animals native to Florida can be seen. The village, which includes a museum of paintings of the Indian way of life, is open every weekday and on Sunday afternoons. Gambling for high stakes at bingo is illegal in Florida, but the Seminoles' reservation is federally protected and they are allowed to run a bingo hall where a player can win more than $100,000. The hall seats 1,400. People pile in from all over Florida and are often joined by visitors from abroad. Bingo is played every afternoon and evening except Sunday.

A Stylish, Sub-tropical City and Unique Wildlife Park

A diverse mix of cultures makes Greater Miami a fascinating city. It contains a number of architectural gems and an American Police Hall of Fame. Parks, beaches and museums will please the adults in your party, while children will love the Seaquarium and hands-on science exhibition. Coral Gables is a gracious city within a city with miles of cycle paths allowing you to fully appreciate its beauty. Of special interest is a lovely park designed for handicapped people. Before you leave, check out the Everglades and you will understand why people fight to preserve this "sea of grass".

Miami is a beautiful city, with its 21st-century skyline. It has architectural diversity, a touch of whimsy, a touch of fantasy, Mediterranean Revival, Italian Renaissance, rainbow-coloured skyscrapers, mirror-glass office towers. Anyone who knew Miami before the 1980s and revisited for the first time now would scarcely recognize it. The building boom of the early 1980s has produced an original and stylish city. Many of the buildings are festooned in

Villa Viscaya, an oceanside home and now a museum, is filled with works of art and antiques that have been collected in Europe.

sub-tropical greenery and blossoms. Some of the most spectacular architecture can be seen along Brickell Avenue. When Florida changed its banking laws in the late 1970s, Miami found itself well positioned to become a new foreign banking centre in the USA. Brickell Avenue, known as the "Wall Street of Miami", really is quite dazzling.

There are 3½-hour organized walking tours of downtown Miami and its historic sites. To arrange to join one of these, or a shorter tour of **Brickell Avenue** or the neighbourhoods of Coconut Grove, Coral Gables, South Beach and Little Havana, telephone (305) 858-6021. For information on tours throughout the historic Black neighbourhoods of Greater Miami, call

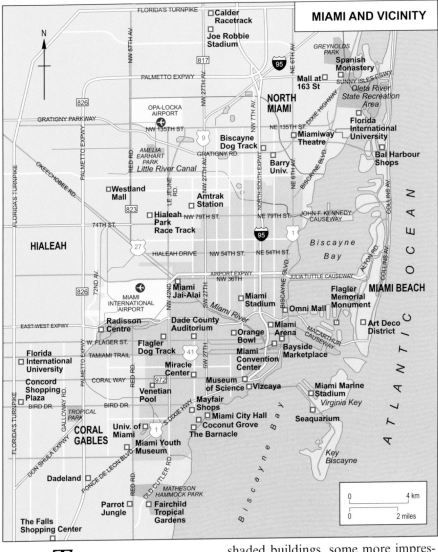

MIAMI AND VICINITY

Town plan of Greater Miami.

the Black Archives (305) 638-6500. The famous Art-Deco district of **Miami Beach**, carefully restored in recent years, attracts many visitors. There are more than 800 ornamented and pastel-shaded buildings, some more impressive than others. **Ocean Drive** is one of the most fashionable Art-Deco streets. To immerse yourself in the decor of the 1930s, stay in one of the several Art-Deco hotels. Miami Beach Police headquarters is also a good example of the period. On Saturday mornings at 10.30 a.m. a 90-minute guided walk of the Art-Deco district is organized. For details phone (305) 672-2041. Each participant is asked to make a few dollars' contribution.

The Development of Miami

One of the causeways crossing Biscayne Bay, part of the Intracoastal Waterway, is named after Julia Tuttle. It was purely a result of her vision and persistence that Greater Miami came into existence. Miami is still the only

*T*he sands of Miami Beach all but disappeared during the 1970s—the result of badly conceived development. Fortunately, the damage was reversed when the Army was called in.

known city in the USA founded by a woman.

Julia Tuttle, the wife of a wealthy industrialist from Cleveland, Ohio, moved south with her two small children. They arrived in what was to become Miami—then just an isolated trading post—by mail boat in 1875. The region was wild and remote, a mosquito-ridden swampland. What Julia Tuttle saw were the ruins of a US Army camp, formerly known as Fort Dallas, an Indian trading post and a couple of plantations along the shore of Biscayne Bay. The area was unsurveyed, and the only inhabitants were a few Seminole Indians. Explorers and hunters were the only visitors.

But in her mind's eye, Julia Tuttle saw a beautiful city with a sub-tropical climate, where people could spend vacations soaking up the sun.

The problem was access. There were only two ways to reach South Florida, by cargo-carrying sloop down the east

The Vanishing Beach

To look at the wide, sandy shores of Miami Beach today, you'd hardly believe that during the 1970s the beach all but disappeared, because of man's interference with nature.

Miami Beach was part of the mainland until 1925, when, in deference to navigation interests, a channel was cut at Bakers Haulover, turning Miami Beach into an island. The natural movement of sand along the shore was interrupted, and the island lost its beach like some men lose their hair.

There were two more contributory factors: sea walls to protect hotels were built at high water-line, moving the shore eastward to expose only low-tide beach. The waves hit harder and the erosion of the shoreline increased. And sand dunes were bulldozed to allow for new beach construction. It wasn't appreciated at that time that dunes absorb energy from breaking storm waves which are a major cause of beach erosion.

So the time came when the beach was reduced to a mere fringe. Not only had the sunbathing possibilities been drastically curtailed, there was also the fear that the sea walls would crumble into the Atlantic, dragging the pool areas of the luxury hotels with them.

Experts devised a beach restoration project. It involved re-creating an eroded bar of sediment in deep, calm offshore water, to cause incoming waves to break farther offshore and dissipate their energy. Also, the level section of beach, formed by wave movement, was extended to a 15-m (50-ft) width, causing large storm waves, which can cause erosion, to break many more times, losing power with each break. Finally, a 6-m (20-ft) wide hurricane dune, built 3.50 m (11.5 ft) above mean low-water level, was installed.

The work was carried out by the US Army Corps of Engineers at a cost of $64 million and completed in 1982, when the soldiers moved on to a similar project at Key Biscayne. Now Miami Beach still has its 16-km (10-mile) stretch of white sand, wide as a football pitch, and feels as proud as a bald man who has found a hair restorer which really works.

coast, an arduous and sometimes dangerous voyage, or by cattle cart, following old Indian trails, a long and comfortless journey. The obvious answer was the railroad. At this time it was 640 km (400 miles) away, having penetrated just south of Georgia's border with Florida.

Julia Tuttle was well aware of Henry Flagler, the railroad tycoon, whose work, as the years went by, was opening up parts of the state. But Flagler wasn't interested in the far southern region, and resisted her powers of persuasion. He even turned down an offer of a gift of 120 hectares

(300 acres) of land. Then, in the winter of 1894–95, 20 years after her arrival in Florida, nature proved to be her ally. The state was in the grip of a rare but relentless frost, which almost wiped out the new citrus industry that had seemed so promising. Only the extreme south-east and south remained untouched by low temperatures. Julia Tuttle sent Henry Flagler a bouquet of freshly picked orange blossom, proving to him that Miami could deliver citrus fruits to northern markets year-round.

Flagler wasted no time. His Florida East Coast Railroad was extended to

Biscayne Bay, and in 1896 it was in operation. Today, the rail tycoon's name lives on in Miami, commemorated in one of the major streets, Flagler Drive. The railroad was rapidly followed by the wealthy. Palatial homes and grand hotels sprang up in Miami Beach, Coral Gables, Opa Locka, Hialeah and other neighbourhoods around Miami, replacing the mangrove and scrub vegetation.

If building soared in the twenties, thirties and fifties, it almost went into

M iami has developed into a stylish city following a building boom in the 1980s.

orbit in the heady 1980s. Skyscrapers, in designs at which one can only marvel, sprang up in downtown Miami and along the boulevards flanking Biscayne Bay. Miami's new harbour suddenly became the world's biggest cruise-ship port. Miami International Airport achieved importance for the number of its international flights. Banks, insurance companies and multinational corporations moved in by the score. In Europe and the Far East, as well as in North America, Miami gained a high profile as a sophisticated modern city with an up-market infrastructure—a great place to set up home and a fun place for a vacation.

Of course not all publicity is good publicity. While TV shows have put Miami firmly on the world map, some

have emphasized the seamy side—the violence and the illicit drugs scene. Like all world-class cosmopolitan cities, Miami has its share of vice—arguably less today than in the past decade or two. But unless tourists go looking for trouble, they are likely to remain unaware of any problems which may exist.

Getting Around Miami

For a general view of what Greater Miami has to offer, take the **Old Town Trolley** which goes to noted spots, including the **Art-Deco** district. There are 14 stops. You can get on and off as you wish, to shop, see the sights, have a meal. Or you can sit tight for the

After a long period of neglect, the Art-Deco buildings of Miami Beach have been restored, and visitors can take a guided walk around the area.

prominent people. The John F. Kennedy Memorial Torch has a perpetual flame at the top of an 5.5-m (18-ft) shaft.

Greater Miami has a multicultural population approaching two million and covers an area of 5,180 sq. km (2,000 sq. miles). There are more than a dozen notable shopping centres and malls open on weekdays and Sunday afternoons. One of the first you come to, driving south from Fort Lauderdale, is **Bal Harbour Shops** in Collins Avenue, known for its world-renowned fashion boutiques and specialty stores—Gucci, Cartier, Saks Fifth Avenue.

Biscayne Bay separates Miami from Miami Beach. It is crossed at intervals by several causeways. There are beautiful homes, beautiful yachts and beautiful views to admire. **Miami Beach** is 22 km (14 miles) from Miami International Airport. It is reached in less than half an hour by car. Downtown Miami is about 13 km (8 miles) from the airport—a 20-minute ride.

For a less conventional form of transport than the excellent Metromover (*see* sidebar), take a rickshaw ride. A company called Majestic Rickshaw operates in Coconut Grove, Bayside and Miami Beach. The charge is per 10 minutes per person—in 1990 it

two-hour narrated tour. There's a trolley every 30 minutes. Also, to link with them, open-air trolley cars depart from Bayside Marketplace on three routes— Port of Miami, Omni International Complex and Coconut Grove.

Just to the south of Port of Miami is **Bayfront Park** of the Americas, a quiet retreat with monuments to

Boom Town Miami

After World War I, northerners flocked to South Florida for vacations. Many decided to stay on, buying winter retreats or permanent homes. Others, in considerable numbers, cashed in on the massive profits that could be made in real estate. Some properties changed hands time and time again, each purchaser paying far more than the last. This was the 1920s boom time. Miami's population soared. In five years it went up from 30,000 to 100,000. Holiday-makers added another 300,000 every winter. (Today 1.8 million people live in Greater Miami.)

It was boom time for con men, too. Their honeyed words made a few acres of swamp sound like a residential paradise. As people realized that many developments were being built without the guaranteed improvements that should have been made, the clamour for property cooled off. Boom turned to bust. In 1929 the stock market crashed and the Great Depression took hold. One neighbourhood, however, which remained less affected than some, was Miami Beach. The new Art-Deco architecture, with pastel colours, ornamentation and the Streamline Moderne style, reflected people's desire for relief from the troubles of the times. Hotels here charged less than the opulent resort hotels elsewhere in the region, and budget-minded visitors enjoyed staying in them.

World War II was followed by another boom. Thousands of American servicemen had undergone their training at Miami Beach, and a lot of them, feeling that their northern home towns compared unfavourably with southern Florida, settled in Greater Miami with their families. A frenzy of development took place to keep up with the demand.

In the early 1960s, following Fidel Castro's coup, the Cubans arrived—265,000 of them. Thousands more Latin immigrants have arrived since. Greater Miami emerged as a world financial centre, a commercial capital of the Caribbean and much of Latin America, as well as being a resort with the aura of the tropics, offering a wide range of activities and attractions and a sophisticated lifestyle.

People Mover

Few places are blessed with such a first-rate public transport system as Miami. Helping to keep countless cars off the road is the Metromover, affectionately known as the People Mover, which was introduced in 1986. Computerized cars stop at nine stations along a double-loop track just under 3 km (2 miles) long, high above the ground and sweeping around the sides of skyscrapers. It covers a 26-block business district and you never wait more than two-and-a-half minutes for a car—often it's only 90 seconds. By 1994 it will have extended north to the Omni International Mall and south along the Brickell Avenue business corridor to Coral Way. The fully automated system operates from 6 a.m. to 9 p.m. on weekdays and from 8.30 a.m. to 6.30 p.m. at weekends. It is extremely cheap to use.

At Government Station it connects with Metrorail, another sleek and low-cost service. This elevated rail transit system serves downtown and some of the suburbs, with 20 stations on the 33-km (21-mile) route. It's fast, and it provides spectacular views, including one of a long, long neon sculpture over the Miami River that is splendid after dark. Metrorail operates the same hours as Metromover. For ground-level travel, there's Metrobus, with 65 routes around Dade County by coach or minibus. Metrobus carries 200,000 passengers a day.

The Port of Miami is the world's biggest embarkation point for cruise ships, from a three-day trip to the Bahamas to a round-the-world voyage.

was three dollars. The rickshaw service runs from 9 a.m. to 2 a.m.

Forget Miami Vice. Miami Nice is the name of a cab drivers' charm school programme introduced a few years ago. Thousands of taxi drivers have received training in courtesy, grooming and cab care on which their licences depend.

Things to Do in Miami

South of Miami Beach are Virginia Key and Key Biscayne, reached by the Rickenbacker Causeway, a toll road. Key Biscayne has 8 km (5 miles) of beaches. Two riveting places to visit are quite close together. One is the Miami Seaquarium, where the sea lions are natural comedians and entertainment is also provided by dolphins and a 4,500-kg (10,000-lb) killer whale. Visitors can watch sharks, manatees and stingrays being fed. There are aquaria full of tropical fish. A lush, tropical area, declared an official wildlife sanctuary, is home to native birds, sea turtles and crocodiles—Florida has a few crocodiles as well as thousands of alligators. Plans to develop the Miami Seaquarium as a recreational and educational marine park should now be in progress.

The other must-see centre nearby is the **Miami Museum of Science and Space Transit Planetarium**—another one the children will enjoy as well as adults. There's enough to keep you absorbed all day and half the night. Hands-on exhibits cover a wide range of subjects, from light, sound and electronics to human biology. Demonstrations of scientific phenomena are given. There's a collection gallery of rare natural history specimens. The Wildlife Centre has live reptiles, giant insects and an aviary. The Space Transit Planetarium has a 20-m (65-ft) dome. State-of-the-art astronomy and laser shows take place daily, with a free show on Thursday evenings. Also, stargazers can visit the Observatory free of charge on weekend evenings. The Museum and Planetarium underwent an expansion programme costing more than five million dollars a year or two ago. To find out times of the Planetarium shows or to inquire what is currently in Miami's night skies, ring the Cosmic Hotline on (305) 854-2222.

Biscayne Boulevard, in downtown Miami, draws the shopaholics. **Omni International Mall** has 125 stores offering a tremendous range of goods. When your feet get tired you have a choice of 17 restaurants and a 10-screen theatre in the mall. If you don't find all the presents you need to take home, try the new **Bayside Marketplace** on Biscayne Bay. Built on 6.5 hectares (16 acres) of waterfront, this shopping, eating and entertainment complex reflects Miami's ethnic and cultural qualities. Craftspeople, inventors and entrepreneurs add to the character of the place at Pier 5. The marketplace opens from 10 a.m. to 10 p.m. Monday to Saturday and on Sundays from noon to 8 p.m.

Gondola rides can be taken from the marina by Bayside Marketplace. Also available are tours of HMS *Bounty*, which is moored at the marina. It is a reproduction of the 18th-century fully rigged merchant ship which featured in the 1962 MGM film *Mutiny on the Bounty*.

Since 1990 Biscayne Boulevard has been the site of another museum, one that is claimed to be unique. Formerly located on Florida's west coast, it is the **American Police Hall of Fame and Museum**. It contains 10,000 artefacts and items from the past and present, including a replica of the electric

140

chair, gas chamber and cells. More than 3,000 police officers who lost their lives on duty are commemorated by a 406,400-kg (400-ton) marble memorial. Photographs, a scene-of-crime room, firearms, uniforms and law enforcement memorabilia are displayed in the museum.

*M*iami's Metrorail *is a fast, cheap, elevated transit system which provides some spectacular views.*

Swimming for his supper. The gentle giant is one of many entertainers at the Miami Seaquarium.

The Bass Museum of Fine Art, Park Avenue, Miami Beach, offers guided multilingual tours to enable you to get the most out of your visit. It has a permanent collection of European works covering seven centuries. Sculptures, textiles, furniture and the decorative arts are represented.

Driving north along Biscayne Boulevard takes you to US 1 and past the extensive Florida International University complex, beyond which is the **Oleta River State Recreation Area** in North Miami. This provides one of many beaches where there are picnic shelters with barbecue grills. A cycle path, fishing facilities and showers are available.

Parks and Beaches

Greater Miami has at least two dozen parks. Some, like Crandon Park on Key Biscayne, have playgrounds, walking trails, boat rental, tennis and golf and a baseball field. Almost all have barbecue and picnic facilities, and there are campsites on several of them.

The **Bill Baggs Cape Florida State Recreation Area**, at the south end of Key Biscayne, is a good picnic beach in a wooded setting. A tall lighthouse built in 1825 is still in operation, having survived not only hurricanes and the Civil War but also an attack by Indians in the Second Seminole War. In 1836 the Indians tried to set fire to the building, with the lighthouse keeper and his assistant inside. A keg of gunpowder was hurled at them from the tower, and the captives were rescued by a passing ship whose crew heard the explosion. The tower—you climb 120 steps to reach the top—dwarfs the keeper's cottage, which has been restored and furnished as it would have been originally. Both buildings can be visited by the public.

More than 560 hectares (1,400 acres) of public beaches belong to Greater Miami. They are known for their variety as well as their dazzling white sand and blue-green waters. Probably the best beach for children who want to do more than bathe and build sandcastles is at **Matheson Hammock Park**, in Old Cutler Road, South Miami. It has lifeguards, boating, guided nature walks, a picnic area, rest rooms and a bait and tackle outlet. A good surfing beach is at the **First Street Beach** area of Miami Beach. The best swimming beach stretches from **South Pointe Beach** northward to 87th Street. Lifeguards are on duty. **Hobie Beach**, on the north side of the Rickenbacker Causeway, is a great windsurfing beach. For improving that tan while lazing in the sun, secluded **North Beach Park** is among the most peaceful. It is between 72nd and 87th Streets at Miami Beach. **Haulover Beach**, at the 72-hectare (177-acre) Haulover Park at Collins Avenue, adjoining Sunny Isles, is named after the place where fishermen used to haul their boats over the beach for repairs.

Nautical sporting events, such as hydroplane races and regattas, and

143

F̲ishermen used to drag their boats over the sand for repairs at Haulover Beach.

summer pop concerts are held in Biscayne Bay at Virginia Key. An open-air Marine Stadium accommodates 6,500 spectators.

Village Life

Coconut Grove, on Miami's Biscayne Bay shore, is one of the fashionable "villages" of the region, with prestigious hotels, nightclubs, restaurants and boutiques, antique shops and pavement cafés. Artists and craftspeople can be seen at work. There's a happy mixture of the bohemian and the chic. The Grove is one of Miami's

Overlooking the bay, and just across the road from the Museum of Science and Space Transit Planetarium, is an Italian Renaissance-style 70-room mansion set in 4 hectares (10 acres) of formal gardens flanked by a dense natural hammock forest. The vegetation gives you an idea of what Florida was like before it was developed. The mansion, Villa Vizcaya, completed in 1916, was the indulgence of the late James Deering, of the agricultural machinery company. He built it as a winter retreat after an extended visit to Europe, where he studied architectural styles and decided to copy his favourite. Vizcaya—the name means "elevated place"—was the result. He filled its rooms with antiques and treasures which he collected during his European tour. The villa has been a museum, open to the public, for some years. An elegant stone barge built in the bay close to the gardens was, according to legend, used as a dock for delivering alcoholic drinks to the villa during prohibition.

Another unlikely place to visit in Greater Miami is a Spanish Monastery (the Cloisters of the Monastery of St Bernard) originally built for Cistercian monks and now billed as the oldest building in the Western Hemisphere. It is on the West Dixie Highway in North Miami Beach. The monastery, dating back to 1141, stood for seven centuries in Segovia, Spain. US newspaper magnate William Randolph Hearst had it transported to the United States in thousands of pieces in 1925. He never got down to the business of unpacking it. That eventually happened in 1954, when developers rebuilt it on its present site. Medieval works of art can be seen at this fine example of Romanesque and early Gothic architecture.

oldest neighbourhoods, with Victorian street lamps on the red-brick sidewalks, and quite a bit of history.

Mayfair Shops in the Grove is a substantial shopping mall in a setting of waterfalls, fountains and tropical vegetation, with shops at different levels. Completed in the 1980s, the mall has a number of restaurants and cafés and 100 boutiques, selling as wide a choice of designer clothes as you'd find

Monroe's House

One of the early settlers in the late 19th century was Commodore Ralph Middleton Monroe, a naval architect who built a house from materials washed ashore after shipwrecks. It was a single-storey building. Monroe was an original thinker. As his family grew more living space was needed, and instead of adding a floor above, he "pushed" the original structure upwards, supporting it on stilts, and put in a new ground floor. It was hardly a trend-setting project, but it was sufficiently different and interesting for it to become, many years later, a state historic site. The house, called The Barnacle, can be seen at Main Highway.

Monroe was also the man responsible for the comparatively natural state of the Grove's bayfront area. He made great efforts to preserve the bayfront from over-development, and today people can still appreciate the parks and marinas.

anywhere. There's also the **Mayfair Hotel**, where you can stay in a suite with a Japanese hot tub. Even newer than Mayfair Shops in the Grove is **Cocowalk**, an entertainment and retail centre on three levels.

Coconut Grove Playhouse, formerly a movie theatre, is now the base of South Florida's leading professional theatre company. Broadway and off-Broadway shows are staged there.

It's worth exploring the Grove's streets of little specialist shops. Many visitors hire bicycles to do this. Young people rent roller-skates or skateboards, both typical means of transport in the area.

Children playing in a park at Coconut Grove, one of Miami's oldest neighbourhoods.

Festivals are popular events in Coconut Grove. Half a million people crowd in for the **Arts Festival** in February. The Grove is *en fête* again in June, when the annual **Miami Bahamas Goombay Festival** is held. This is where the Grove's strong Bahamian influence is celebrated, and these fun-loving Black people, whose families built Bahamas-style frame houses on Charles Avenue at the back end of the last century, don't do things by half measures. Street parades in bright costumes, native foods, a marching band and native music played on kazoos, whistles, cowbells, skiffleboards—anything that can add to the noise and the rhythm—attract around a million people out to enjoy themselves.

Those who prefer a quieter life can hire a sailing dinghy or a windsurfer from a marina at Dinner Key, where 60 years ago Pan American Airways had a seaplane landing base and terminal.

Coral Gables

West and south of Coconut Grove is Coral Gables, a city of shady streets and tropical landscaping. There are some 17,000 residences in the city, including some of the most expensive homes in the world, fetching up to $15 million. You can't build just anything habitable in Coral Gables. Architectural standards are strict. But you could become extremely confused if you were escorted blindfold around the residential areas and were periodically allowed to see where you were. You might guess Holland, France, South Africa or the Far East. Yet most of the

---

George Merrick's Dream City
The visionary who originated this city within a city, George Edward Merrick, erected a main entrance, La Puerta del Sol, at the north-eastern approach. With a 30-m (90-ft) bell tower and a 12-m (40-ft) archway, the gateway has earned an entry in the national register of historic places. Never a man to do things by halves, Merrick also developed an extensive Venetian Pool, fed from a natural spring and carved from coral rock. Arched bridges, waterfalls, palm trees and caves completed the picture. It was finished in 1923, and countless people since have been delighted to cool off in the clear water.

Merrick named Coral Gables after the home where he grew up. His father, a Congregational minister, moved with his family from Massachusetts to Florida in 1898, buying 65 hectares (160 acres) of undeveloped land to the south-west of Miami. The family operated several orange, grapefruit and avocado groves which flourished, and young George Merrick saw it transformed in his mind's eye into a residential suburb of Miami. By 1921 he had assembled enough parcels of land around the family plantation to begin developing his dream city. He gathered together a team of notable designers who created a model suburb with broad avenues, fountains, monumental gateways and architecture with the basic Mediterranean theme. In the six months from October 1923 to March 1924, £7 million-worth of property was sold. More than 600 homes were built, with 105 km (65 miles) of road and more than 130 km (80 miles) of sidewalk. Fifty thousand trees and shrubs were planted and 45 km (28 miles) of the city was lit by street lamps.

GREATER MIAMI AND THE EVERGLADES

architecture is distinctively Mediterranean. This is because George Merrick, the man who thought up Coral Gables—and had the money to see his dreams come true—wanted its gracious homes built in the Mediterranean style. As time went on, little bits of European, South African and Oriental influence were given an odd corner here and there.

To look at Coral Gables today, you may imagine that it was born to prosper. In fact, there were probably some who were established before the suburb became the next best thing to Utopia who intoned: "Pride cometh before a fall." For in less than five years of Merrick starting to turn his dream into reality, the worst happened. The combination of uncontrolled land speculation and the hurricane of 1926 brought about the collapse of the Florida land boom. Although Coral Gables was well planned, with its major investments completed, it was bankrupt and unable to pursue new projects. With the Great Depression of 1929–34, the real estate business fell to bits. Poor George Merrick and his wife moved out to run a fishing camp, which was destroyed by another hurricane in 1935. He returned to Miami in 1940, and worked as Postmaster of the city until he died two years later.

As the Western world emerged from the Depression, financial reorganization ensured that Coral Gables flourished once more. In 1973 Coral Gables became the first city in Florida to bring in an Historic Preservation Ordinance to safeguard its unique heritage.

Miracle Mile is the city's noted downtown shopping district, and has been since 1945. Two of the shops opened then, Carroll's Jewellers and the J.P. Baldi Beauty Salon, are still in their original position and serving a third generation of customers.

Coral Gables has miles of cycle paths—it is linked to Coconut Grove by one. Free maps are issued to visitors who want to discover the city by bicycle or take the 32-km (20-mile) self-guided tour organized by the city authority. Alternatively, there are tour buses.

The University of Miami, the Lowe Art Museum and the Ring Theatre are at Coral Gables. A number of new hotels have gone up in recent years, with the business and conference market in mind, and the original Mediterranean-style Biltmore Hotel, built by Merrick for $10 million, underwent a $40 million renovation programme in the late 1980s. The hotel encompasses the Metropolitan Museum and Art Centre.

On SW 72nd Avenue, west of Coral Gables, is a 26-hectare (65-acre) park specially designed and equipped for handicapped people. This is the **A.D. Barnes Therapeutic Park**. It has a solar heated swimming pool, nature centres, playground, tree house, walking trails, picnic areas, a basketball court and baseball field, and it's all wheelchair-accessible. Entry to the park is free. A small charge is made for the pool.

You can wander along winding paths to a rainforest, admire a sunken garden and read the labels on the plants, shrubs and trees at the **Fairchild Tropical Gardens**, south of Coral Gables. The 33-hectare (83-acre) botanical garden has a vine pergola and thousands of tropical plants from many parts of the world, including 400 species of palm. There are several lakes. The Tropical Garden can be toured by tram, on which a commentary is given. The tram leaves every hour.

Next door to Fairchild is the **Matheson Hammock Park** in Old Cutler Road. Two hundred and two hectares (500 acres) of beach curve around a salt-water lagoon. Some of Greater Miami's 241 km (150 miles) of bicycle paths are in Matheson Hammock Park. Fish bait is on sale. birdwatchers particularly enjoy this park, November and December being the most rewarding time of year for them.

Birds provide the entertainment at another nearby attraction—the **Parrot Jungle and Garden**s at South Dade. Established more than 55 years ago, the Jungle has well over 1,000 parrots, macaws and related species. Some of them are so tame that they happily perch on you while you pose for your friends' cameras. Have a bit of bird seed available and several extra birds will insist on being in the picture. Their colours are amazing. Even more amazing are the shows they give six times a day. They ride tiny bikes, go roller-skating, play poker and answer the phone. Many of the birds fly free in the 5 hectares (12 acres) of tropical gardens. As well as parrots, there's a large population of flamingos; giant tortoises, iguanas and great-grandfather-size alligators are on display.

South Miami has a number of the region's crowd-pullers, like Metrozoo, Monkey Jungle, Orchid Jungle, Coral Castle and air and rail museums. Visitors are caged and the primates roam free at **Monkey Jungle**. One section is

an Amazonian-style rainforest. In another, crab-eating monkeys swim in a pool. Trained chimpanzees and monkeys give daily talent shows.

At the cageless **Metrozoo**, the animals, including koala bears and rare white Bengal tigers, live on islands similar to their respective natural habitats, and people view them across a moat. Metrozoo is one of the world's largest zoos, with more than 200 animal species. Included in its 117 hectares (290 acres) is a 0.6-hectare (1.5-acre) aviary 20 m (65 ft) high in which 300 exotic bird species can enjoy extended flights. Visit on a Sunday and you may

Look, no hands! This resident of the Parrot Jungle loves to demonstrate his cycling routine.

find your admission price includes a ticket to a musical presentation—Country 'n' Western, classical, rock or jazz may be on the menu. In 1990 the Asian River Life exhibit was added to the zoo. There are several Asian otters and one of the world's largest lizards—a 2-m (6.5-ft) long Malayan water monitor. To add authenticity to the Asian River Life exhibit, man-made mist swirls around the jungle setting and sound effects provide jungle noises and distant drumbeats.

Entertainment

Elsewhere in Miami you can track down the music of your taste, whether it's pop—the internationally acclaimed Miami Sound Machine is known for its pop with a Latin beat—or opera. The world-class Greater Miami Opera was founded some 50 years ago.

On the dance scene, there's everything from conga and rumba to modern ballet and flamenco. The New World School of the Arts Dance Ensemble is comprised of high school and college students performing a mixture of ballet, modern jazz, Spanish, new wave and Afro-Caribbean numbers.

Plans are afoot to develop a performing arts centre, bringing Greater Miami's orchestral, opera and ballet companies under one roof.

Located in the Metro-Dade Cultural Center is the **Historical Museum of Southern Florida**, providing a fascinating insight into the region's past. Those wanting a guided tour in English or Spanish must arrange it in advance—tel: (305) 375-1492. Canoe trips

at sunset and by moonlight, and walking and cycling tours, are organized by the museum authorities. In the same building is the **Center for Fine Arts**. Major exhibits from museums and art collections around the world are displayed. Jewellery, posters and gifts are on sale in the Center Art Store.

To the south, on Sunset Drive, children will find that learning is fun at the **Miami Youth Museum**. Guided tours, which are available on weekdays between 10 a.m. and 4 p.m., are by reservation only—tel: (305) 661-2787. Another place the youngsters will love is Malibu Grand Prix, on NW 8th Street, west of Miami International Airport, It's an amusement park with sprint racing carts, miniature golf, video arcades and rides. It opens until 11 p.m. Mondays to Thursdays, midnight on Sundays and 3 a.m. on Fridays and Saturdays.

You will soon notice that a lot of Spanish is spoken in Miami. Spanish-speaking people who have settled here come from throughout Latin America and the Caribbean. Calle Ocho, a 30-block strip on SW 8th Street is known as Little Havana.

It was the arrival of large numbers of Cubans in the early 1960s after Castro's take-over of their country that enhanced the international flavour of Miami. Many of them set up shops and restaurants, and cigar factories. Little confections and savouries are sold from street barrows, with tiny cups of very sweet Cuban coffee. Nightclub entertainment in the area offers the excitement of energetic salsa and flamenco dancing, with brightly coloured Spanish costumes. Visitors are warmly welcomed. In March an Hispanic

When thousands of Cuban refugees settled in Miami in the early 1960s they brought their skills with them.

street party dominates the large-scale celebrations known as **Carnaval Miami**. More recent newcomers to Greater Miami, the Haitians, have added their music, dancing and art to the local culture in Little Haiti. Try their Creole food, like griot (fried pork) or tassot (fried goat). Their main festival is in May. Take photographs of these various immigrants and their events and you could fool the neighbours into believing you'd been farther afield than Florida.

Opa Locka is a predominantly Black community whose city has Moorish architecture with domes and minarets on some of its homes as well as on major buildings like the City Hall. The main streets, in the shape of a crescent moon, are named after characters from *The One Thousand and One Tales from the Arabian Nights.*

Black people from the Bahamas and Jamaica contribute to the cosmopolitan scene with their cheerful brand of music, singing and dancing. Greeks, Germans, Italians and Scots are represented, and there's a Polish-American Club. The Irish are there in strength, making their presence felt with a St Patrick's Day parade and festival. It's a good mix, and residents as well as visitors like to join in the fun provided by immigrant communities. They enjoy tasting the food of the different nations, too, in the multitudinous restaurants.

One of the best places to sample a true local speciality is **Joe's Stone Crab**, first opened some 80 years ago in Miami Beach. Stone crabs are one of the great Florida dishes. You eat only the claws, and being so delectable they are not cheap. Although there are other items on the menu, Joe's closes from mid-May to mid-October, the close season for stone crabs

Attractions Around Miami

A ride through 5.5 km (3.5 miles) of scenic south Miami can be enjoyed during a visit to the **Gold Coast Railroad and Museum**. The train is pulled by a 1913 steam locomotive, and the ride lasts half an hour. Displays include steam and diesel locomotives, railroad cars used by past presidents of the USA and other historic railroad cars.

Air transport, from the days when planes were first invented to the end of World War II, is the theme at **Weeks Air Museum**. More than 35 aircraft on display—most of them still in flying condition—have been restored and preserved. Exhibits include engines and propellers.

People from many different countries have visited Miami especially to see the Orchid Jungle, one of several unusual attractions at **Homestead**, which is the southernmost part of Miami. Nowhere else in the world is there a bigger variety of orchids, and there are different ones according to the season. But you don't need to be an orchid specialist to appreciate this tropical site. Orchids, some with curious formations and markings, have a fascination all of their own. The **Orchid Jungle** has blossoms from almost every part of the world. Some grow on huge trees in the jungle terrain. There's an orchid laboratory with glass walls, through which a tissue culture cloning process can be watched. Complimentary flowers are presented to lady visitors, and there's an irresistible gift shop.

The ingredients for Momma's Apple Pie and countless other recipes grow in an 8-hectare (20-acre) park in the Homestead area. The full title is the **Preston B. Bird and Mary Heinlein Fruit and Spice Park**. This is a museum of living plants, a botanical garden with 500 varieties of fruit, nuts and spices from around the world.

Coral Castle

The most incredible attraction in Homestead—indeed surely in the whole of Florida—is Coral Castle. In a way its creation is as big a mystery as that of the Egyptian Pyramids and Stonehenge, because one 44.5-kg (7-stone) man worked alone to move blocks of native coral bedrock, each weighing up to 30,480 kg (30 tons), to build the structure. He used only primitive hand tools, and carved groups of statues demonstrating his regard for astronomy, magnetism, Florida, the concept of the family and the girl he loved.

It was in 1923 that the slightly built Latvian immigrant, Edward Leedskalnin, began work on his extraordinary edifice. The story goes that his fiancée jilted him hours before they were to have been married. Presumably, building the Coral Castle provided him with a much-needed distraction. It was a monument to his love. The girl missed out on having the ultimate in do-it-yourself husbands. Edward used 1 million kg (1,000 tons) of coral. He provided solar-heated bathtubs, outdoor coral furniture, a 20,320-kg (20-ton) 6-m (20-ft) telescope pointing to the North Star, and a sundial which gives the exact time and indicates the solstice and equinox days as well. Scientists today still wonder not only how he moved the enormous lumps of coral but also how he achieved the perfect balance of a 9,144-kg (9-ton) swinging gate.

The work continued for 20 years. The subtle colours of the coral and the greenery around the castle, enhanced by clever lighting, make this a pleasant place to visit in the evening. Coral Castle, which was placed on the USA's national register of historic places in 1984, is open daily from 9 a.m. to 9 p.m.

There's also a herb and vegetable garden. Fruits and spices can be bought fresh, dried or canned.

A short drive north of Coral Castle, on the North Dixie Highway, is a charming little state historic site called **Cauley Square**. It is a renovated 1904 railroad village where special events are often staged. The arts and crafts stores and speciality shops reflect the pioneer era of Southern Dade County. There's a garden tearoom and an aviary on the 4-hectare (10-acre) site.

You've travelled around Miami and seen a lot of the sights. How about a trip offshore to see the wonders of the deep? Go 14 km (9 miles) east of Homestead along Canal Drive and you come to **Biscayne National Underwater Park**. This is America's newest underwater park, and also its largest, with more than 72,000 hectares (180,000 acres) of islands and reefs. Canoe rentals, scuba-diving and family snorkelling trips can be organized, or you can get a splendid view of 7.6-m (25-ft) high coral reefs with masses of exotic fish and sea life from the comfort of a 16-m (52-ft) glass-bottom boat. The journey to the reefs takes you through wilderness mangrove creeks. Snorkelling and scuba-diving from the boat are also options.

Homestead could be regarded as Miami's country cousin, in the nicest possible way. It is agricultural country with "Pick Your Own" fields where you can stock up with strawberries, limes, tomatoes and avocados. Rodeos provide spectator sport, with the local lads and lasses demonstrating their skills in the saddle in exciting contests. Hot-air ballooning and skydiving are available.

Follow US 41, known as the Tamiami Trail—a combination of Tampa and Miami—to the Miccosukeee Indian Village in the Everglades, 40 km (25 miles) west of Miami. The route, straight as an arrow, goes alongside the Tamiami Canal, where you may see aquatic wildlife, including alligators. During the week you may see only a few other vehicles on the road, and if you are driving right across the state through the Everglades there may be moments when you wonder whether all human life, apart from yours, has disappeared from the face of the earth.

At the **Miccosukee Indian Village**, located at Mile Marker 70 on US 41, you can watch craft workers busily wood carving, basket weaving, making dolls and patchwork items and doing bead work. These and many other native products can be bought in the gift shop. An Indian museum features films and artefacts from different tribes. Wrestling—alligator versus Indian—is demonstrated. You can see the unique and fragile ecology of the **Everglades** by airboat, and learn from the Miccosukees about their folklore. At the village you'll see their chickees—a roof of palm fronds on cypress pole supports, providing welcome shade and maximum breeze. One chickee is used for cooking, another is for sleeping in and others are used for craft work. Every year, for a week after Christmas, more than 40 Indian tribes gather at the village to exhibit their crafts and to entertain with singing and dancing at the Indian Arts Festival. At the end of July there's an annual three-day International Music and Crafts Festival.

The Everglades, known as the "Sea of Grass", provides a habitat for all Florida's indigenous animals.

The Everglades

Of particular interest to nature-lovers, the Everglades is an area of outstanding importance. In or around the Everglades live all of Florida's indigenous animals, although they, and the area which supports them, are in constant danger from the needs of man. Pick up a leaflet and a map and see what you can identify as you work your way round the "Sea of Grass". Anyone interested in getting an introduction to the complex and fragile make-up of the Everglades should spend some time at the **Everglades National Park Royal Palm Visitor Center** just west of Homestead. Here you can study what you're going to see and pick up some literature and a map, so that when you're on site you'll have a better understanding of what it's all about. Follow the road 61 km (38 miles) to its dead end and you'll find yourself at another visitor centre near Flamingo, where, incidentally, there are extensive camping facilities. By then you'll have had some hands-on experience of the unique ecosystems of the Everglades, because along the route there are boardwalks, trails and observation posts from which you can see (and possibly identify, if you have the right books) an amazing number of species of grasses, plants and trees, birds and other wild creatures. **Chakika State Recreation Area**, north-west of Homestead, is a 260-hectare (640-acre) slice of the Everglades which has a spectacular waterfall.

The **Everglades** area, flat and at most 3 m (10 ft) above sea level, is known as the "Sea of Grass". There are also hardwood hammocks, cypress stands, mangrove islands, palm groves and pine trees. The region, which forms a variety of interrelated ecosystems, is 160 km (100 miles) long and up to 112 km (70 miles) wide.

All Florida's indigenous animals exist in or close to the Everglades, although some species, like the saltwater crocodile and the Florida panther—which is now extremely rare—are seldom seen. There are bears, bobcats and wild hogs. The Everglades is virtually a huge and slow-moving, very wide shallow river, flowing southward from Lake Okeechobee to the Gulf of Mexico. At its western extremity it meets the salt water of the Gulf. Here the Ten Thousand Islands form a "buffer zone". Among these islands you have a chance of seeing alligators, manatees, porpoises, sea turtles and sharks, and some beautiful birds, including the roseate spoonbill, osprey and bald eagle.

Tours

You can't avoid seeing alligators with Everglades Airboat Tours. The company, operating from Homestead, offers airboat rides in the Everglades all day, and there's an alligator farm with

at least 2,000 of the reptiles in residence. Be warned: airboats are noisy
machines, but they get you right into
the Everglades as they skim over the
"river of grass". The wildlife must have
got used to the din.

For a more in-depth study (and a
more expensive one, but worth while
for the serious student of this unique
region) a company called Florida Everglades Tours Inc., based at Homestead, offers a lecture on the ecology
followed by a 70-minute aerial tour.
Alternatively, expert naturalists will ac-
company you on a two-hour ground
tour, or you can do the lot—air and

ground safari and have a good packed
lunch into the bargain.

Yet another way of penetrating the
interior is to go with Shark Valley
Tram Tours. The base is 56 km (35
miles) west of Miami on US 41. You
get a 24-km (15-mile) two-hour ride
with an expert interpretation and a
midway break viewing the wilderness
from a 15.5-m (50-ft) observation
tower.

Exploring

Driving through the Everglades, mile
after mile, you may find the roadside
scenery lacking in variety. It is only

when you get right into it, on foot along the boardwalks, or by canoe, or on an organized group trip, that you can appreciate the significance and fascination of the area.

The Everglades cover an area of 566,500 hectares, (1.4 million acres) which took more than six million years to develop. Modern man being what he is, the whole ecosystem started to fall to pieces when he interfered. Some predict that the primitive wilderness region, most of which is publicly owned by the state or federal government, will not last far into the 21st century. Man-made drainage systems have adversely

affected natural water-levels and much of the water that fed the Everglades has been diverted to the cities that have mushroomed in the 20th century. The sugar-cane industry is blamed for problems concerning water quality.

However, now that man is aware of the trouble he has caused to the 'Glades environment in recent decades, action is being taken to try to stop the situation getting worse and, if possible, to reverse it. A coalition of some 25 state and national environmental organizations has been meeting regularly since 1985 to address major issues. Among these are the conversion of wild land to citrus groves, and oil exploration work in the Big Cypress National Preserve, adjacent to the Everglades.

Big Cypress was established as a National Preserve in 1974. It was long ago denuded of most of the big cypresses that gave the swampy region its name—the timber was used for boat building and coffin-making among other things—but those that still stand are reckoned to be up to seven centuries old.

When the Everglades was proclaimed a World Heritage Site in 1979, the United Nations described the region as "a place to be cherished for all mankind; a place to preserve for all time." We'll have to wait and see what happens.

Although it is a noisy form of transport, the airboat provides a mobile vantage point for viewing wildlife in the Everglades.

Beauty Above and Below the Sea

Home of America's only coral reef, the Keys is a wonderland of lagoons, of turquoise seas and bright skies. Take a crash course in scuba-diving or put on a snorkel mask so that you can fully appreciate the fascinating diversity of life beneath the gentle waves. Explore the wreck of a treasure ship, and if you find you like it down there, why not stay in an underwater hotel? Life is informal, the people are relaxed, the atmosphere almost Caribbean, and the cuisine of the area has developed a strong individual character, borrowing ideas from Dixieland, Cuba and the Bahamas.

Driving Down

There really is something special about the **Florida Keys**—a gentle, laid-back, almost rustic ambience that sets the area apart from the rest of Florida, let alone the United States—and you become aware of it as soon as you reach US 1, just a few miles south of Miami International Airport. At first, the roads you take are the usual tagliatelle twists, winding around and over each

A performer at the Theater of the Sea on Islamorada in the Florida Keys.

other through seemingly endless miles of suburb: shopping malls, business centres, car showrooms and housing estates. Then the buildings begin to thin out, US 1 shrinks almost to the dimensions of an English country road and you start to look for the first of those famous green-and-white mile marker posts—126 of them in all that count down the distance between Florida City on the mainland and Monroe County Courthouse at Key West. The markers are useful indicators of your precise location. The people who live in the Keys, who call themselves "Conchs", after the strange shellfish which forms a substantial part of their diet, use the mile markers as addresses. Thus your hotel might be at Islamorada MM 83.5.

159

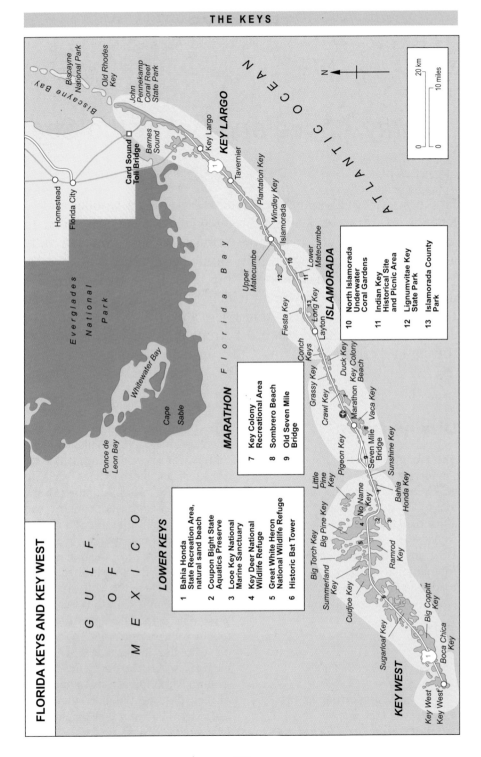

FLORIDA KEYS AND KEY WEST

LOWER KEYS

1 Bahia Honda State Recreation Area, natural sand beach
2 Coupon Bight State Aquatics Preserve
3 Looe Key National Marine Sanctuary
4 Key Deer National Wildlife Refuge
5 Great White Heron National Wildlife Refuge
6 Historic Bat Tower

MARATHON

7 Key Colony Recreational Area
8 Sombrero Beach
9 Old Seven Mile Bridge

ISLAMORADA

10 North Islamorada Underwater Coral Gardens
11 Indian Key Historical Site and Picnic Area
12 Lignumvitae Key State Park
13 Islamorada County Park

For a time the highway traverses a typical Everglades landscape—sawgrass swaying to the distant horizons, punctuated by the occasional bump of jungly hammock and clumps of tropical trees. Then mangroves and stretches of water become more apparent, and the road narrows again, to a single lane in each direction. Warning signs appear, urging drivers to be patient—the next overtaking section is only three minutes away. Then the road does a dog's leg turn, crosses a bridge over a more open stretch of water, and you are on **Key Largo**, largest and most northerly of the chain of islands linked by a road that snakes across the blue and green hues of the Atlantic Ocean and the Gulf of Mexico to stop just 145 km (90 miles) short of Havana, the capital of Cuba.

Driving is the best, indeed, the only way to travel through the entire Keys. There are air connections between Miami and Key West, and there are airports at Key Largo and Marathon, and the best option is to fly one way and drive the other, though this might be expensive for a family. However, you can drive from Key West to Miami, or vice versa, in less than four hours, school buses, trucks and accidents permitting, so you have the choice of combining a slow trip with a fast one, or of alternating leapfrog stops through the islands in each direction.

Conchs are proud of the climate of the Keys, and they will tell you about

*M*ap of the
Florida Keys.

the natural air-conditioning system that keeps it surprisingly temperate. Although the average daytime high temperature is 27.7°C (81.9°F) and the night-time low 22.8°C (73°F), ocean breezes keep the atmosphere generally comfortable. There are basically two seasons—winter and summer, or "dry" and "wet". Winter brings day after day of clear blue skies, while the summer brings short, unpredictable tropical showers. It is never too cold for shorts.

Earlier Days

The first European residents of the Keys—a corruption of the Spanish word "cayos", meaning "small islands"—were Spanish Conquistadores and seamen whose vessels had been wrecked among the shallows and coral reefs of the surrounding waters. Their captives were the Calusa Indians who had moved from the mainland because of the abundance of seafood and hardwoods from which they could construct their homes. The Spanish chronicler Antonio de Herrera was travelling with the explorer Ponce de Leon when the Keys were sighted on Sunday, 15 May 1513. Without going ashore, they named the line of islands and rocky islets *Los Martires* (The Martyrs) because "they looked like men who were suffering". Herrera later thought it was an apt name in view of the many who had been lost there.

Pirates were the first people to set up shore bases, which could be hidden away among the complex pattern of channels, creeks and mangrove-fringed islands. They were driven away by the US Navy's Pirate Fleet, established in the Keys in the early 1820s. Settlers moved in and began farming productive groves of Key limes, tamarind and breadfruit. In the Lower Keys, pineapple farms flourished and a factory soon supplied canned pineapple to most of eastern North America. Later, a shark factory was established on Big Pine Key. It hired workers to catch sharks, and the hides were salted down and sent north to New Jersey where they were processed into shagreen, a tough leather.

Settlers at Key West and Islamorada became wreckers, salvaging goods from ships that foundered on the nearby reefs—some say the ships were deliberately lured ashore—and Key West became the wealthiest city in the United States.

In the early 1900s travel between many of the islands was possible only by ferryboat or private vessels, then Henry Flagler extended his East Coast Railway 210 km (130 miles) from Homestead to Key West. It was completed in 1912 after seven years of very hard work.

Construction of the Overseas Highway was itself an incredible engineering feat. It consists of 181 km (113 miles) of roadway and 43 bridges, one

Rail Tragedy
In 1935 more than 64 km (40 miles) of the railway were destroyed in a 322-kph (200-mph) hurricane, which blew a train off the tracks as if it were a toy and killed more than 600 people. The Overseas Highway, as US 1 is called in the Keys, is partly built on the bridges and trestles of the old railway. Some parts of the railway remain as a skeletal monument to the tragedy of 1935.

of them almost 11 km (7 miles) long. A $185 million improvement programme in 1982 replaced 37 narrow bridges with modern, wide-track spans. The highway threads through the islands, changing from country lane to main street to fairground ride, and rarely out of sight of water as it jumps from Key to Key.

Boating and Fishing Paradise

The islands are grouped into five regions: the Upper Keys, which cover Key Largo, Tavernier and Plantation Key; Islamorada, with Windley Key, Upper and Lower Matecumbe, Fiesta Key and Long Key; the Middle Keys, covering Marathon and a number of smaller keys; the Lower Keys, the largest and least developed area, which includes Big Pine Key, noted for its miniature Key deer; and Key West, which stands alone, basking in such descriptions as "the end of the world", "Margaritaville", "the place where time stands still". Don't be misled into thinking that the Florida Keys consist only of the islands linked by the Overseas Highway, or that they come to an end at Key West. In fact, there are hundreds of islands, many not much bigger than a bus, others substantial but still uninhabited, scattered from just south of Miami, across Florida Bay and out 110 km (68 miles) beyond Key West to the Dry Tortugas, a cluster of coral islands reached by seaplane or charter boat.

Each of the inhabited Keys is different in some way from all the others, and each has some feature which is

Game fishing is a way of life throughout the Florida Keys.

used as a kind of identity tag. Thus, Key Largo is "Diving Capital of the World" while Islamorada claims that distinction for its sport fishing. Marathon, "Heart of the Keys", is a mini-metropolis with superb boating facilities. The Lower Keys are noted for wildlife, fishing and getting away from it all. Key West, a touch gay, a little fey, a tropical Bohemia yet not as cosmopolitan as it likes to think it is, has an eccentric, easy-come-easy-go ambience with wide appeal, and it is easy to understand why figures like the writers Ernest Hemingway, Tennessee Williams, Robert Frost and Carson McCullers, and President Harry S. Truman chose to stay there. The separate identity of the Keys as a whole is emphasized by the fact that Monroe County—to give the area its official political title—is often referred to as "the Conch Republic".

With the sea rarely much more than a stroll away, it follows that water-borne activities play a major part in the Keys' way of life. Highways else-where are lined with car showrooms and petrol filling stations; US 1 is fringed with boat yards and marinas on the outskirts of the communities through which it passes. Conditions for boating—under power or sail—are generally excellent, with lots of scope for exploring along America's only coral reef and in the Back Country, as the hundreds of islands not connected to US 1 are known. The Keys are renowned for diving and game fishing, but there is little in the way of beaches for those who are content to lie back on the sand and get a tan. The coral reef that makes the Keys unique has prevented the build-up of sand, al-though there are a few beaches, some of them man-made.

The waters of the Gulf of Mexico and the Atlantic surrounding the Keys are ideal for scuba-diving or snorkelling and, for those who prefer not to get their feet wet, there are glass-bottomed boats from which hundreds of tropical fish and other forms of marine life may be observed. Key Largo is said to be one of the finest places in the world for underwater nature study, and diving is certainly the island's major pursuit. The **John Pennekamp Coral Reef State Park** (MM 102.5) contains more than 300 species of fish and more than 40 species of coral. Combined with the **Key Largo National Marine Sanctuary**, it covers nearly 520 km^2 (200 square miles) and was established mainly through the persistence of a crusading journalist who wanted to preserve a pristine patch of offshore reefs from the encroachment of man.

The Key Largo area has more than 25 independent dive operators, all providing daily trips as well as training schemes for visitors wishing to learn scuba-diving. A popular attraction is the famed Christ of the Deep, a statue submerged in 8 m (25 ft) of water at Key Largo Dry Rocks. A couple of barracuda who appear to guard the statue are always handy to add scale and drama to underwater photographs.

Key Largo, however, is not the only diving destination in the Florida Keys. Reefs and wrecks around the entire area offer opportunities for novices and experts alike. **Looe Key National Marine Sanctuary**, near Big Pine Key, in the Lower Keys, offers what is claimed to be some of the more spectacular shallow-water diving in the world, and is the setting for an annual underwater music festival in summer.

Sailfish, blue marlin, white marlin, kingfish, cobia, amberjack and dolphin are just a few of the fighting fish that have attracted sportsmen to the

Reef Relief
With all the underwater activity in the Keys, there is, naturally, concern for the fragile environment of the coral reef. Reef Relief, based at Key West, is an organization with only 700 members, yet it has earned Presidential recognition of its efforts to preserve the corals of the Keys. Founded by Craig Quirolo in 1986, the group has organized the installation and maintenance of 83 mooring buoys at six reef tracks near Key West. The buoys allow boats used by fishermen and divers to tie up rather than drop anchor on the fragile reefs. Reef Relief also runs a public education programme, alerting people to the threat caused by diver damage, offshore oil development and pollution, and providing information on what individuals can do to help improve the quality of the reef. President Bush, a keen fisherman and frequent visitor to the Keys, has presented the organization with a "Point of Light" award for its continuing efforts on behalf of reef preservation.

Mankind has also given the barrier a helping hand by developing artificial reefs. The Florida Keys Artificial Reef Association has organized the sinking of redundant vessels which form a framework on which nature can build new coral reefs. The 88-m (287-ft) freighter *Eagle* was blown up and sunk off Islamorada in 1985, and two Coast Guard cutters, pensioned off in 1987, were sent to the bottom off Key Largo. All three wrecks attract the attention of dozens of scuba-divers each week and also benefit sport-fishing enthusiasts.

Keys. Ernest Hemingway helped to establish the area's fishing reputation in the 1930s, and President Bush is helping to sustain it today with his well-publicized bone-fishing trips to Islamorada.

Keys Cuisine

As in the rest of Florida, seafood forms the major part of any Keys menu. The Keys' cuisine, however, has a character of its own, influenced strongly by the dishes of Dixieland, Cuba and the Bahamas. Conch is served everywhere, mainly in the form of fritters, and also as burgers. It forms the basis of a tasty chowder, can be grilled, or eaten raw in a salad or a Mexican-style ceviche when it is served in a spicy marinade. Other seafood staples are spiny lobsters, pink shrimps, stone crabs, yellowtail and mutton snappers, giant grouper and a fish called grunt—which brings us neatly to *lechon*, which is roast pork flavoured with garlic and the tart local oranges. Other dishes with their roots in Spain are *ropa vieja* (it literally means "old clothes") a concoction of leftover beef; *vaca frita* ("fried cow"), and *picadillo*, a hamburger-style concoction with capers and raisins. Another local favourite is Bahamian fish stew served with grits. Raw bars serving oysters, clams and squid—to say nothing of conch—are to be found throughout the Keys. Specialty desserts served in all types of establishment include a caramelized custard flan, guava shells with cream cheese and, of course, Key lime pie which achieves its unique flavour from the rind of the small piquant limes which flourish in the area.

You may be dismayed to find dolphin on the menu. This is not the intelligent, friendly mammal that performs so well in places like Sea World, but the dorada, a fish plentiful in the warm waters of the Gulf Stream. No one seems to know why it is confusingly called dolphin when served as food.

There are three dolphin centres in the Keys where members of the public can swim freely with the bright-eyed mammals. The **Dolphin Research Center** at Grassy Key, near Marathon, maintains links with university research programmes and independent investigators throughout the world, and also looks after sick and injured dolphins. At the **Dolphin Plus** complex on Key Largo visitors not only get to swim with the dolphins but are also given a full educational programme on the plight of endangered marine life. Visitors to the **Theater of the Sea** on Islamorada can also join the dolphins in the water.

Entertainment

Night-life in the Keys is more rough and ready than you'll find in Miami or Orlando, with local talent rather than big names filling the bill. That said, however, the area has produced the occasional performer of international status. Pop star Jimmy Buffet began by strumming and singing in the bars of his home town, Key West.

Small bands, combos, trios, singles and some excellent solo pianists are the rule in hotels, bars and restaurants throughout the area, and there are even sporadic comedy routines. Dance floors range from postage-stamp size to one or two of ballroom proportions. For the younger set there is plenty of rock, pop, soul and cha-cha-cha. Country 'n' Western music is big in Marathon, and Cuba's musical influence is very detectable in Key West, where Latin ensembles perform the rumba, the merengue and the samba. Key West also boasts its own brand of jazz blues. Conchtown Rhythm is a blend of New Orleans jazz and calypso. Local stars in this genre are

Coffee Butler—he's billed as "the southernmost Louis Armstrong"—and Sylvia Shelley.

Attire at any time in the Keys is never expected to be more than informal. The **Pier House Hotel**, one of the best at Key West, even has a topless beach. Any man found wearing a tie anywhere in the area is likely to have it cut off, and the phrase "Key West

A typical bed and breakfast establishment in Key West—a traditional "gingerbread house".

formal" that appears on invitation cards means any colour shorts but khaki.

Shopping

Souvenir hunters will find plenty to keep themselves busy throughout the Keys. Twisted, whitened pieces of driftwood, *au naturel* or artistically fashioned, coconut products, beautiful seashells, straw items and handwoven palm fronds formed into hats, basketry or wall hangings can be found in shops and on market stalls set up in a number of places along US 1. Seashell art—some sophisticated, some frankly junk—predominates and there is a wide choice of mobiles, jewellery, lamps and bric-a-brac for sale. Key West has complete shopping facilities ranging from sidewalk vendors to expensive boutiques in historic buildings. Locally produced specialties in Key West are stylish hand-printed fabrics and perfumes extracted from native flora.

Accommodation

The Keys offer a wide range of accommodation—everything from the Edwardian opulence of Henry Flagler's **Casa Marina Hotel** on Key West, now under the Marriott flag, to other resort hotels of international status, condominiums, guesthouses, motels and camping grounds. Key Largo even has an underwater hotel where guests pay around $180 a day, all in, for staying in a 3 m by 2.50 m (10 ft by 8 ft) room with private bath 10 m (5 fathoms) down in Bora Bora Lagoon. The **Jules Undersea Lodge**, formerly a scientific research base, has a multi-purpose chamber which serves as dining room and entertainment centre with television, computer games and stereo. It can take six guests at a time, and they can explore the lagoon day or night using tethered breathing equipment. Before checking in, guests must complete an orientation session and provide proof of qualification in basic scuba-diving skills.

Camping

Outdoor types who prefer to breathe fresh air directly into their lungs will find campsites to suit all budgets and gear, from tents to the most luxurious recreational vehicles. Recent years have seen a major updating of camping facilities throughout the Keys, and reservations are recommended, especially in the popular winter season. The **John Pennekamp Coral Reef State Park**, Key Largo, has some 50 pitches in a most attractive location with full watersport facilities, nature walks and camp-fire lectures given by camp rangers. Nearby Barefoot Key (MM 106) has woodland sites with water and electricity hook-ups and caters mainly for teenage tenters.

Between mile markers 101.5 and 95 are several resort camps offering RV amenities, and in the Middle Keys is the popular **Long Key State Recreation Area** with waterside pitches, guided nature walks and lecture programmes conducted by rangers. At Fiesta Key (MM 70) KOA, the American camping organization, has a huge resort, and another well-known facility is **Outdoor Resorts** at Long Key (MM 66).

Below Marathon, which also boasts a couple of campgrounds, is the **Bahia**

Honda State Recreation Area with attractive pitches and rare sandy beaches fronting both the Atlantic and the Gulf of Mexico.

The Lower Keys has a number of campgrounds—including **Venture Out** at Cudjoe Cay, where only vehicles with full hook-ups are accommodated, and **Lazy Lakes Resort** which has nearly 100 pitches on Sugarloaf Key.

Key West itself has only three locations—**Leo's Campground** in Suncrest Road, **Boyd's Key West Campground**, Moloney Avenue, and **Jabour's Trailer Court** in Elizabeth Street, within walking distance of Old Town.

Upper Keys and Key Largo

Dozens of red flags with a white diagonal stripe waving from atop buildings and flapping on roadside poles might lure the first-time visitor to Key Largo into thinking that the "Conch Republic" really is an independent state, but the flag is the international signal that diving operations are being carried out, and Key Largo, remember, calls itself "The Diving Capital of the World". Humphrey Bogart, Lauren Bacall and Edward G. Robinson, who helped lift the place to international fame in a 1948 film about a hurricane, seem to be regarded very much as bit players in the island's history. True, you'll find a little Bogart/Bacall nostalgia in the Caribbean Club Bar at MM 104, where some of the film is said to have been shot, but there are no references to the black-and-white movie drama in any of the locally produced tourism literature.

Queen of the Silver Screen

Key Largo's major movie star is the grubby little steamer from *The African Queen*, shot in 1951, with Katherine Hepburn and Humphrey Bogart. The vessel is docked at the Key Largo Resort Holiday Inn, when not on tour all over the world. In Britain she has cruised on the River Thames and the Clyde and attended the London International Boat Show. Needless to say, her destruction by explosion at the end of the classic film was faked.

Built at Lytham St Anne's, Lancashire, in 1912, the *Queen* is an authentic steam launch. Her original name was *Livingstone*, after the great explorer, and she was dismantled and shipped to East Africa where she was used to carry everything from explorers to gun runners, cattle to gin, along the river routes between Lake Albert and Murchison Falls, so her role in *The African Queen* was very much a case of type-casting. In 1951 she was still working the African river routes, her steam engine replaced by diesel, when the film company found her. Steam was re-installed and the *Queen*, officially renamed, was transported to a tributary of the River Congo to play her part in the film that won Bogart his only Oscar. Filming over, the *Queen* remained in Africa for the next 17 years, until an American movie buff bought her for $700 and shipped her to San Francisco, where she fell into disrepair, was sold again, and spent a brief spell as a carnival attraction. In 1982 Jim Hendricks, a salty property owner in Key Largo, bought the *Queen* for $65,000, and it's Jim you will see to this day lovingly steering her as she chugs along the short canal that runs out to sea between the Holiday Inn and the Best Western Suites on Ocean Drive.

Named Cayo Largo (Long Island) by Spanish explorers, the island is the largest of the Keys, some 48 km (30 miles) long, and the number of diving shops and boats—to say nothing of all those flags—testify its main preoccupation. The reason for this are the coral reefs—the only living reefs in the continental United States—which lie close offshore and continue throughout the length of the Florida Keys.

Information on the area can be obtained from the Key Largo Chamber of Commerce and Florida Keys Welcome Center located in a new shopping centre at MM 103.5. A kilometre and a half (1 mile) down the road is the **John Pennekamp Coral Reef State**

Park, the first underwater park in the United States. The park and the **Key Largo National Marine Sanctuary** which adjoins it are 34 km (21 miles) long and 13 km (8 miles) wide and cover about 490 km² (190 square miles). The area contains 55 varieties of coral and is home to more than 600 species of fish, as well as crabs, sea urchins, snails, lobsters, shrimps, molluscs, starfish, sea cucumbers, sand dollars, barnacles and sponges. There are seagrass beds and mangrove swamps, and there is as much wildlife to see on land as there is under the ocean, with tropical vegetation and shore birds to be observed on a nature trail and among the many interesting channels through the mangroves.

The park is named after John Pennekamp, a journalist who wrote campaigning articles in the *Miami Herald*, urging preservation of the Florida reef. He also played a major role in establishing the Everglades National Park. The Pennekamp Park is furnished with first-class facilities—a visitor centre with aquarium exhibits and audio visual presentations, picnic sites, marina, the inevitable dive shop, motorboat, sailboat and canoe rentals and a sandy beach, albeit man-made. But it is the coral formations and their marine life that most visitors want to see and experience.

Visitors waiting to board a trip boat in the John Pennekamp Coral Reef State Park on Key Largo.

Diving

For scuba-divers, a boat named *Dive Master* leaves at 9.30 a.m. and 1.30 p.m. each day for trips to two different dive sites. Depending on conditions, the sites are Molasses Reef, French Reef or the Benwood Wreck. Molasses Reef is the most popular in the sanctuary, with high coral ridges, tunnels and almost every kind of coral formation, including elkhorn, staghorn, star and brain, and fish of every size and colour. Benwood Wreck is the remains of a ship that sank in about 12 m (35 ft) of water in 1942, and there are other wrecks at French Reef, where there is also a deep cave. Scuba-diving instruction is available for novices.

El Capitan, a 20-m (60-ft) dive boat with a convenient platform on the stern, takes snorkellers out three times a day on two-and-a-half hour trips, which allow about an-hour-and-a-half of actual time in the water. Most of the trips are to Grecian Rocks, an area so shallow that the coral sometimes breaks surface at low tide. Visibility is excellent and there are plenty of fish, many of them very photogenic. *El Capitan* leaves the Pennekamp marina at 9 a.m., noon and 3 p.m.

Those who don't like to get their feet wet can join the *My Discovery*, which has a windowed underwater hull and takes passengers out to Molasses Reef, also at 9 a.m., noon and 3 p.m. There are also trips to Key Largo Dry Rocks where divers and snorkellers can view the 3-m (9-ft) statue of Christ set among the coral formations in about 8 m (25 ft) of water.

A newer attraction, offering glimpses of life beneath the surface, is the

Key Largo Undersea Park, set in a 0.4-hectare (1-acre) lagoon. This is the site of that strange underwater hotel, Jules' Undersea Lodge, and here also is the **MarineLab Undersea Habitat** where snorkellers can watch scientists conducting underwater research projects. They may also join marine archaeologist R. Duncan Mathewson III as he leads a team of students searching shipwrecks for cannon, anchors and other sunken artefacts. Mathewson played a key role in the discovery of the *Atocha*, a Spanish galleon which sank off Key West in 1622, laden with gold and silver worth millions of dollars.

Ashore, there isn't really much to Key Largo itself. South of John Pennekamp Park the loose straggle of shops, boat yards and restaurants gradually coalesces into a downtown area, with hotels, a couple of supermarkets, liquor stores, bars and eating places. **Mrs Mac's Kitchen** at MM 99.3, on the right as you are heading south, is a piece of classic Americana, an old-fashioned roadside diner with more space to sit at the bar than there are seats at the tables. The food is simple, good, cheap and quickly served, and the atmosphere is so all-American you might expect Mickey Rooney and Judy Garland to dance through the door. Mrs Mac's is where the locals gather, not only for a bite to eat and a drink, but also to catch up on the gossip, which can be very entertaining and informative. The banter between customers and staff can be hilarious—if you can follow it.

Tavernier

At the southern end of Key Largo, **Tavernier** was a centre for wreckers in the 18th century, and there is a tale that it owes its name to the taverns frequented by sailors from the wrecking fleet. It was first settled in the 1860s by two Bahamian farmers from Key West. Early pioneers grew fruit and vegetables and developed pineapple and coconut plantations. For a time the area was called Planter, then it became known as "Lowe's Place", after Amos Lowe, who received a grant of land from President Chester A. Arthur in 1864. Tavernier is the only "old" neighbourhood outside Key West where descendants of original first or second generation settlers still live.

Much of old Tavernier was restored and designated in 1986 as an Historic District. More than 50 buildings—railroad stations, pioneer homes, churches, a school and several offices—have been documented, and along US 1 between MM 92 and MM 91 you'll see the Old Post Office (1926), the Tavernier Hotel (1932), the Albury House and the Old Church Community Center/Visitor Center (1936). Their white timber walls and tin roofs are typical of island architecture but, if you don't stop, your most enduring recollection of the place is likely to be of a typically small Florida town skirting a highway—Harry's Liquor Bar, a power station, a shop selling handbags, another selling carpets, and a couple of boat yards. Information can be obtained from the Old Church Visitor Center.

Close to Tavernier is the **Harry Harris Park**, a waterfront recreation area with a sandy beach, enclosed natural salt-water pool, children's playground, picnic facilities and barbecue grills. There is a launching ramp for boats and there is fishing from the sea wall. Named after a local businessman who served as Mayor and as a County Commissioner, the park is administered by Monroe County and is the place where you will find local people enjoying their own facilities. There are paved bike paths and grassy areas shaded by buttonwood trees, and a softball field gets lots of use. Open-air concerts are staged frequently. Access to the park is from US 1 at MM 92.6.

At MM 91 the highway crosses Tavernier Creek to reach **Plantation Key**, named for a 19th-century pineapple-growing enterprise. This is an attractive little island with a number of narrow waterways and many boat yards. Mostly residential, it comes to an end at Snake Creek, where there is a US Coast Guard station.

Islamorada

Crossing Snake Creek leads to Windley Key, first of "The Purple Isles" (Islas Moradas) as the early Spanish explorers called them because of a species of violet-hued sea snail once found on the shores—at least, that is one story. Another theory is that the islands owe their name to the profusion of orchid trees and bougainvillea blooms. Either way, the images most likely to remain in a visitor's mind are of the turquoise sea, verdant foliage, a rich blue sky—and a sign that shrieks, "Welcome to Islamorada, Sporting Fishing Capital of the World".

Anyone with even a smattering of Spanish should forget the pronunciation that springs readily to the lips. The locals say "Eye-lamorada" and give strange looks to those who pronounce it in any other way.

Windley Key

Once two islands named the Umbrella Keys because of their shape, they were joined by a causeway and renamed **Windley Key** to honour an early settler. In 1908 Henry Flagler's railway company began quarrying on Windley for the huge amounts of limestone needed for embankments. Now disused, the quarry attracts geologists from all over the world who come to study the exposed patterns of fossilized coral.

The quarry now belongs to the state of Florida and is scheduled to become a state park.

Another old quarry on Windley Key has been turned into the **Theater of the Sea**, opened nearly 50 years ago and one of Florida's oldest attractions. Apart from being one of those places where visitors can swim with the dolphins—you'll need to make a reservation for the experience, by the way—the theatre presents a continuous show of marine creatures, including sea lions, sharks, rays and turtles.

Fishing

The Whale Harbor Channel separates Windley Key from Upper Matecumbe Key, where the town of Islamorada is situated. Everything changes as soon as you reach the bridge that crosses the channel. The intimate, almost rural character of Windley Key and Plantation Key gives way to a holiday resort atmosphere, and as you reach the other side of the broad stretch of water you see at once why the Islamoradans make such a fuss about their

*T*riumphant anglers pose with their catch at Whale Harbor Marina, Islamorada.

fishing activities. **Whale Harbor Marina** positively bristles with charter fishing vessels and their tall lookout towers. You can sense the excitement of deep-sea game fishing just by taking a stroll along the dockside. Be there when the boats come in and you realize that the graphic claims made on the moorings are not empty promises.

Dedicated sportsmen charter a boat for themselves and go out after tuna, sailfish, tarpon. You'll also see them in the shallows, close to the shore, punting a small skiff, silent, with its motor raised, as they stalk the wily bonefish. Anyone—even complete beginners—can join Captain Ray Jensen's 11-m (65 ft) party boat *Caloosa* which sails from the marina daily at around 9.30 a.m., returning between 4.30 and 5 o'clock in the afternoon. Twice a week—on Wednesdays and Saturdays—the *Caloosa* goes out on a night trip, from 7 p.m. to midnight. No tackle? No problem—you can rent it on board for a very modest sum.

The *Caloosa* moors right beside the **Dockside Restaurant** which opens for breakfast daily at 6 a.m. and continues to serve hungry tourists and famished fishermen throughout the day. Upstairs is the salty **Harbor Bar**, which also serves food and has live entertainment in the evenings. This is the bar the local anglers and charter boat captains use, and it is here you will first encounter the prototypes of Ernest Hemingway's oddly adolescent adventurer, Harry Morgan. Here are the grizzly features, the scale-smeared shorts, the battered caps and the incomprehensible dialogue of *To Have and Have Not*. You'll find it all again at Key West, where the story is set. Oddly, though, it is more noticeable here—and somehow more real too.

Accommodation and Amenities
Right next to the Whale Harbor Marina is the **Chesapeake Motel and Villas Resort**. The word "motel" belies the property's up-market standards, for the Chesapeake is used as the headquarters for President Bush's entourage when he goes on bonefishing trips to Islamorada. The resort has well-furnished rooms in three-storey stilted buildings with parking space

underneath, and luxury villas with kitchens set privately among tropical trees. There is a beach, swimming pool and a lagoon, with good mooring facilities, and a launching ramp which was blasted out of the limestone by Flagler's railroad builders.

The Chesapeake is just one of a number of quality resort properties in the Islamorada area. The best-known is probably **Cheeca Lodge** at MM 82. This is a luxury hotel, set in 11 hectares (27 acres) of grounds with

*T*he Chesapeake Motel and Villas Resort on Islamorada is used as headquarters for President Bush's entourage when he goes on bonefishing trips.

330 m (1,100 ft) of private and natural beach, more than 200 rooms, suites and villas, two ocean-front dining rooms and a cocktail lounge. There are six tennis courts, two pools and a 161-m (525-ft) fishing pier. Said to be one of the most beautiful resorts in Florida, the Cheeca Lodge also has a par 3 golf-course.

Resorts apart, there is a wide range of accommodation in the Islamorada area, including modest hotels, motels and bed and breakfast guest-houses. There is also a wide variety of eating places. The local chamber of commerce has an information centre in an old railway coach at MM 82, in downtown Islamorada, where there are a number of roadside stalls and stores, selling shells and other souvenirs. There are also three art galleries featuring original watercolours and acrylics by local artists.

The area has a total resident population of not much more than 2,000, but Islamorada is the fourth largest town in the Keys. Originally, it housed only a few farming families, but the Florida East Coast Railway changed its character. By the time the Overseas Highway opened in 1938 Islamorada had become a well-known fishing centre and resort. The area has always had a progressive attitude towards leisure and was one of the first to provide a nature walk among the indigenous plant life and to provide a pathway for cyclists.

South of the town of Islamorada, as Upper Matecumbe narrows, you begin to appreciate that you are travelling along a narrow spine of quite small islands. The road looks as if it has been squeezed out of a tube across the

> **Free Trolley Tour**
> The Islamorada Trolley Tour provides a free trip between MM 80 and MM 103—that's from the southern end of Upper Matecumbe Key all the way to the northern end of Key Largo and back. It's a good opportunity for drivers at least to take in the sights at leisure and for everyone to learn something about the area from an expert.

surface of the sea, and the first of the long, graceful Keys bridges appears. Across the delightfully-named Teatable Key Channel a wayside picnic area at MM 78.5 is also the embarkation place from which the 24-passenger pontoon *Monroe* takes visitors to two remarkable offshore state parks.

Lignumvitae Key

On the Gulf side is the 115-hectare (280-acre) **Lignumvitae Key**, which boasts the highest point in the Keys— 5.5 m (18 ft). Scientists say some of the vegetation on the island is more than 10,000 years old. Apart from the dense *lignum vitae* ("wood of life") tree from which it gets its name, the key also abounds with mahogany, mastic, poisonwood, gumbo and other rare trees. In 1919 the island was purchased by William J. Matheson, a prominent Florida financier, who built a house of coral rock, a windmill and a small jetty. Apart from these, the Key is in pristine condition. It has been owned by the state since 1972.

Indian Key

A 5-hectare (12-acre) island on the Atlantic side of US 1 is named **Indian Key**. In the 1830s there was a thriving village of wreckers, under the leadership of Jacob Housman. In 1836 the

174

community actually became the seat of government for Dade County, which now comprises the Greater Miami area. The settlement was almost wiped out in 1840 in a bloody raid by Indians outraged at the take-over of their territories. They left the village in crumbling ruins which can still be seen.

San Pedro Underwater Park

Just over a mile south of Indian Key is the **San Pedro Underwater Archaeological Park**, where the remains of a Spanish galleon wrecked in 1733 lie in 5.5 m (18 ft) of water. The site has been laid out as a submarine historic trail, with a marked route for divers through the vessel's wooden hull and ballast stones. Seven replica cannon have been lowered on to the wreck to re-create its appearance at the time of its discovery by scuba-divers in the 1960s.

> **Spanish Treasure Ship**
> The *San Pedro* was a treasure ship in a fleet of 21 military and merchant vessels which set sail from Havana on favourable westerly trade winds on Friday, 13 July 1733. They were bound for Europe heavily laden with gold, silver and other valuable cargo. The *San Pedro* alone was packed with 16,000 pesos of silver and many crates of Chinese porcelain. Just one day out of port, the winds shifted from the ease and a storm sprang up, scattering, sinking and swamping the convoy along the Middle and Upper Florida Keys. Only one ship survived, limping back to Havana to sound the alarm.
> Since their discovery, almost all the wrecks have been plundered by treasure and souvenir hunters and most have been badly damaged by erosion.

The *San Pedro* was chosen as the site of an Underwater Park because of her favourable situation, excellent condition and the abundance of marine life she shelters. This is one of the Keys' oldest artificial reefs and gives scuba-divers and snorkellers at all levels of experience an opportunity to explore an historic shipwreck.

A shady place for picnicking in the Long Key State Recreation Area.

The *Monroe* takes visitors to Indian Keys at 8.30 a.m. Thursday to Mondays. Lignumvitae is visited on the same days at 1.30 p.m. Both Keys and the San Pedro Underwater Archaeological Park can also be visited by trip boats from local marinas.

Caloosa Cove

At the southern end of Lower Matecumbe Key is **Caloosa Cove**, a renowned tuna-fishing location and one of President Bush's favourite relaxation spots. A nearby beach area has been turned into a park by the county authorities and is ideal for family picnics, swimming and fishing. Also

The Golden Orb Nature Trail takes walkers through a variety of terrain in the Long Key State Recreation Area.

nearby (MM 73.8) is the medium-priced **Caloosa Cove Resort** which has condominium accommodation in 80 ocean-front units equipped with self-catering facilities.

Long Key

The Overseas Highway lives up to its name as it leaves the Matecumbes and zigzags across open water by way of Craig and Fiesta Keys to reach **Long Key**, as good a place as you will find anywhere in Florida to take a break or make an overnight stop. Don't miss the **Long Key State Recreation Area** (MM 67.5) which has excellent camping facilities and a reasonably good beach with picnic tables, shaded by Australian pines. There are two nature trails—one a boardwalk route through mangroves—and hiking and canoeing facilities. There is an abundance of marine and birdlife, as well as tropical hammock trees—notably, gumbo

Boot Key Harbor is a maze of channels, inlets and islets at Marathon.

limbo, poisonwood, mahogany, Jamaica dogwood and crabwood. Gumbo limbo is also known as "the tourist tree" because its smooth bark is red and always peeling.

Allow an hour or so during your stay at the Recreation Area for the **Golden Orb Nature Trail**. This is named after a type of spider—harmless, you may be glad to know—that is prolific in the area and weaves large webs. The trail takes walkers along the shoreline, through tropical scrubland, and skirts areas of mangrove. The shoreline scenery is stunningly Caribbean and evocative of hidden treasure and pirates carousing over barrels of rum, and the silence is disturbed only by the rustlings of small creatures—marsh rabbits, perhaps, or geckos—or the sudden hammering of a colourful but cheeky pileated woodpecker.

Camping enthusiasts are well catered for in the Long Key area. Apart from the 60 pitches in the state recreation area, there are 418 more with full facilities for RVs at Outdoor Resorts (MM 66) and another 350 for tents and vehicles at the Fiesta Key KOA site (MM 70). The beautifully located **Lime Tree Bay Resort** (MM 68.5) has 29 moderately priced rooms, a freshwater pool, tennis, boat rentals, snorkelling and 300 m (1000 ft) of tropical waterfront overlooking Florida Bay.

Marathon and the Middle Keys

Built in 1982, the second longest bridge in the Keys, named after a US Congressman, Dante Fascell, takes US 1 on a 3.7-km (2.3-mile) leap to Conch Key and the start of the Middle Keys.

Picturesque **Conch Key** looks as if it has been transported from the shores of New England: a tiny harbour village with whitewashed houses and jetties strewn with nets, fishing gear and lobster traps. **Duck Key**, the next along, was once a centre for making salt by evaporating sea water. The enterprise came to a halt when the proprietor died, and in 1937 the 26-hectare (65-acre) island was abandoned. Development started again in 1955 when the causeway linking it to US 1 was built. Duck Key today is a place of well-groomed homes and the posh Hawk's Cay Resort and Marina (MM 61).

Hawk's Cay Resort on Duck Key has a private lagoon, a marina with slips for 70 boats, four restaurants, two lounges, 12 luxury suites, more than 160 spacious rooms and, for those who have to mix business with pleasure, 930 m² (10,000 ft²) of meeting space. The resort offers coral reef diving, fishing—it has its own charter fleet—sailing, tennis and private sandy beaches. It is also one of those place where visitors can enjoy a swim with dolphins and witness a sea-lion training programme.

Grassy Key, the next island down, is home of the **Dolphin Research Center**, where serious scientific endeavour runs in tandem with public entertainment, and tourists again get the chance to frolic with the friendly mammals.

Grassy Key merges into **Crawl Key**, named from a corruption of the Dutch word "kraal" (or the Spanish "corral") meaning an animal enclosure made of rocks or logs. In this case, the enclosures were pens in which large sea turtles were held until they were butchered for food. The meat was used as steaks or as the foundation of real turtle soup. Today, the turtle is protected.

Fat Deer Key contains the only incorporated city in the area of the Middle Keys. **Keys Colony Beach**, on the Atlantic side of the island, was a 36-hectare (90-acre) mangrove swamp in 1954. Now it is a thriving residential and business community covering 115 hectares (284 acres), with a range of tourist accommodation, a golf-course and a marina.

The people of **Marathon** will tell you that the city suffers an identity crisis because it is the only place in the entire chain of islands which does not have the magic word "Key" to add to its name. They forget that the land on which their community stands is officially known as Vaca Key. "Vaca" is Spanish for "cow", though it is more likely that the Spanish explorers who gave the island its name did so because of an abundant population of manatees (sea cows) rather than the doubtful presence of bovines.

With a population of 11,000, close on 50 hotels and an airport with scheduled services to Miami and Key West, Marathon has a big city feel. But it is rooted very much in the waters of the Atlantic Ocean and the Gulf of Mexico, owing its origins to fishermen from Mystic, Connecticut, who discovered its magnificent

178

harbour and sheltered backwaters in 1818. Some of their descendants can be found to this day among crews who sail Marathon's modern fishing fleet.

Vaca Key's economy extended into agriculture when Bahamian farmers arrived in 1850 to plant vegetables and fruit. Evidence of early Bahamian settlement is to be found at **Crane Point Hammock** (MM 50), a 26-hectare (64-acre) botanical preserve which also houses the **Florida Keys Museum of Natural History** and the **Children's Museum of the Florida Keys**, a 260-m² (2,800-ft²) indoor and outdoor facility with ten interactive exhibits demonstrating the Keys' unique ecology.

Originally a private estate, Crane Point Hammock now belongs to the Florida Keys Land and Sea Trust, a private, non-profit organization that acquires natural areas in the Keys for habitat protection, historic conservation, open-space preservation, and recreational use. The site contains archaeological digs, an "Indian and hurricane-proof" home built with 60-cm (2-ft) thick walls in the late 1800s and rare artefacts, including weapons, tools, an ancient Indian dugout canoe and pottery some 5,000 years old.

Highlights of the Natural History Museum include a wall-sized, colour-enhanced enlargement of a Skylab photograph of the region which reveals many details about the island chain, a shipwreck display, ancient objects in gold and silver, ships' cannon and everyday objects from the past. After learning about the Keys' ecology at the two museums, visitors to Crane Point Hammock can follow a nature trail that winds through endangered native

> **Marathon Effort**
> Marathon gained its name from the frantic efforts to complete Henry Flagler's Florida East Coast Railway. Below Vaca Key was an 11-km (7-mile) stretch of almost totally open water, calling for tremendous engineering skills and enormous effort from the 5,000 construction workers on the job. Flagler, getting on in years and afraid he might not live to see his enterprise completed, appealed to the workers to put everything into their task. The newly thriving community was named in honour of their marathon efforts.

foliage, unusual geological features, and mangrove, palm and hardwood hammocks.

Calling itself "The Heart of the Keys", **Marathon** makes much of its position at more or less the centre of the islands, and it is true that tourists could well settle themselves in here and take comfortable trips in either direction. It takes only an hour or so to reach either Key Largo or Key West, and Marathon itself has most of the things people might need of a holiday destination. It is a diving and snorkelling centre in its own right. It has intensive charter-boat fishing operations—its waters are renowned for tarpon and marlin—and there is excellent rod and line angling to be enjoyed on the **Seven-Mile Bridge**, which has been closed to traffic since renovation of the Overseas Highway was completed in 1982. Locals describe the bridge as the world's longest fishing pier. **Sombrero Beach**, a mile or so out of town on the ocean side, is more like the Florida you'll find further north, with fine sand, picnic and barbecue facilities.

179

The town has supermarkets, specialist shops, restaurants and bars. One of the best of these, especially at sundown time, is the **Dockside Lounge**, a waterside pub on Sombrero Boulevard. The bar extends on to a jetty with benches and tables and mooring posts for visitors who arrive by boat. It's a good place for tourists who like to view the local scene and catch up on the gossip. At sunset the view across Boot Key Harbor is stunning.

Boot Key Harbor, which is a maze of channels, inlets and islets, is more than 3.2 km (2 miles) long—much more than the length of downtown Marathon itself—but you may not realize it is there at all as you drive along US 1. The harbour, surrounded by a network of lanes with intriguing bars and restaurants, is hidden by the shops, offices and hotels on the Atlantic Ocean side of the highway. The tastiest of the harbourside eating and drinking places are reached from 15th Street. One of the more popular of these is the **Upper Deck** restaurant and cocktail bar, where local people and visitors alike gather to watch the Keys' sunset. The menu includes sandwiches and snacks, as well as full-service meals, and you can buy wine by the glass.

The Upper Deck is part of the **Faro Blanco Marine Resort**, an extensive complex of garden cottages, luxury three-bedroom condominiums and floating stateroom suites located on both the Gulf and ocean waterfronts. The floating staterooms, very spacious indeed, are in the same dockside area as the Upper Deck. The resort's

*F*aro Blanco Marine Resort at Marathon has accommodation in these floating staterooms.

amenities include four restaurants, three entertainment lounges, an Olympic-size freshwater swimming pool, charter fishing, boat rentals and a courtesy shuttle bus to the shops. At the opposite end of Boot Key Harbor the **Sombrero Resort and Lighthouse Marina,** on Sombrero Boulevard, has similar amenities and 124 de luxe suites offered, the management claims, at "hotel prices". Its **Good Times Lounge** is another favourite watering hole.

Marathon offers a full range of accommodation—everything from bed and breakfast and modest self-catering establishments to motels and the best luxury hotels.

Join in the Sunset Celebration

Sunshine Key hosts many plant and animal species of Caribbean origin, giving it a unique environment. The three parks in Big Pine Key offer a measure of protection to the miniature Key Deer, rare and endangered species of birds, and marine life. A sanctuary for humans is Key West, a lively, vibrant island which you can cycle around in half a day. The richest city per capita in the 19th century, the area has concentrated on making its visitors so welcome they can't bear to leave. An open-air aquarium includes a "touch tank", but the major attraction is Hemingway House, where the author wrote some of his most famous novels. Join in with the locals' sunset celebration and cheer as the sun goes down.

Few places in the world can have such a spectacular gateway as the Lower Keys. The Seven-Mile Bridge—actually only 6.79 miles (10.93 km) long—leaves Marathon and Vaca Key at MM 47 to fly straight as an arrow across turquoise waters rich in game fish. Flagler's old bridge, now accessible only to those on foot, runs alongside, taking a slightly more devious route to include **Pigeon Key**, a tiny island which was originally a camp for the railroad builders. Some of its original houses still stand, capturing the

The power of sail on a cruise in the waters around Key West.

attention of artists and photographers. For some 20 years the island was a marine research centre for the University of Miami, but the lease recently reverted to Monroe County and there are plans to open it as an historic cultural site with the Keys' first railway museum.

Sunshine Key

The new bridge comes to earth at Sunshine Key, a 30-hectare (75-acre) island given over to a completely self-contained camping resort (MM 39). There are more than 300 pitches with full hook-up facilities, and the **Sunshine Key Camping Resort** has a beach, marina, dive shop, store, recreation room,

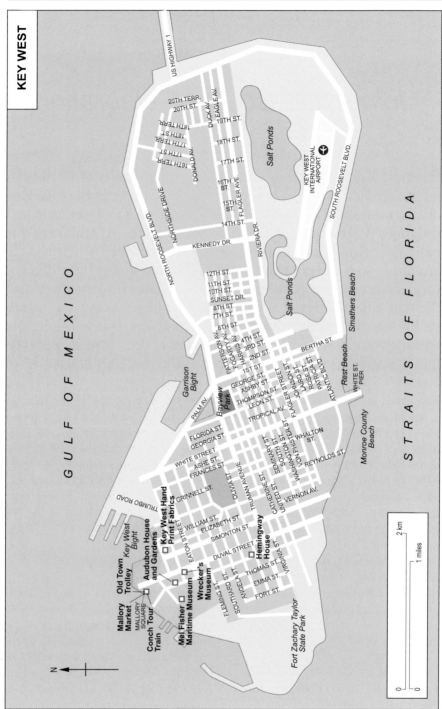

KEY WEST

Bahia Honda Park

Bahia Honda is Spanish for "Deep Bay", and the park covers 255 hectares (635 acres) of which 210 hectares (510 acres) are under water. Scuba-diving and snorkelling opportunities are excellent and the 10-m (30-ft) deep water beneath the old and new bridges attracts tarpon and other large game fish. The park also offers good swimming and natural, sandy beaches, one of which is included in the top one per cent of American beaches in a survey published in 1991 by the University of Maryland. The beach was assessed for the quality of its sand, water and air temperatures, amenities, ease of access and the annual total of sunny days.

fully lit tennis courts and a freshwater pool. There are further camping facilities in the Bahia Honda State Recreation Area, which also has accommodation in bayside cabins. The park is Florida's southernmost recreation area and has a natural environment unique in the continental United States. Its biological communities include dunes, coastal berm, mangroves, tropical hardwood hammock and underwater habitats, and host many plants and animal species of Caribbean origin. Among the rare plants found in the park are yellow satinwood, manchineel, silver palm, key thatch palm and the endangered small-flowered lily thorn. There is abundant birdlife, including white-crowned pigeon, great white heron, roseate spoonbill, reddish egret, osprey and least tern.

Town plan of Key West.

Big Pine Key

US 1 crosses Spanish Harbor Keys to reach Big Pine Key, where it makes its first significant bend—a sharp right-hand turn—since leaving the mainland, now more than 105 km (65 miles) away. Big Pine, No Name and neighbouring keys constitute the **Key Deer National Wildlife Refuge**, home to about 300 miniature deer, which are protected by a hunting and overnight camping ban, strictly enforced traffic speed limits and dog leash regulations. A sub-species of the Virginia white-tailed deer found on the mainland, the Key deer reaches a height of not much more than 0.60 m (2 ft). At one time their number was reduced to about 50, largely through hunting. The best time to see the deer is early morning or late afternoon, though they are likely to wander on to the highway at any time, hence the need for caution when driving. Visitors are urged not to feed them because wild animals can be placed in jeopardy if they lose their timidity.

At the northern tip of Big Pine Key is **Watson's Hammock**, a popular nature preserve within the deer refuge. Named after Jack Cotrell Watson, first manager of the refuge and a man who was ready to use his gun to defend the deer from poachers, the preserve harbours a variety of plant and animal species. The **Pine Woods Nature Trail** leads walkers through the hammock, and the area can also be explored by canoe. Nearby is the **Blue Hole**, the largest body of fresh water in the Keys. Formed as a result of rock-quarrying operations when the island's first roads were being built, the Blue Hole has become an important source of drinking water for the Key deer and marsh rabbits. It also supports such birdlife as little blue herons, green-backed herons and gallinules. Aquatic wildlife includes largemouth bass, bluegills and killifishes, but the star of the show is "Granpa", a large Florida alligator, one of several who have made their home in the former quarry.

The waters adjoining the Big Pine Key section of the deer refuge form the **Great White Heron Refuge**, which offers protection to a number of rare and endangered species and is the winter resting site for many migratory birds. Also offshore from Big Pine, about 13 km (8 miles) to the southwest, is **Looe Key National Marine Sanctuary**, a coral reef with a wealth of plant and animal life. Named after *HMS Looe*, a British frigate wrecked there during a storm in 1744, the sanctuary has several distinct habitats, with seagrass beds, patch reefs and sand flats. It is easily accessible by boat, and skin-divers and scuba enthusiasts, at all levels of ability, can arrange trips with dive centres on Big Pine, Ramrod and Summerland Keys. Excellent water clarity and generally moderate sea conditions allow all Looe Key's features and inhabitants—there are thousands of brightly coloured fish—to be viewed from the surface.

More Lower Keys

Summerland Key has considerable residential development, with its own post office and airstrip. Neighbouring **Cudjoe Key** (Cudjoe is said to be a Southern short form of Cousin Joe) is a

---

Perky's Tower
In 1929 Richter C. Perky was trying to develop a fishing camp on a site he had purchased from an Englishman, C.W. Chase, whose efforts to establish a sponge fishery there had failed. Perky's own enterprise was being hampered by swarms of ferocious mosquitoes which were driving the anglers away. His solution was to build a wooden tower—it looks like a windmill without arms—and smear it with $500 worth of smelly guano to lure a defending corps of insect-eaters. Nothing happened. Perky rounded up a squadron of bats and installed them in the tower. Like the anglers, they fled—local legend says the mosquitoes ate them—and poor Perky went bankrupt. But his tower endures at MM 17 behind the Sugar Loaf Lodge resort. The mini-tower in front of the resort is not the real thing.

---

more sparsely settled island with a US missile tracking station, which is the home of *Fat Albert*, a big white balloon frequently seen in the sky. **Sugarloaf Key**, so called because an ancient Indian midden found there resembled an old-fashioned loaf of sugar, is the site of the **Perky Bat Tower**, monument to a project that must have seemed like a good idea at the time.

The Overseas Highway runs next through the **Saddlebunch Keys**, a group of islands predominantly covered with red mangroves and largely uninhabited, except for one large residential development and a US Navy communications site. **Big Coppit Key** houses the families of service personnel stationed at a naval airbase on the next key, **Boca Chica**. **Stock Island**, where herds of pigs and cattle were once kept, now has a country club and a golf-course.

At its far end is a 49-m (159-ft) bridge—the last on US 1—and the totally different community of Key West.

Key West

The Last Resort, as some wags dub Key West, instantly presents a dilemma to visitors arriving by car. For the first time since leaving the mainland the highway divides, but it doesn't matter which way you go— both routes lead to Old Town, and the worst that can happen is that you will

finish up back at the bridge. The island is only 6.4 km (4 miles) long by 3.2 km (2 miles) wide, so no one is likely to be lost for long. The road to the right is North Roosevelt Boulevard. To the left is South Roosevelt Boulevard.

North Roosevelt enters the city through the latest area of Key West to be developed. It is not much different from the outskirts of most American cities—hotels, motels, filling stations, garden centres and supermarkets. Until the 1950s the land here was salt marsh, a habitat for many shore birds. The road continues to pass the Key West Yacht Club, many of whose members live on their craft all the year round, and the city docks at Garrison Bight Marina. Turning right at the traffic lights here will lead to the area

Souvenirs for sale at a roadside stall in Key West.

where charter-boat fishing trips can be arranged. N. Roosevelt soon becomes Truman Avenue, and the next set of traffic lights are at the intersection with White Street, the edge of Old Town.

From the bridge again, S. Roosevelt—the road to the left—takes a more restful route along the ocean side of the island, passing a community of residential houseboats, the airport and the East Martello Tower, one of three Civil War forts on Key West. Next comes a stretch of land where salt was extracted by evaporation from ponds in the 1830s. Some 20 hectares (50 acres) here have been designated as the **Riggs Wildlife and Bird Preserve**. Smathers Beach is one of several public beaches on the island, and there are rental facilities here for sailing catamarans, windsurfing boards, deck-chairs and air-beds. At the far end of Smathers Beach the road swings sharply inland. The first turning on the left, Atlantic Boulevard, leads us parallel with the shore again, towards Higgs Beach where parasailing and water-skiing are available. The White Street fishing pier is the signal to turn right; in a dozen blocks or so we again reach the intersection with Truman Avenue and the start of Old Town.

Origins and Development

Key West is a corruption of the Spanish, *Cayo Hueso*, meaning "island of bones". The key was discovered by Ponce de Leon in 1513 and gained its name because of the many human bones found by early explorers. The bones were believed to be the remains of warriors killed in battles between rival groups of Indians and left unburied either for religious reasons or because

the limestone ground was too hard for grave-digging. The island changed hands a number of times. Between 1763 and 1783 it was a British possession, acquired with the rest of Florida under the First Treaty of Paris negotiated with Spain at the end of the Seven Years' War. At times it was in private ownership. Between 1815 and 1822 it was the property of a Spanish cavalry officer who sold it for $2,000 to John Simonton, a businessman from Alabama. Simonton sold shares in the island to John Fleming, Pardon C. Greene and John Whitehead, and all four are commemorated to this day in Old Town street names.

The consortium did not own Key West for long. In 1822 the US government took charge, opening a customs house and sending in the navy to rid the area of pirates, who had been a scourge since soon after the arrival of the first Europeans. Another early occupation—one that brought great prosperity to Key West—was wrecking. Many a ship came to grief on the poorly marked reefs, and local seamen amassed fortunes from salvage operations. Sometimes, it is claimed, a ship would be lured to destruction by a light tied to the tail of a cow or mule. Some of the older houses in Key West have "Widows' Walks" on their roofs from where, it is said, the wives of sea captains would watch for the return of their menfolk. It is just as likely that the walks were used as lookout posts from which newly wrecked vessels could be spotted.

As a result of wrecking, combined with the more acceptable industries of salt extraction and cigar-making (a Cuban import), Key West became the richest city per capita in the United States, a position it enjoyed for much of the 19th century. By 1888 its population had reached 18,000, making it the largest city in Florida. During the Spanish–American War of 1898 it was an important naval centre, and when the conflict ended it became a first-rate shipping port, competing seriously with New York City. Flagler's Overseas Railroad put the icing on Key West's rich cake, and the little island's fortunes continued to soar during World War I when naval operations again intensified. Then came the Armistice, and it all fell to bits.

With the war over, the US Navy decided to close down its Key West base. The cigar industry, which had prospered in spite of a disastrous fire in 1886, pulled up its traps and resettled in Tampa after a long period of labour troubles. The sponge fisheries were already in ruins, and pineapple processing no longer thrived because American consumers preferred the sweeter variety now available from Hawaii. Then came the stock market crash and the Great Depression. Key West, once America's richest city per capita, became the poorest with more than half its people—now reduced to around 10,000—on relief. The city went bankrupt.

State and federal advisers decided that Key West's future lay in tourism—there were good beaches, attractive scenery and a super climate—so work started on sprucing the place up and on mounting an advertising campaign to promote the "new" tropical paradise nationally. The work was all but completed and the islanders ready to welcome crowds of holiday-makers when the great hurricane of 1935 struck the island chain. Key West itself escaped the worst of the storm, but its hopes of economic recovery were ruined, along with Flagler's railroad.

Completion of the Overseas Highway and the return of the navy during World War II got the city back on its feet. During the late 1940s extensive shrimp beds were discovered nearby and to this day "pink gold", as the locals call it, makes a valuable contribution to the island's economy.

In post-war years, Key West, which had received some publicity spin-off from Ernest Hemingway's period of residence, gained another boost when President Harry S. Truman began taking holidays there and became so fond of the place that he established a "Little White House" at the US Navy base fronting on Whitehead Street. The Cuban Revolution of 1959 and the 1963 Missile Crisis which had President John F. Kennedy and the Soviet Union's Nikita Kruschev in eyeball-to-eyeball confrontation ensured Key West—only 145 km (90 miles) from Havana—a spotlit space on the world stage. Boat people, refugees from Fidel Castro's Cuba, began turning up on America's Caribbean doorstep.

The 1960s saw Key West becoming established as a great sport-fishing area, and in the 1970s drug smuggling increased to the extent that cargoes of marijuana were openly unloaded on city docksides. Today's residents of Key West are more likely to be involved in smuggling chilli seeds. They enjoy food with a zest and they also enjoy gardening, especially growing their own chillies, of which there are dozens of varieties in Latin America. The Conchs will go to almost any length on a trip abroad to obtain new varieties of seed and bring them home, in spite of US Customs regulations which forbid agricultural and horticultural imports.

Naval cutbacks at the end of the 1970s again hit the local economy, but one beneficial result this time was that some land—always a scarce resource on small islands—became available for development. Nevertheless, Old Town was in a sorry state, with shops and bars closed and buildings in disrepair. Government grants were pumped in and Key West was again marketed strongly as a tourist destination. The campaign also brought in many new residents from cities in the north, people who were attracted by the laid-back lifestyle of a place in the sun and a community with liberal attitudes. The latest newcomers, however, also had a sense of social responsibility and they began restoring the properties they purchased and launching civic improvement schemes to burnish the city's image. Many old Key West residents readily pay tribute to the efforts of the gay community that replaced the lackadaisical hippies who had made the place their home since the mid-1960s.

After spending millions of dollars to get Key West's tourism industry going again, the federal government brought it all to a halt by setting up a checkpoint at Florida City on the mainland to search for drugs and illegal immigrants. The roadblock frequently caused a tailback up to 32-km (20-miles) long, and tourists began to look elsewhere. Key West's response was typically eccentric, though effective. Prompted by a local radio station's initiative, bar room pollsters voted to secede from the Union and declare war on the United States. The Conch Republic, as Key West—and indeed the whole of the Florida Keys—was to be renamed, would then surrender and demand foreign aid. Instead, the United States capitulated and the checkpoint was removed.

What to See and Do

Key West today is a thriving community whose population of around 30,000 is frequently doubled by tourists. It is a community of individualists who happily acknowledge their economic dependence on tourism, but are determined not to let it spoil their special place. Development controls are strict—even to the extent of dictating the type and colour of paint that can be used externally on buildings considered to be of historic importance. In **Old Town** that means almost every building. Here are whole streets of Conch houses, attractive 19th-century homes reflecting the architectural styles of New England, New Orleans and the Bahamas. Many of them are known as gingerbread houses because of the flat cut-out shapes of railings on their verandahs and garden fences. Another type of home found in the shady streets of Old Town is the shotgun house—long, narrow buildings where, it was said, you could fire a gun from the front door and the shot would go clean through the back door, exactly in line at the other end. No one seems to know why anyone would want to do that.

Bikes are the most popular form of transport in Key West.

Amsterdam Curry Mansion

On Caroline Street, the Curry Mansion is open to the public and gives visitors an opportunity to see the inside of a classic Key West home. Now owned by Edith and Albert Amsterdam, the house was built by William Curry who became Florida's first millionaire through selling ships' supplies, timber and salvaging wrecks. The oldest part of the house dates from 1855, and the front part was added in 1899. It is beautifully furnished, with many valuable antiques, and there is a widow's walk with a splendid view of the city. The Curry Mansion is also a guest-house.

Most of the action in Old Town takes place on Duval Street, moving south for about eight blocks from Front Street and spilling over for a street or two on either side of Duval. Almost everything you need to see is comfortably within walking distance, and the whole island can be explored easily in a leisurely half-day bike ride. There are many cycle rental agencies in Old Town. The best way for newcomers to familiarize themselves with Key West, though, is to take a tour with either the Conch Train or the Old Town Trolley. Both are familiar sights all over the island, especially the **Conch Train**, a long line of open railway-style carriages pulled by a "loco" complete with cowcatcher and tall smokestack. The loco is actually a disguised jeep, powered by butane gas for environmental reasons. The people of Key

West are proud of their clean air and anxious to keep it that way.

The Conch Train, which has been touring the streets of Key West for more than 30 years, departs from the Art Center at Mallory Square every half-hour throughout the day. The newer **Old Town Trolley**, an old-style bus, also departs from Mallory Square, though passengers can get on and off

The Conch Train, pulled by a butane-powered jeep disguised as a locomotive, takes tourists on a round-trip of Key West.

as they choose at sixteen stations around the island. Both tours last 90 minutes and are well worth the few dollars fare. Commentaries by the driver-guides are informative, entertaining and individual, with much tooting and bell-ringing along the route as friends and neighbours are greeted.

Duval Street, Old Town's artery, has a European feel, with open-air cafés and bars, boutiques, souvenir shops and art galleries. It is very much a street for strolling along. Locals call it the longest main street in the world because it runs from the Atlantic Ocean to the Gulf of Mexico. Much of the eastern half of its length is residential, interspersed with the premises of purely domestic businesses. The

downtown shopping area really starts around the intersection with Angela Street where there are good examples of Art-Deco architecture and an old Cuban-style music hall. The major landmark in this area is the **Holiday Inn La Concha Hotel**, built in 1925, renovated in 1987, and the tallest building in the city—but still reaching no higher than seven floors. Its rooftop bar is a popular watering hole with a panoramic view of Old Town.

One block down from La Concha, on the corner of Duval and Eaton, is **St Paul's Episcopal Church**, a monument to mankind's persistence in the face of the elements. The church has been destroyed three times by hurricanes. After the last disaster, in 1919, it was decided to rebuild it in stone. Next, at 322 Duval, near the Caroline Street intersection, comes the Oldest House, a dwelling of 1829 in which the **Wreckers' Museum** is housed. Exhibited as the home of a wrecker captain, the museum displays documents and artefacts, including a wrecker's licence and regulations, a blacklist of wreckers caught working an insurance racket, and model ships. Antique furnishings and children's playthings help to convey the atmosphere of a specialist businessman's home during a time of great prosperity.

The next three blocks are the real heart of Old Town, with the greatest concentration of shops and bars. Here, on the corner of Duval and Greene, is Sloppy Joe's Bar, a shrine for fans of Ernest Hemingway.

The end of Duval Street is signalled by a set of traffic lights covering a wide intersection with a Conch Train station on the right and a large, ornate

*T*he architecture of Cuba is reflected in this old music hall on Duval Street.

brick building on the left. This is the bank that was robbed in Hemingway's *To Have and Have Not*. These days the bank appears to be held up mainly by the back of a young top-hatted Black man sleepily waiting in the shade to tell fortunes. Beyond the traffic lights Duval Street peters out with the Ocean Key House and Pier House hotels facing each other, and straight ahead the

193

Sloppy Joe's

Sloppy Joe's Bar is a big, noisy place, plastered with photographs of Hemingway and "Papa" bric-a-brac. There is live entertainment day and night and younger people, especially, like to be seen there drinking margaritas and living it up as they imagine the writer must have done. But this is not the original Sloppy Joe's. In Hemingway's day it was called the Midget Bar and although he certainly used it from time to time the place where he arm-wrestled, drank and told yarns after a hard day's writing at his home on Whitehead Street was about half a block down Greene Street on the opposite side of Duval. It is now called Captain Tony's Saloon. The Sloppy Joe who ran it in Hemingway's time moved to larger premises as his business prospered—boosted no doubt by the master's patronage—and he took the title with him.

jetty where tourists board the Fireball glass-bottomed boat for two-hour cruises to the coral reef.

The road that crosses Duval at the lights is Front Street. To the right, passing the Conch Train station, Front Street continues for three blocks, with resort hotels and restaurants on one side and shops on the other. It comes to an end at Key West Bight, overlooking the harbour where commercial fishing and shrimping vessels are moored. Nearby, in the William Street

Sloppy Joe's Bar attracts the Hemingway fans with live music and margaritas—but it is not the place "Papa" habitually used.

Waterfront Marketplace, is the **Hurricane Museum** with exhibits, photographs and memorabilia testifying to the dramatic weather conditions which have to be faced in this area from time to time.

Key West Bight is definitely a tourist attraction (*see* sidebar). This is where most of the trip boats are to be found—the sunset cruise catamarans and schooners, the charter fishing craft—but it is also a working harbour, where shrimp boats slip unfussily from their moorings and head purposefully towards the Dry Tortugas. There are souvenir shops, of course, but these are squeezed in among sheds where powerful marine diesels are serviced and the rakish working craft of Caribbean design are scraped down and patched up.

At the foot of Margaret Street you will find the turtle kraals (corrals) where green sea turtles were kept in

*C*aptain Tony's Saloon is the original Sloppy Joe's in which Ernest Hemingway arm-wrestled, drank and told yarns.

Key West Bight

This is one of those waterfront areas unique to North America. The smell of the sea and fish, the haphazard coils of rope and chain, the hints of tar and salt are the same as you would find anywhere in the world—from the Hebrides to the Falklands, Manila to Cape Town—but only in Canada and the United States, it seems, do seafaring communities have the ability to create an extra dimension of fantasy. Perhaps it is the timber they use, but the boardwalk jetties and mooring posts undulate and lean rather more precariously than elsewhere; the dockside buildings tilt comically, clearly designed by hammer and nail rather than pencil and paper. Popeye, you feel sure, is only just around the corner.

---

the past before being butchered for meat. The veal-like flesh was a favourite in chowders and as steaks, or even turtle burgers, on Key West menus. Turtles have been protected by federal law since the early 1970s, and the site of the kraals is now a restaurant and marina with sea creatures on display. Among them are a number of

195

Sunset cruises under sail leave every evening from Key West Bight.

turtles, including Hawkeye, who weighs 80 kg (175 lb) and is known to be more than 30 years old. She luckily escaped death before the protection law was introduced. Another first-rate restaurant in the area is the **Half Shell Raw Bar**, as much a favourite with the locals as it is with tourists. It's a big

rambling place with a large central bar, and as workaday as any of those marine engine workshops. The menu is extensive, imaginative and reasonably priced. Bar snacks include oysters and clams, served by the dozen, at cheaper than fish and chip prices in the UK. If you like a spicy start to a meal try the stuffed jalapeños—best with a mug of cold draught beer.

Turning left on to Front Street, at those lights back on Duval, leads to the **Mallory Square** area, renowned for its daily sunset celebration along the dockside. This is another manifestation of Key West's uninhibited way of life. Anywhere else, an event like this would be hyped up by the marketing people into a stunt. The sunset celebration is pagan, unself-conscious. People just gather on the dockside to watch the nightly spectacle of sundown, and if it's an especially good one they clap and cheer. True, there are jugglers and sword-swallowers, magicians and a bagpipes player. Certainly, there are stalls selling cold drinks and ice creams, teeshirts, baubles and bangles. But no one has to be there; you don't have to eat and drink, nor buy a teeshirt. No one is forced to drop a dollar bill or two into a juggler's cap or the piper's Tam O'Shanter. And you know darned well that even if there were no tourists, no vendors, the people of Key West would still be there, drinks in hand, cheering as the sun goes down.

Mallory Square itself is a delightful place, tree-shaded and colourful with market stalls and boutiques. Pirate Alley, a narrow lane with little shops and bars, is as full of character as its name implies. The **Key West Hospitality House** and the **Chamber of Commerce** are to be found in the square, and both places dispense tourist information and literature. Also in the area are the **Art Center**, the old cigar factory and the **Aquarium**, the first tourist attraction built in the Florida Keys.

The Half Shell Raw Bar at Key West Bight is a favourite eating place with locals as well as tourists.

Mallory Square's nightly sunset celebration is pagan and unselfconscious.

Restaurants in the Mallory Square area are for purposeful diners rather than pleasure seekers, and the bars are for people who like to talk or listen rather than sit stupefied by amplified music. However, fun worshippers with a penchant for Country 'n' Western will doubtless head for the **Hog's Breath Saloon** at 400 Front Street. It's a noisy, happy place with live entertainment that draws crowds emerging from the sunset celebration, and a notice in the bar makes the mystifying

The Conch Train stops in Mallory Square during its round of Key West.

and arguable declaration that "Hog's breath is better than no breath at all". Front Street turns into Whitehead Street, which could just as well be called Heritage Highway because it passes between so many buildings significantly linked with the city's past. The first place you come to is a big, brick building, the old **Customs House** built in 1891. Its steeply pitched roof, designed to prevent a build-up of snow in ·northern winters, was installed at the insistence of pedantic government architects. Locals point out that the roof has certainly done its job. Not once in the past century has snow settled on it.

The Aquarium

In 1932 the Aquarium opened as part of the efforts to breathe new life into the island's depressed economy, and it was the first open-air aquarium in the United States. Exhibits include a living coral reef, several tanks of sharks and a turtle pool. The reef offers a fascinating view of a struggling coral system and the sea life that makes its home in such waters, including barracuda, a hammerhead shark and colourful angelfish and parrotfish. The quality of water and the weather in the area are considered ideal for coral to be reproduced in what amounts to captivity. A "touch tank" contains creatures that can be handled safely by visitors, especially children, and another tank displays the flamboyant Florida spiny lobster in a habitat authentic even to the point of including lobster traps of the sort used by local fishermen.

Next, on the corner of Whitehead and Greene, comes Mel Fisher's **Maritime Heritage Museum**, which houses

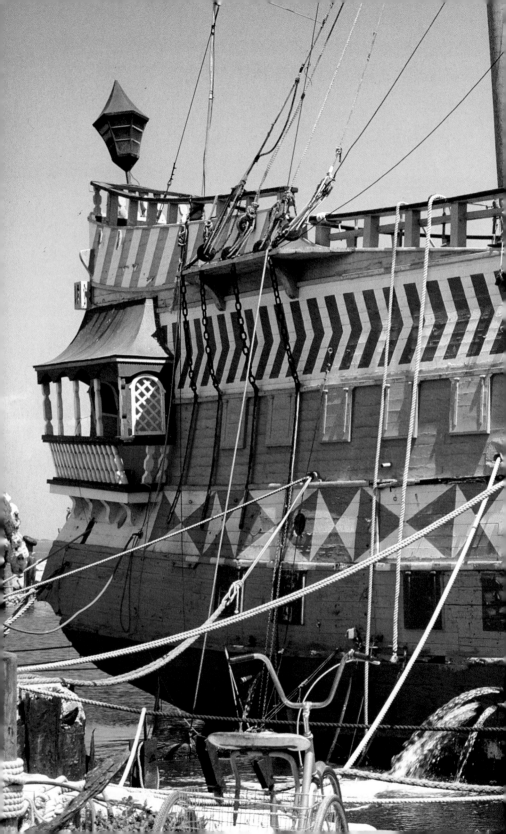

SEE THE
TREASURE
OF THE
ATOCHA

A reconstruction of the wrecked galleon Nuestra Señora de Atocha *from which a fortune in treasure was recovered by Key West's Mel Fisher (previous page).*

Audubon House
The house, opposite the Fisher museum, was named after the peripatetic ornithologist and painter John Audubon, who visited Key West for a few weeks in 1832. As elsewhere in Florida—and indeed many other parts of the United States—Audubon worked hard, studying and drawing birds in their natural habitat. Each day he would explore the mangroves in search of native birds, starting off as early as 3 a.m. and frequently working late into the night.

At that time the house belonged to Captain John H. Geiger, a salvager and harbour pilot with whom he stayed. In 1962 the house became the property of a prominent Miami businessman who dedicated it as a public museum. Completely restored, the Audubon House retains its original hinges, hardware and wood used by the ships' carpenters who built the place. All fastenings in the house are with wooden pegs—no nails have been used anywhere—and it took more than two years to research and complete the restoration, which inspired a civic preservation trend in the 1970s.

The house contains numerous original engravings by John Audubon, including many from his famous *Birds of America* "double elephant" folio produced between 1826 and 1838. The rooms are furnished with 18th- and 19th-century pieces from all parts of the world.

an awesome collection of gold, silver, and other treasure, recovered from Spanish galleons wrecked long ago along Florida's reef. The collection, worth millions of dollars, was recovered by teams of divers led by Mel Fisher, a persistent and painstaking man who has come to be acknowledged as America's master treasure hunter. He earned the title in 1971 when he brought up the first part of a sensational cargo from the galleon *Nuestra Señora de Atocha*, wrecked during a hurricane in 1622. There is also a fortune in artefacts recovered later from the *Atocha*'s sister ship, *Santa Margarita*, which went down in the same storm. Other salvaged spoils—this time from the merchant vessel *Isaac Allerton*, which sank in 1856—are on show at the historic Key West **Shipwreck Museum,** a few blocks away at 510 Greene Street. More than 400 wreckers salvaged the ship which helped Key West to become the richest city per capita in the US.

Between Greene and Fleming streets, the western side of Whitehead is taken up by the former Truman Annexe Navy base, which includes President Harry S. Truman's **Little White House.** In 1986 the entire waterfront tract was purchased for $17 million by a Boston developer who has since spent a further $108 million on the restoration of some 20 historic buildings, including the Little White House, and on the provision of a marina, yacht club, beach, restaurants, shops, offices and parks. Just beyond the post office, on Eaton Street, is the Monroe County Courthouse, in front of which is a splendid kapok tree and Mile Marker 0, the official end of US

1, though people with a poetic turn of mind prefer to regard the end as the Southernmost Point, which is at the far end of Whitehead Street.

A right turn on to Southard Street leads to **Fort Zachary Taylor**, one of four red-brick forts built in the latter half of the 19th century to protect America's strategically important southernmost shore. Work on the three-storey Fort Zachary Taylor, intended to guard all entrances to Key West harbour, began in 1845 and ended 21 years later. In 1850 it was named after the 12th US President, who had died in office that year. The fort was still unfinished when the Civil War broke out—yellow fever, hurricanes, shortages of material and manpower and Key West's remoteness had hampered progress—and during the conflict the incomplete building was controlled by Union forces who successfully blockaded Confederate ships, shortening the war by a year, according to some historians.

Fort Zachary Taylor fell into dereliction and became buried under tons of windblown sand. When the site was being considered for development as a sewage treatment plant in 1968, local historian Howard England, who worked as a civilian architect at the naval base, enlisted the support of his two sons and started digging. Within the next ten years England and other volunteers excavated thousands of bullets as well as cannonballs and cannon from seven of the fort's 24 gun rooms. The fort, opened as a state historic site in 1985, with picnic facilities, swimming and fishing, is believed to hold the largest number of Civil War artefacts in the United States. Thousands of visitors are attracted to the site, mainly because of its 21-hectare (51-acre) beach.

The other forts are the East Martello Tower on South Roosevelt Boulevard, the West Martello Tower on Atlantic Boulevard and Fort Jefferson, 112 km (70 miles) west of Key West in the Dry Tortugas. The building of the East and West Martello Towers was authorized by Congress in 1844 to protect Fort Zachary Taylor from enemy attack. Construction of the fortifications began in 1861, but new military equipment soon made them obsolete. The Key West Art and Historical Society runs **East Martello Gallery and Museum**, where folk art collections and exhibits of early Key West life are on display. Nine art galleries, photographic displays and hundreds of local artefacts are on show in 13 vaulted rooms with brick arches. Visitors may climb the 48 steps of the winding staircase to the top of the Citadel, the fort's central tower, which provides a sweeping view of the island and ocean. **West Martello Tower** houses a garden centre and the Key West Garden Club.

Fort Jefferson, known as the Gibraltar of the Gulf, was built in the mid-1800s on Garden Key in the Dry Tortugas, a cluster of seven coral reefs. Today, the national monument's unspoilt environment is home to rare migratory birds and an abundance of marine life. It attracts divers and nature lovers from all over the world, who come to examine staghorn coral, French angelfish, loggerhead turtles, the sooty tern and noddy tern. During the Civil War, the fort was held by the Union and served as a prison for

captured deserters. It remained a prison for ten years after the war. Its most famous inmate was Dr Samuel Mudd, the physician from Maryland who unwittingly set the broken leg of John Wilkes Booth, the man who assassinated President Lincoln. Fort Jefferson can be reached by charter boat from Key West, and there are daily flights by seaplane. Camping is allowed in certain areas, but facilities are sparse and reservation is suggested for overnight stays.

About halfway along Whitehead Street, on the right, is the Key West **Lighthouse and Military Museum**. The lighthouse was built in 1825 and the museum contains maritime and navigational exhibits. Energetic visitors who climb the 88 steps to the top of the lighthouse will be rewarded with a lofty view of the city.

Directly opposite the lighthouse, at 907 Whitehead Street, is the place many people regard as Key West's major attraction: the **Hemingway House**. It is certainly an attractive house in a large, restful garden surrounded by a wall said to have been built by Hemingway and his cronies. Conch Train Tour guides comment wryly that judging from the wall's uncertain lines they must have had a great time building it.

Built in Spanish Colonial style from rock quarried in the grounds, the spacious house has furnishings, rugs, tiles and chandeliers brought from Spain, Africa and Cuba. There is some argument about whether or not the items were ever owned by the Hemingways or have been brought in since. However, there is no doubt that Hemingway owned the place for 30 years from 1931, when he bought it for $6,000. Here he wrote some of his best-known novels and short stories, including such works as *A Farewell to Arms, Death in the Afternoon, The Snows of Kilimanjaro, For Whom the Bell Tolls* and, of course, *To Have and Have Not*.

Hemingway worked in a study on the first floor of a utilities building at the back of the house, writing from 6 a.m. to noon then setting off for Sloppy Joe's. He lived in the house

> **The Hemingway Days Festival**
> July each year sees Key West celebrating the Hemingway Days Festival, a week-long carnival which includes competitions for budding journalists and short-story writers, a storytelling contest and Hemingway trivia quizzes. Non-literary activities include kayak tours of the Keys' back country and mangroves, a sailing regatta, fishing tournament and a mini-marathon. The most bizarre event is the annual Hemingway look-alike competition, which brings in throngs of grizzly beards and level gazes. The irony is that Hemingway himself, who arrived in Key West looking like Clark Gable, probably modelled his subsequent image on the appearance of the Key West locals. The festival is rounded off with an arm-wrestling championship, a Street Fair and Food Fest and a 1930s theme party staged at the Hemingway Home and Museum.

The house at 907 Whitehead Street, Key West, which Ernest Hemingway owned for 30 years. Here he wrote some of his best-known novels and short stories.

with his second wife Pauline and their two sons for about ten years. He left, after obtaining a divorce, to marry the journalist Martha Gelhorn. Pauline and the boys stayed on at Key West.

Many of the trees and shrubs in the garden were planted by Hemingway.

Southernmost Point— the end of continental USA—is also the end of Key West's Whitehead Street.

The swimming pool was the first to be built in Key West, installed on Pauline's orders while Hemingway was away. It cost $20,000, and he was not pleased. Chastising his wife for the extravagance, he took a one-cent piece from his pocket and pressed it into the still unset mortar of the brickwork patio. "Here," he snorted, "take the last penny I've got." The coin is still there.

When Hemingway died in 1961 the house was sold to a local family, who had so many visits from people wanting to visit the home they decided to establish it as a memorial to the writer. The place is still occupied by about 45

descendants of the cats who lived there at the same time as the author. About a third of them have seven toes, a phenomenon not unusual, apparently, all along America's eastern seaboard. There are guided tours of the house daily from 9 a.m. to 5 p.m.

Sidewalk stalls selling shells and coconut souvenirs and a large, red-and-white striped buoy mark the end of Whitehead Street—and the end of mainland America. This is the Southernmost Point where a sign indicates that Cuba is 145 km (90 miles) away.

A popular excursion for many Key Westers—and for some it's the last trip

they ever make—is to the City Cemetery, a shady, restful square bordered by Frances, Petronia and Olivia Streets and Windsor Lane. It's a place for a quiet stroll and to reflect on the island's past. At a special memorial rest the bodies of seamen who died when the Battleship USS *Maine* was sunk in Havana Harbour in 1898 at the start of the Spanish–American War.

The cemetery also demonstrates that some of the islanders, at least, have a grave sense of humour. The 8.5-hectare (21-acre) cemetery is renowned for the sometimes startling epitaphs carried on its tombstones. A tablet commemorating B.P. Roberts (17 May 1929–18 June 1979), for example, complains: "I told you I was sick". Carved into another nearby headstone is this laconic message from a grieving widow: "At least I know where he's sleeping tonight".

Nicknames are widely used among Key West residents and they are to be found adorning many of the stones. Bunny, Shorty, The Tailor, Mamie, Bean K. Lito and many others are all there. José J. Abreu's marble memorial lists 17 nicknames: Mr Clean, Baldy, Joseito, Jojab, Jacinto, Josellilo, Diablo, Uncle Tio, Cousin, Loco, Kojak, Gamba, Calvito, Pepito, Skinhead, Primo and Nuts. There are also two messages: "The buck stops here" and "Call me for dinner". The memorial is an example of one Key Wester's forward thinking. At the time of writing, José Abreu, a US Navy pensioner, was still alive.

Key West Cemetery is open from dawn to dusk. Guided tours are available on Saturdays and Sundays at 10 a.m. or 4 p.m.

Relax and Unwind in
Beautiful Surroundings

Take things easy in a part of Florida which offers a more sedate pace of life. Here you will find the gladiolus capital of the world at Fort Myers, where Thomas Edison and Henry Ford lived next door to each other. The history of the Native Americans in the area is well documented and here you will probably come across several Indian villages.

One of the most difficult questions to answer about Florida is: "Which is your favourite part of the state?" Each region is distinctive and each has its special appeal. The south-west has a completely different ambience from the south-east. The Lee Island Coast, though accessible by air and road and offering a range of excellent accommodation, is less well known than the Gold Coast of the south-east. Those

Although the population of Naples has increased considerably in recent years, the city has managed to retain a small-town atmosphere.

seeking the quiet life, sailing to uninhabited islands and private coves, collecting shells, visiting wildlife sanctuaries, playing the odd game of tennis or golf, taking a boat trip with smiling dolphins leaping alongside, will want to return to the south-west again and again. Nature can be enjoyed in a civilized setting. There are country inns and restaurants where you may meet the locals—mostly people from many parts of the USA who spend part of the year in a house or condominium—the "semi-natives".

It is only in recent years that upscale resorts on the islands of Sanibel and Captiva have featured in tour operators' brochures on Europe's side of the Atlantic, and they are mainly in the programmes of small specialists.

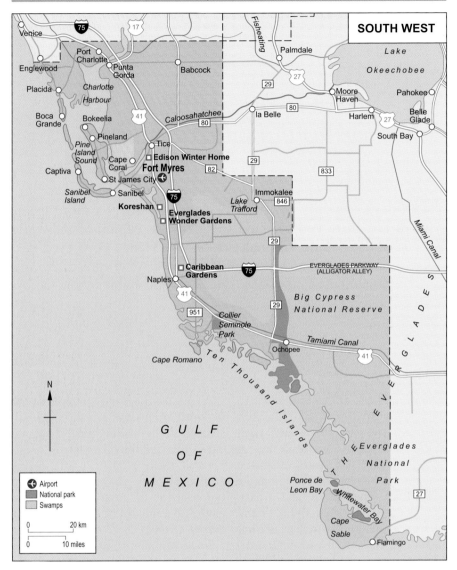

*F*lorida's south-west,
the Lee Island Coast.

International visitors to the Lee Island Coast will probably fly into Miami, Tampa or Orlando, particularly if they are planning a two-centre holiday.

They will either pick up a car at one of the airports, or make a short flight to the South-west Florida Regional Airport at Fort Myers. Motoring to Fort Myers from Tampa takes about two-and-three-quarter hours, and from Miami about three hours. The car journey from Orlando takes about three-and-a-quarter hours.

Driving Down

If you're driving from Miami, be sure to check your tank, because if you see a gas station in the Everglades or the Big Cypress National Preserve, it's probably a mirage. On the way to Naples, the most southerly of the Gulf Coast resorts, you'll go by several Indian villages. One of them is **Osceolas**, a picturesque settlement where you can learn some authentic Indian history. There's a small entry charge.

*M*onroe Station provides a rare encounter with civilization along the Tamiami Trail.

Ten-and-a-half kilometres (6½ miles) through the swampy **Big Cypress Preserve** there's a Ranger Station on the right, with rest rooms. This is the base of the emergency helicopter service which patrols the region, searching for lost canoeists and stray birdwatchers.

The next landmark is on the left, a few miles down the road. This is **Monroe Station**, and coming across it is like encountering an oasis in the desert. A big, illustrated notice-board outside the ramshackle building provides a good read. One of its messages says: "Marriages performed here. Bring your own guy or girl." Another warns: "Armed guard on duty four days a week. Pick your day." Compass points are marked: "Miami, Naples, Heaven, Hell". The building itself is a grocery

store, cool and shady, and it is also a bar, with plenty of chairs and tables. You can sit down and enjoy a hamburger with your cold beer or Coke. You may muse how such a remote business can prosper. Few motorists are on the road, but the answer could be that almost all of them call for something. Monroe Station's very remoteness perhaps compels the over-civilized people of the 1990s to stock up on groceries and to take some refreshment while they can. The signposts tell you you're on your way to Naples—but can you really believe that you'll reach it by nightfall?

Behind the wheel again, follow the straight road between miles of wilderness—you really have no option apart from turning back the way you came. Stop at one of the picnic areas—the only places where you can pull off the road—to stretch your legs and see what unfamiliar birds you can spot.

Thirteen kilometres (8 miles) past Monroe Station is a roadside notice: "Panther crossing next five miles". But you'd be extraordinarily lucky to see one. A few minutes later you come to another Indian village on the right, **Ochopee**, and a few miles after that there's a place where for a few dollars you can take a swamp buggy trip into the wet wilderness. That's if there's anyone around operating the buggy. It goes out only when there are enough takers to make it worth while. Winter is probably peak time. We found the weird machine with its huge stern wheel, and the swathe it had cut through the vegetation, but neither sight nor sound of human life.

A couple of minutes' drive past the boundary of the Big Cypress National Preserve, there's a left turn (State Road 29) to Everglades City, with an **Everglades National Park** visitor centre, and access to the Park along the Chokoloskee Causeway over the swamp. Beyond this, on the right, is a Seminole village with a craft shop selling tomahawks and other crafts.

Ten Thousand Islands

Beyond Everglades City are the Ten Thousand Islands. Ten Thousand Islands is a bit of a misnomer. Nobody knows exactly how many islands there are—the number is constantly changing. The islands of mangrove trees are formed from pieces of shell, driftwood and seaweed that get trapped in the tangled roots. It is estimated that there could be as many as 20,000.

If you're thinking of spending a bit of time at the largest of these, Marco Island, 24 km (15 miles) south of Naples, return to US 41, drive north and take Route 951 on your left. Marco Island is more developed than any of the other islands, some of which are just humps of mangrove and other vegetation. To get among the islands, you can hire a boat, but if you do this you would be well advised to take a guide along. It's the easiest thing in the world to get lost in this region. Probably the best way for the casual observer to enjoy the magnificent scenery is to go for a two-hour 22-km (14-mile) cruise aboard the *Island Princess*, operated by Island Nature Cruises.

About 9.6 km (6 miles) long and 6.4 km (4 miles) wide, **Marco Island** is one of those Florida locations that has hurled itself into tourism in the space of a few years. Any former resident returning after a long gap would be astonished, and no doubt dismayed, to see the tall condominiums around the shoreline. There's a wide variety of restaurants and good golf and tennis facilities. Visitors can tour the island aboard an old-fashioned trolley and listen to a narration. There are ten trolley trips daily. The windsurfing off Marco Island is good and the fishing excellent, as the warm Gulf Stream pours into the local waters.

The island has an interesting Indian history. Calusa Indians lived there from 500 BC to AD 1700. They were said to be over 2 m tall (up to 7 ft) and resisted enslavement by the Spaniards in the late 16th century. There are ancient Indian shell mounds. The island boasts the highest point in south-west Florida—Caxambar Pass is 15.54 m (51 ft) above sea level.

The town of **Marco**, right in the north of the island, is known as Olde Marco. It has good shops, restaurants and cafés.

But what effect has the steady tide of tourism had on the island's wildlife? According to the tourism authority, because of its unique ecological balance Marco shines as an environmental example, with its prolific bird sanctuary. The 26-hectare (64-acre) breeding ground at Barfield Bay attracted five nesting pairs of bald eagles in 1990, and more than 200 bird species have been noted there, including ospreys, terns, egrets and blue herons.

If you're touring the Lee Island Coast, or exploring two or three resort areas, you'll need to get back on the Tamiami Trail (US 41) via Route 951 to Naples.

Near Marco on the mainland is the **Collier Seminole State Park**, where there are opportunities for basic camping, fishing and boating. Canoes can be hired by the hour or by the day. In the 2,630 hectares (6,500 acres) of marshland which form the park is a 340-m (1,100-ft) boardwalk through the mangrove swamps. Rare species which are claimed to have been seen in the park include Florida black bears and panthers, crocodiles, mangrove fox squirrels and wood storks.

The **Collier County Museum** reveals the local history from prehistoric times. An archaeological laboratory, a steam locomotive and a Seminole village exhibit can be seen in the historical park.

Back on US 41 is a prestigious development, a gateway to the Ten Thousand Islands, where you may want to spend a night or two—the **Port of the Isles Resort**. It was built in the Spanish style in the 1960s, but fell into disrepair while it stood vacant for many years. The 200-room property, in extensive grounds, was sold at auction in 1980, restored and equipped with a range of facilities. These include a spacious marina, skeet shooting, a spa, acres of sub-tropical woodland and a private airstrip, not to mention the sort of fishing that anglers rave over. According to their style of fishing and the time of year, they may be after anything from trout to a small shark. Or it may be snapper, grouper, redfish, catfish or tarpon. A freshwater river runs through the property, feeding a harbour which has been designated a manatee sanctuary. Self-catering accommodation is available as

well as hotel rooms. Telephone number for reservations: (813) 394-3101.

Naples

Port of the Islands is a half-hour drive south of Naples. When you see the South Shores Country Club on your left you are within minutes of the resort. Continue straight along US 41. Soon the road becomes a divided highway. After crossing a bridge, with a view of boats on the water, stay in the left lane for downtown Naples. You'll find yourself in Fifth Avenue South, the "Millionaires' Row" of stately mansions. This is no upstart of the last decade or two. Naples was recognized by visiting yachtsmen as a centre of gracious living in beautiful surroundings, with a good climate, more than 100 years ago.

The population of **Naples** has increased considerably in recent years, with new settlements along the coast and a number of tall condominiums, but it has managed to retain something of an unhurried small-town atmosphere, at the same time being considered trendy. It has some fashionable stores and designer outlets at **Third Street South**, but be sure also to look around **Naples Depot**, the old railroad station where restored storerooms and boxcars make a quaint place to shop.

Port of the Islands Resort is a gateway to the Ten Thousand Islands (previous page).

The first people attracted to Naples in the late 19th century—it was then a village—were wealthy North Americans, politicians and celebrities among them. There were gentlemen hunters and fishermen, too. They had to travel there by boat from Fort Myers. One of the early discoverers of Naples's charm as a winter retreat was General John Williams, a Confederate soldier from Kentucky, who first saw it soon after the Civil War. It was he who gave it its name, in memory of his service to the King of Naples, Italy. Now Naples has a population approaching 21,000, with golf, tennis and watersport activities to keep its residents and visitors happy.

The pier at Naples juts out 310 m (1,000 ft) into the Gulf of Mexico. It replaces one which was destroyed in a hurricane in the 1960s. It is a popular haunt of the fishing fraternity, obviously, but it is also a place where people gather to watch the sunset.

One of the local attractions is **Jungle Larry's Zoological Park** at Caribbean Gardens. It was formerly known as the African Safari Park. You can give your feet a rest and take a 30-minute tour by tram. There are animal shows, a petting zoo and a conservation programme for endangered species. Facilities for the handicapped include free use of wheelchairs. Strollers (or buggies) are provided free for toddlers.

Nearby, **Bonita Springs**, with its bays, lagoons and network of waterways, is regarded as a bit of Old Florida, where the pace is easy. Boating, golf and fishing are the main pursuits, and the local dog-racing track draws the crowds from October to August. You have to be over 18 years old to attend. Canoes can be hired on the short but scenic Imperial River, which runs from Estero Bay to Corkscrew Swamp. Bonita Beach is beautiful, with smooth white sand. Much of the local accommodation is in waterside motels or condominiums. There are "U Pick" farms along US 41, with tomatoes the main winter crop. Melons are sold at roadside stalls.

Field sports are played at the 24-hectare (60-acre) Bonita Springs Community Park, which has a playground, a spacious lake and picnic facilities. Golf Safari is an 18-hole miniature golf-course amid tropical gardens and waterfalls, open daily from 10 a.m. to 10 p.m., and there are good courses for "full-size" golf in the area, too. They reckon you can count on good golfing weather year-round, the average temperature being 25°C (77°F).

To see Everglades animals, birds and reptiles in their natural habitat, go to the **Everglades Wonder Gardens** in downtown Bonita Springs. There are bears, otters, deer, alligators, snakes, birds of prey and wading birds.

March sees the **Bonita Springs Tomato Festival**—three days of sports, competitions, live entertainment, seafood snacks and a display of arts and crafts. **Derby Day** at the dog track is also in March, when greyhounds enter the $20,000 championship race, and a parade is held afterwards. The track is operated by the Naples/Fort Myers Kennel Club. In October the pioneers who originated Bonita Springs are honoured at a **Pioneer Day** celebration, with arts and crafts exhibited, games and a food fair, and with an irresistible aroma of barbecued chicken hanging on the air.

About 24 km (15 miles) south of Fort Myers is a novel entertainment, **Waltzing Waters**, with water, light and music shows. The brilliance of lasers and the movement of fountains combine to give fantastic effects of colours and patterns. Allow at least an hour for the programme and to experience other attractions on site—Rainbow Golf (an 18-hole putting course), a gift shop selling items from all over the world, and the Hanging Gardens. The Waltzing Water shows are on the hour from 10 a.m. to 9 p.m., indoors in the daytime and part inside and part outside in the evening.

At **Fort Myers Beach** on Estero Island you may see people parasailing between December and August if wind conditions are right. Water-skiing,

Koreshan State Historic Site

At Estero, on the banks of the Estero River, is the Koreshan State Historic Site. It is a restored village where a Chicago physician, Dr Cyrus Teed, and his followers settled in what they saw as a Utopian-style religious commune in 1894. The sect believed that the earth was a hollow sphere, with all life, the planets, moon and stars within it. They shared property and practised celibacy, the sexes being separated. Teed died in 1908. By 1961 membership had dwindled to four people, who left the property to the state. The local tourism authority reports, mystifyingly, that Koreshan publications are still being produced by descendants of members of the commune. Guided tours are given through the historical area (minimum of four people). Visitors can camp in the park in their recreation vehicles or tents. A nature trail and picnic area are available, and craft can be rented to follow the Estero River Canoe Trail.

*F*ort Myers Beach is a great place for Hobie Cat sailing.

windsurfing, boating, sailing, shell collecting, charter-boat fishing, tennis and golf are among the outdoor pursuits. Three-and-a-half hectares (9 acres) of water and numerous bunkers present a challenge at the 15-hectare (37-acre) Bay Beach Golf Club, open daily to the public. Less challenging but good fun is the Jungle Golf miniature course on the San Carlos Boulevard—18 interesting holes offering encounters with life-size and life-like models of jungle animals.

Overlooking Estero Bay is the **Matanzas Pass Wilderness Preserve**, which can be explored by elevated boardwalk. It is a peaceful place for bird and plant study, or just strolling along the wild oak hammock and mangrove shoreline.

Estero Beach itself is claimed to be the safest in the world, though no clue is given as to how this was assessed. Certainly the shore slopes gently, there's no undertow, and porpoises sometimes patrol the water, as though keeping an eye on swimmers like watchful lifeguards. The only trouble with some of the beaches is their unwieldy names. The **Dwight Lynn Hall**

*T*he Lee Island Coast is protected by its barrier islands.

Memorial Park is a beach with bathhouse, free public pier and bait shop. The **Carl E. Johnson Recreation Park**, with beach, good swimming, picnic area, nature trails, a canoeing and fishing bay and snack bar is on its own small island, which can be reached on foot or by a tractor-drawn tram across Oyster Bay. **Lover's Key** is a lovely and sometimes deserted spot which is said to be the place to find romance.

Mound Key, near the southern tip of Fort Myers Beach, is a shell mound constructed more than 1,000 years ago by Calusa Indians.

On the way northward to Fort Myers on US 41, children will want to cool off at the Aqua Slide, open from 11 a.m. to 5 p.m. As well as the water slide there are go-carts and electronic games.

Fort Myers

Aptly named City of Palms—the wide main street is lined with them—Fort Myers is known as the winter home of inventor Thomas Edison, and also as the gladiolus capital of the world. Some of the original settlers in the area were flower growers from Holland, Belgium and Luxembourg, and they did well with their gladioli in Fort Myers.

It is a beautiful little city which grew up on the banks of the Caloosahatchee River. Everglades Jungle Cruises of about three hours can be taken up the river. There are also two-day river trips up to Lake Okeechobee, and two-day coastal cruises to St Petersburg.

Edison built his winter home, now a museum, on a 5.6-hectare (14-acre) riverside site at McGregor Boulevard. The property straddles the highway, with some exhibits displayed in a building across the street. Guided tours of the house, botanical gardens and museum take place all day. The museum contains Edison's collection of 170 gramophones, his cars and his first electric light bulbs. The original equipment he used for rubber research from 1925 to 1931 can be seen in the laboratory.

If you have to wait a few minutes for your guided tour, don't worry. You will be in the shade of a truly massive banyan tree. It has put down so many "suckers" that take root like new tree-trunks that it resembles a forest. The one tree has spread to a circumference of more than 123 m (400 ft) in 60 years to become the biggest banyan tree in Florida.

Edison's tropical gardens contain some 6,000 tree and plant species which he collected from many parts of the world. The house was built in 1886 and its furnishings represent the early 1900s period. Thomas Edison had enjoyed a cruise on the Caloosahatchee River in or around 1885, and was so delighted with the Fort Myers area that he decided to establish a home there. The story goes that he was 39 when he moved into the house in 1886. He had been told that his health was failing. Living there every winter must have suited him—he died at the age of 84. In 1947 his widow left the property to the city as a memorial to the inventor. Every February, Fort Myers celebrates his life with a **Pageant of Light Festival**. It lasts 10 days, finishing with a parade and fireworks.

It was Edison who founded the Fort Myers tradition of palm-lined streets. There are more than 100 varieties of palm in the city, including the royal palms which Edison established on McGregor Boulevard.

For those devoted to the early 20th century, which by European standards is comparatively modern, there's a third river-front home, in addition to the Edison and Ford houses (*see* sidebar), built at the turn of the century, which has been renovated and opened to the public. Bought by the Burroughs family in 1918, it is called "The Burroughs Home". It is on the US National Register of Historic Houses

Edison and Ford

One of Edison's closest friends was Henry Ford, the motor manufacturer, who made the first mass-produced motor car. In 1916 Ford and his wife, Clara, bought a 1.2-hectare (3-acre) estate next door to Edison's, and lived there until Edison died in 1931. There was a boundary fence which both families referred to as the Friendship Gate. Ford's estate, called "Mangoes", was sold to a private buyer in 1945, and in 1988 the city of Fort Myers bought it for $1 million. Two years later, with house and gardens renovated and restored to the 1920s period when the Fords lived there, the estate was opened to the public for daily guided tours. Visitors taking a combined tour of the Edison and Ford properties get a dollar off the price.

and is considered the first luxury home in Fort Myers. It is built in the Georgian Revival style and is credited with starting the building boom in the area. Special features are its Palladian windows, wrap-around verandah, solid oak mantel, electric bells and lights and indoor plumbing. Local people hire the house for weddings and other functions.

Calusa and Seminole Indian civilizations are depicted at **Fort Myers Historical Museum** on Peck Street. The area's past from 1200 BC to AD 1913 is documented. It was because of the seven-year Second Seminole War, in which hundreds of American settlers were slaughtered, that the fort which gave Fort Myers its name was set up. A scale model of it can be seen in the museum. Early medical and transportation exhibits, and a glass collection, are displayed in the Spanish-style depot, and there's a refurbished 1930

railroad car. The museum is closed on Mondays.

The **Nature Center of Lee County**, at Ortiz Avenue, has permanent and changing exhibits. A boardwalk leads visitors on a tour of the native Florida swamp environment. A new 90-seat planetarium on the site has changing shows with laser effects.

Lakes Park, in Gladiolus Road, South Fort Myers, is a 112-hectare (277-acre) recreation area with a marina where paddle-boats, canoes and fishing boats can be rented. In the park are paved nature trails, freshwater swimming, showers and picnic sites with barbecue grills.

For live entertainment, the new Edison Community College/University of South Florida **Performing Arts Hall** is the place. It is on the campus of the Edison Community College on College Parkway. Broadway musicals, dance performances and popular and classical music concerts are held. Next door is the **ECC Gallery of Fine Art**, with work from internationally known artists displayed. The **Lee County Arts Center** on McGregor Boulevard features local artists' and craftsmen's work. Recitals and concerts are given, and classes and workshops held. The Center is closed on Fridays in summer. Weekday opening is from 9.00 a.m. to 5.00 p.m. Admission is free, and the Centre is accessible to wheelchairs.

North Fort Myers has a number of attractions of its own, the **Shell Factory** being one which hardly anybody misses, particularly if they have already caught the shell-collecting bug. Seven kilometres (4 miles) north of Fort Myers on US 41, the Shell Factory houses

Corkscrew Swamp Sanctuary
For a drive out of town to see a particularly interesting natural preserve, take the rural SR 82 approximately 25 km (15 miles) south-east to the Corkscrew Swamp Sanctuary. The Sanctuary, at Immokalee, is maintained by the National Audubon Society. Rare orchids, endangered bird species and bald cypress trees, reckoned to have stood for seven centuries, can be seen from a raised boardwalk, as well as alligators and many other wildlife species and native plants.

what is said to be the world's largest collection of shells and coral. Admission and guided tours are free. Jewellery and novelties, footwear, imported resort wear, hand-made leather goods, brassware, lamps and other items are available as well as shell products. Opening times are 9 a.m. to 6.30 p.m. in winter and spring, and 9.30 a.m. to 6 p.m. in summer and autumn.

Next door to the Shell Factory is the **Fantasy Isles** attraction, where children can meet nursery-rhyme characters. Mother Goose is the hostess, and fairy-tale characters line waterside banks connected by bridges. Amusement rides, an aviary, a petting zoo and a wax museum keep the little ones happy. Fantasy Isles opens every day of the year, and a single admission charge covers all the entertainment. Facilities include a gift shop and restaurant.

Also of special appeal to children, and something of a nostalgia trip for older visitors, is **Nature's Wonderland Children's Museum**, south of the Shell Factory. Hundreds of playthings from the past and present are displayed in the doll and toy room. There's a

reconstruction of a barrier reef and exhibits of fossils and seashells. The museum opens only in the afternoons, from noon until 4 p.m., daily except Mondays.

More aspects of the wild side of Florida, with a possibility of sighting wild turkeys and buffalo, can be seen in a guided tour by swamp buggy among the woods and waters of the **Telegraph Cypress Swamp**. Babcock Wilderness Adventures runs the tours into the extensive Babcock Ranch, due north of Fort Myers on Route 31. Reservations are necessary (tel: (813) 656-6104).

Fort Myers has the southernmost bonded winery in the continental United States. The **Eden Vineyards Winery** has for a long time supplied restaurants, but a few years ago it was decided to invite the public for free tours. A charge made for sampling the wine includes a souvenir glass.

ECHO Experimental Farm
Of interest to gardeners, farmers and anyone keen to see what is being done to help solve the problem of the hungry peoples of the world, is ECHO (Educational Concerns for Hunger Organizations). Experiments with unusual crops and different ways to grow food are carried out by a non-profit-making Christian interdenominational ministry working to help the undernourished. Agricultural conditions typical of those in countries where many people go hungry are re-created, and edible plants are produced. These include rice, sesame, black pepper, chives, vanilla, lemon grass and fruit trees, such as jaboticaba, mango, mulberry and atemoya. Free tours are given by appointment (tel: (813) 543-3246).

222

The fastest period of population growth for Fort Myers and adjacent Cape Coral was in the 1970s. Like much of Florida, it was a perfect retirement area, and Cape Coral's development was particularly fast. With water on three sides and a 640-km (400-mile) network of canals and waterways, Cape Coral attracts the fishing and boating fraternity. At Christmas there's an illuminated boat parade along the canals, and in May they hold the **International Water Festival and Parade**. Competitive events, with boat-racing teams, high-school bands and other participants provide the entertainment.

Also in Cape Coral, for three weeks in May, is a major offshore powerboat racing event, the **Lee County Regatta**. It is claimed to be the world's largest event of its type. The boats go out the mouth of the Caloosahatchee River into the Gulf. Hydroplane races are held on Lake Kennedy, where there is a park with picnic area, fishing and swimming. There are at least half a dozen other parks in Cape Coral, some with a nature trail or jogging track, and there's a BMX bike track. The main recreation centre, the **Cape Coral Yacht and Racquet Club**, at Driftwood Parkway, has a 190-m (620-ft) fishing pier, bait and tackle shop, a yacht basin and marina, a senior citizens' centre, swimming pool, tennis and racquetball courts and public golf-courses.

The city's polygon-shaped **Art Studio** offers art shows that rotate periodically. You stay still as the works displayed come into view. Admission is free.

East of Fort Myers is **Lehigh Acres**, another boating and fishing resort. It

has 16 lakes. The community began nearly 40 years ago as a place for retirement, but younger people moved in to provide support services, liked it, settled there and produced families. As a result, the place isn't top-heavy with senior citizens, and the annual calendar of events includes a **Miss National Teenager Pageant**. Held in August, it is televised nationwide and attracts teenage contestants from throughout the United States. Lehigh Acres has three country clubs with 18-hole championship golf-courses, professionals' shops, driving ranges and locker rooms. The winter season brings top-name performers from the entertainment world to the resort's 1,500-seat Lehigh Auditorium, during the **Festival of Stars**, from January to the end of March.

To enjoy the scenery between Naples and Fort Myers from a different viewpoint, take the **Seminole Gulf Railway** excursion train and have an enjoyable meal during the three-hour journey. The "dinner train" seats 150, and leaves Naples daily from Wednesday to Saturday. A five-course meal is served during the 71-km (44-mile) journey. On Sundays there's a brunch excursion and a two-hour supper trip.

The Barrier Islands

Now for a look at the barrier islands of the Lee Island Coast, which shelter Pine Island Sound from storms in the Gulf of Mexico. Pine Island, the biggest, is reached by SR 78 from Cape Coral, and Gasparilla Island is approached from the north over a toll bridge from Placida. Pine and

Gasparilla Islands are only minutes apart by water, but by road the journey takes more than an hour. Sanibel and Captiva are reached by toll bridge from Fort Myers Beach. For Cabbage Key, Cayo Costa and Useppa Island, you'll need a boat.

The Lee Island Coast features nearly 965 km (600 miles) of shoreline, 80 km (50 miles) of beaches and more than 100 barrier islands which attract the boating and sailing set. Average temperature is 22°C (73°F), though in summer it is usually about 30°C (in the

*L*ife goes on at a leisurely pace on the islands of Sanibel and Captiva.

upper 80°s F). Parts of the region, notably Captiva and Sanibel, are expensive compared with most of the rest of the state, but accommodation costs may be reduced by up to 40 per cent in the low (summer) season.

Sanibel and Captiva

If you want to spend a few days pottering about, cross the causeway to **Sanibel** and **Captiva** and discover the possibilities. Hire a bicycle, collect shells, learn to sail, canoe in a wildlife refuge—or see it from your car—follow a nature trail, wander around a marina, admire the private homes, fish for red snapper, take a boat trip with an escort of dolphins, or join a lunch or dinner cruise. Whatever you do, it can be done at a leisurely pace. This is the place to forget about life in the fast lane and unwind as never before.

South Seas Plantation Resort lies at the northern tip of Captiva Island.

Until the 1960s, a few residents had the two beautiful islands to themselves. The only visitors arrived by private yacht, cruiser or mail ferry. Then, in the face of some understandable opposition, the causeway was built and the world drove across it. At first it was mainly North Americans, but in the mid-1980s Sanibel and Captiva began to appear in a few European and UK tour operators' brochures. There is a choice of accommodation—motels, apartments, cottages and full-scale resort hotels and condominiums. Sanibel has considerably more accommodation and restaurants than Captiva. Many developments are discreetly hidden behind trees, and buildings are kept below treetop height. Periwinkle Way is part of one long road which leads through Sanibel, across a bridge to smaller, narrower Captiva Island.

At the northern tip of Captiva Island, jutting out into the Gulf of Mexico and 48 km (30 miles) from Fort Myers, is the world-class **South Seas Plantation Resort**, which has 4 km (2½ miles) of private beach and its own deep-water yacht harbour for craft up to 30 m (100 ft) long. A smaller

*W*ild dolphins show off
*to tourists on a boat trip off
Captiva Island.*

marina takes boats up to 8 m (26 ft) long. The 130-hectare (330-acre) resort has nearly 600 units of accommodation—villas, cottages, hotel rooms, self-catering villas and suites and beach homes with up to four bedrooms. There are 22 tennis courts, 17 fresh-water swimming pools, a nine-hole golf-course, restaurants, a pub, a ballroom, a video game centre and a gallery of shops and boutiques. Cycles and sailing boats, jet skis, water-skis and windsurfers can be rented, excursions are organized, luncheon and dinner cruises by party boat to Cabbage Key or Useppa Island leave daily, and there is a supervised programme for children. Game-fishing charters, with fishing tackle and guides, are available, and guided shelling expeditions are arranged.

Watersports include skin-diving, scuba-diving, aquacycling, water-skiing and jet-skiing. Guests can have instruction in windsurfing and offshore sailing. Seminars and workshops are held on such activities as fitness workouts, wine-tasting and Polynesian dancing.

Captiva is scarcely more than a block wide, and another popular resort, **'Tween Waters**, is at the narrowest part, between the Gulf of Mexico and San Carlos Bay. Swimming, sailing, taking boat trips, fishing, shelling, tennis and enjoying good food are the main activities. Sunday brunch is a tradition perpetuated at the 'Tween Waters, which retains the Florida Victorian style it was given when it was built some 70 years ago. The **Crow's Nest**, a popular place for informal eating, is open from noon to midnight and is a favourite nightspot, with dancing and entertainment.

Skiffs powered by outboard motor can be hired for fishing in the well-stocked Pine Island Sound. Trout, redfish and snook are the most frequent catches. Deep-water fishing in the Gulf, with a guide, can be arranged at 'Tween Waters Marina. Boat trips include tours of Useppa Island, visits to Boco Grande on Spanish Island, shelling excursions to deserted beaches, and a luncheon cruise to Cabbage Key. Accommodation at 'Tween Waters is in apartments, spacious de luxe rooms, cottage rooms, cottage efficiencies (self-catering) and cottages with up to three bedrooms.

According to legend, the pirate José Gaspar used Captiva as his hideout between raids, and kept female captives there. Gasparilla Island also got its name from the buccaneer. Many colourful tales are told about his exploits, but there is considerable doubt as to whether he actually existed.

A Conchologist's Paradise

The easiest thing in the world for anyone visiting the Gulf beaches of Sanibel and Captiva is to become a compulsive sheller. There are no offshore reefs to break up the shells. Every tide brings in a generous assortment of collectible items, and at low water everybody's out there on the best beaches, backs bent in the joyous pursuit of the rare lion's paw, or brown-patched junonia shells. Experts say Captiva and Sanibel have the best shelling beaches in the western hemisphere.

Captain Mike Fuery, a man with one of the rarest jobs in the world, operates shelling charters from 'Tween Waters, taking people out to promising beaches and sand bars. He has been sharing his vast knowledge and experience of conchology with visitors since 1976, and writes a shelling column in the local newspapers. For the novice, almost every shell is an unfamiliar gem. Some of the commonest ones are in beautiful pastel shades, or richly patterned. To preserve the various species, the number of live (occupied) shells a collector may take is restricted, but Captain Fuery recommends that no live shells at all should be taken, and apparently most people refuse to take live shells on principle.

There are such quantities of attractive and varied specimens of non-live shells—more than 400 varieties have been found—that anyone can have the beginnings of a respectable collection after a few days on Sanibel and Captiva. Those who are really hooked—and there are a lot of them, residents and visitors alike—are out at daybreak with their buckets, seeing what new gifts have been deposited on the shore, and some stay out after dark, searching in the beam of a flashlight. The problem is not in collecting, but in finding the space to display the collection. Checklists can be bought locally to help beginners identify their shells. The four-day **Sanibel Shell Fair** is held in March, with shell crafts, shell displays and contests.

Captiva and Sanibel have a good choice of restaurants, almost every menu offering excellent local seafood. **Chadwick's**, the most formal of the South Sea Plantation's eateries, seats 220 in four dining areas decorated in the Old Florida style The restaurant is named after Clarence Chadwick, who originated the plantation in 1900 and planted thousands of coconut palms,

A shady boardwalk leads through part of the J.N. "Ding" Darling National Wildlife Refuge on Sanibel Island.

many of them remaining to this day. It was he who built the Manor House, warehouse and workers' cottages which still stand.

A Captiva restaurant which attracts tourists, and not only for its good, low-cost food, is **The Bubble Room**, and it has a bubbly personality. Huge cartoon-type characters and racing cars dangle from the ceiling. Trains rush back and forth, and jokey slogans abound. You're not likely to fall asleep over the coffee. The Bubble Room gets a lot of awards and media mentions.

Blind Pass is where Sanibel and Captiva meet, with a short bridge to cross. There is a good public beach here. Sanibel is much bigger—20 km (12 miles) long—and has much more holiday accommodation than Captiva. Again, development has been restricted to below treetop level. An area of 2,000 hectares (5,000 acres) to the north of the island has been devoted to a wilderness preserve, with an 8-km (5-mile) scenic drive, nature trails and canoe trails. This is the **J.N. "Ding" Darling National Wildlife Refuge**—nobody ever seems to abbreviate the title. It commemorates Jay Norwood Darling, a political cartoonist who signed his drawings "Ding". He was winner of two Pulitzer prizes for his cartoons. A pioneer conservationist, he spent a lot of time on the islands and was a regular visitor for 30 years. During 1934 and 1935, as Chief of the US Biological Survey—forerunner of the US Fish and Wildlife Service—he started many wildlife management systems that led to the establishment of more than 420 refuges nationally.

The refuge, which has an informative visitor centre, was set up in 1945 to combat the threat to wildlife by increased human development, which tourism had dictated since the 1930s. Sanibel's wildlife habitat was beginning to be destroyed long before that, when agriculture was introduced in the early 1800s, though the 1926 hurricane destroyed much of this. Wildlife management was vital if indigenous flora and fauna were to survive. The refuge authority defines this management as "a combination of science and practical experience that strives to work with people, wildlife populations and habitat for the benefit of wildlife".

The **Wildlife Drive** is closed between sunset and sunrise. Much more wildlife is likely to be seen just after dawn and before dusk. Allow yourself plenty of time, and take with you binoculars and field guides if possible, and the refuge's booklet which tells you what you are likely to see at the numbered marker signs along the route.

There is freshwater on the left of the one-way drive, providing habitat for alligators—most of those in the refuge are 2–2½ m (6–8 ft) long. Wilderness areas and salt water are to the right. The refuge provides a place for nearly 300 bird species, more than 50 types of reptile and amphibian, and more than 30 different mammals. Feeding any of the wildlife is prohibited.

The drive starts at the visitor centre. The **South Dike Trail** for walkers starts at the same place, offering a chance to see otters and ospreys. The distance all round is about 7 km (4 miles). White pelican, wood stork, bald eagle, manatee and the Atlantic loggerhead turtle are among wildlife sighted in the refuge. There is an unusual variety of plants seen in profusion—sea grapes,

wax and salt myrtles, red mangrove, cabbage palm, gumbo limbo trees, strangler figs, coffee and papaya trees and wild orchids. All facilities at the refuge are free.

Along the road outside, at 333 Sanibel-Captiva Road, is the headquarters of the **Sanibel/Captiva Conservation Foundation**, a nature centre introducing visitors to the rare character and fragile ecology of the islands. There are 7 km (4 miles) of nature trails within a wetlands tract of more than 80 hectares (200 acres). Guided tours are available, lectures are given, research areas can be viewed and a native plant nursery offers plants for sale. A small entry charge is made.

Many of the resorts and holiday complexes along Sanibel's Gulf Coast have private beaches, but there are also good public beaches, one of the most popular being at the southern tip of the island. Sanibel Lighthouse, erected in 1884, stands on this beach. Sanibel also has at least two public golf-courses where clubs can be rented. There's a campground for trailers and tents at the Periwinkle Trailer Park.

A favourite boat excursion for visitors to Sanibel and Captiva is to the 40-hectare (100-acre) **Cabbage Key**, where nature trails lead through jungle-like terrain. One of the few buildings is an inn and restaurant built on the top of a Calusa Indian shell mound for American playwright and novelist Mary Roberts Rinehart in the 1930s. The only way to get there is by water.

Accommodation at the inn is limited to half a dozen guest rooms, and there are a few cottages, but over the years countless people have taken the trip

from 'Tween Waters or South Seas Plantation on a luncheon or dinner cruise. A long-standing tradition at Cabbage Key is to stick an autographed dollar bill on the wall. It is said to have been started by local fishermen who wanted to be sure of having the price of a drink handy, and now there are tens of thousands of dollar bills displayed in the public rooms.

Other islands which can be reached only by boat include North Captiva, Useppa and Cayo Costa. **Cayo Costa**, a long, narrow bead in the necklace of islands between North Captiva and Gasparilla Islands, has been developed in recent years as a state park. It has a small population, augmented by day-trippers who arrive in their boats or by public ferry to go fishing, shelling, sunbathing and to enjoy their picnics. There are some rental cabins, and camping under canvas is permitted. Much of the island provides a peaceful habitat and nesting site for birds. Sea turtles lay their eggs on the beaches. Cayo Costa is a real away-from-it-all sub-tropical island, with miles of beaches, mangrove swamps, oak palm hammocks and pine forest.

Tiny **Useppa**, next door to Cabbage Key, is one of the many small islands between Cayo Costa and the largest of the barrier islands in the region, Pine Island. It is the site of the **Useppa Island Club**, an up-market resort which had its origins in the 1920s, when a millionaire, Barron G. Collier, bought

*C*abbage Key, *accessible only by boat, is a favourite spot for day trippers (previous page).*

the island, built himself a mansion on it and added accommodation to rent out as a holiday retreat for the wealthy. Edward Roosevelt and Herbert Hoover went there to relax. Collier died in 1939, World War II broke out and the development fell into decline. It wasn't until the 1970s that it was restored and opened as the Useppa Island Club, with the mansion, now an inn and restaurant, as its centrepiece.

Assuming you are travelling by car and want to see more of the islands, you have to get back over the causeway to Fort Myers Beach, cross the Caloosahatchee River and pick up SR 78, which goes over the Matlacha Pass to the biggest of the barrier islands, Pine Island. The first place you come to is Matlacha, which has a lot of accommodation in hotels, motels and resorts. The main population centres are Bokeelia, at the northernmost point, and St James City, a former fishing village about 36 km (20 miles) away in the south. These and other centres offer a range of accommodation, including campgrounds and parks for recreational vehicles.

Pine Island

Arrangements can be made for guided tours led by naturalists living on Pine Island. They take a look at aquatic birdlife, eagles' nests and the Calusa Indian mounds for which the area has been placed on the National Register of Historic Places.

At **Pineland**, on the north-west coast, is a small historic park which has become a favourite sunset-watching site. Another place to visit is a mango grove. One of the oldest in

Florida, it was planted in the 1920s. The tour of the **Sunburst Tropical Fruit Company** is by trailer, with a commentary by the owner on the grove's history and the techniques of growing mangoes and other tropical fruits. The mango season runs through the summer. After the tour, visitors can sample mango chutney, tropical fruit preserves and fresh fruit in season. Products can be bought direct or by mail order. Tours, which are limited to 15, have to be booked in advance (tel: (813) 283-1200).

With many of the visitors arriving by boat, the island is rich in marinas, which between them provide docking for hundreds of vessels. Some offer boat rentals and charters, and have restaurants and accommodation. Tennis, golf, boating, nature-watching and sports fishing are the main pursuits—

the island is said to be excellent for big tarpon and other challenging species.

At the south end of Gasparilla Island (*see* panel below) is the **Boca Grande Lighthouse**, built in 1890. It is within the island's State Recreation Area, which offers picnicking, swimming, fishing, nature study and a wide beach. Shelling is especially good in the winter months.

Although Gasparilla's resident population isn't very numerous, the island generally, and **Boca Grande** in particular, has, like much of the west coast, been "discovered" in recent years, and the tourism infrastructure has developed to some extent. However, the laid-back charm is still there. The railroad depot is now a collection of little shops and boutiques, and **Banyan Street** is a glorious, green, shady tunnel of banyan trees.

Gasparilla Island

The farthest north of the barrier islands, Gasparilla Island claims to be "Tarpon Capital of the World". According to the local Tourist Development Council, tarpon are more abundant off Florida's west coast in the May to September spawning season than anywhere else in the world. The species migrates in spring to spawn in the warm waters of the Gulf of Mexico from as far away as Nova Scotia and South America. The tarpon annually roam throughout the waters of the Lee Island Coast, from Sanibel to Bonita Beach, but the most experienced fishermen claim Pine Island Sound and the water off Gasparilla's main centre, Boca Grande, are the best areas. The most dedicated sports fishermen compete in tournaments held at weekends at Boca Grande from May to July.

The reason for the fish being so plentiful here is that in the centre of Boca Grande Pass, at the southern tip of Gasparilla Island, is a huge hole about 275 m (300 yds) long, 92 m (100 yds) wide and 20 m (21 yds) deep. Here the tarpon lie, feeding on crab, shrimp, minnows and other bait fish swirled around the hole by tide and current. The appeal to anglers is the fight put up by the tarpon and the size of the fish—in Boca Grande Pass the usual weight is 30–39 kg (65–85 lb). When hooked, the silver creature slices the surface of the water, "standing" on its tail. Professional guides have perfected the art of preventing the tarpon landing on the deck, where it could smash equipment. Strong releasing hooks are used to catch the tarpon, which for all its weight is a bony fish, not designed for good eating, so it is released from the hook to live to fight another day.

Gentle Days on the Suncoast

Tampa city is one of Florida's largest cities: an exciting metropolis where you can find the world-famous Busch Gardens, a family entertainment centre where endangered species are featured in their natural habitat. Visit the Salvador Dali museum in St Petersburg. Small communities live contentedly along the coast of Central West Florida. The suncoast has an average of 361 days of sunshine annually, which provides ample time for fishing, boating, water-sports, or wandering through its eight resort communities. Buy a sponge to remember America's Sponge Capital—Tarpon Springs. And meet the Birdman of Pinellas, who runs a sanctuary devoted to healing sick and injured birds.

Florida's western region has an altogether different character from the Atlantic side. The coastline is much more indented, but not "rugged" as it has so many sandy beaches and a climate bordering on perfection. There are the estuaries of such rivers as the Suwannee, the Waccasassa and Caloosahatchee. There are scores of natural harbours, a couple of huge, well-protected bays and strings of islands, some of them positively idyllic.

With the exception of the Tampa/St Petersburg conurbation, communities in the main are smaller and more widely spaced than those on the eastern seaboard. Even Sarasota and fast-growing Fort Myers maintain a small-town ambience, and life throughout the region moves at a leisurely slow pace.

The key to this whole area is Tampa, as it has been since the 1880s when the railroad baron Henry B. Plant drove a line there from Richmond, Virginia, and built the imposing Tampa Bay Hotel.

Plant's railroad and hotel introduced tourism to the area. Today, the tourists mostly arrive by air. Tampa International Airport has been repeatedly voted the airport most favoured by members of the International Airline Passenger Association.

Spectacular sunsets are a nightly feature along the Pinellas Suncoast.

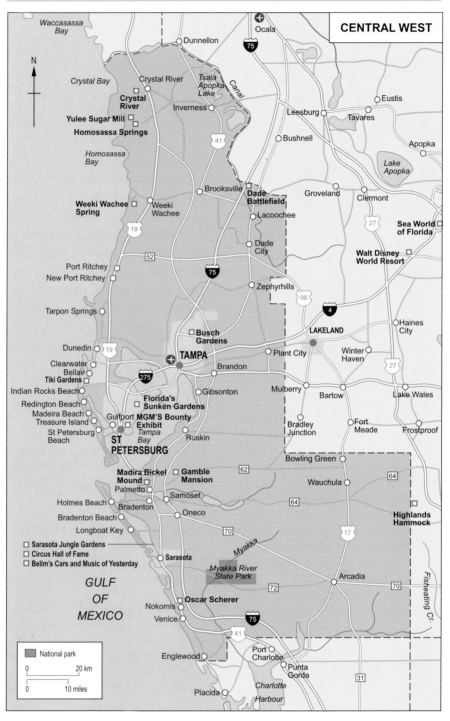

CENTRAL WEST

N

Waccasassa Bay

Dunnellon

Ocala

75

Crystal Bay

Crystal River

Crystal River

Tsala Apopka Lake

Canal

Eustis

Inverness

Leesburg

Tavares

Yulee Sugar Mill

Homosassa Springs

41

Bushnell

Apopka

Homosassa Bay

Lake Apopka

Weeki Wachee Spring

Brooksville

Dade Battlefield

Groveland

Clermont

Weeki Wachee

Lacoochee

27

Sea World of Florida

19

Dade City

Walt Disney World Resort

52

Port Ritchey

75

New Port Ritchey

Zephyrhills

98

4

Tarpon Springs

LAKELAND

Haines City

Dunedin

19

Busch Gardens

Plant City

Winter Haven

27

Clearwater

TAMPA

Bellair

Brandon

Tiki Gardens

Indian Rocks Beach

275

Gibsonton

Mulberry

Bartow

Lake Wales

Redington Beach

Florida's Sunken Gardens

Madeira Beach

Gulfport

MGM'S Bounty Exhibit

Bradley Junction

Fort Meade

Frostproof

Treasure Island

St Petersburg Beach

Tampa Bay

Ruskin

ST PETERSBURG

Bowling Green

Madira Bickel Mound

Gamble Mansion

62

Palmetto

Wauchula

64

Holmes Beach

Samoset

Bradenton

64

Bradenton Beach

Oneco

Highlands Hammock

Longboat Key

70

17

Sarasota Jungle Gardens

Myakka

Circus Hall of Fame

Bellm's Cars and Music of Yesterday

Sarasota

Myakka River State Park

Arcadia

70

GULF

72

OF

Oscar Scherer

Fisheating Cr.

MEXICO

Nokomis

Venice

75

41

National park

0   20 km

Englewood

Port Charlotte

0   10 miles

Punta Gorda

31

Charlotte Harbour

Placida

Tampa

The city of Tampa is the third largest in Florida and has the gleaming skyscrapers we have come to expect of prosperous, businesslike America. But there is fun here, too—the fun, for example, of an annual pirate invasion when the normally sober-suited inhabitants of those tower block offices don colourful, outfits, with pistols and cutlasses, and storm the city in a 305,000-kg (300-ton) pirate ship, the *José Gasparilla*, named after a buccaneer who probably never even existed.

Now the seventh largest port in the United States—important in both the cargo and cruise-liner markets—Tampa began as a military settlement with the establishment of Fort Brooke in 1824. After the Second Seminole War (1835–42) local government elections were held, a courthouse was built and commerce began to prosper. The opening of Plant's railway in 1885 spawned new industry. In 1886 Vincente Martinez Ybor led a movement of Cuban cigar manufacturers into the area. The industry flourished, resulting in a strong, vivacious Latin community in what is now known as Ybor City.

Cigars are still crafted by hand, and Ybor City's Cuban culture is as vibrant as ever. The scent of freshly baked Cuban bread wafts from cafés, and the area's heritage is reflected in red-tiled roofs, wrought-iron balconies, elegant fountains and street-corner shops. One of the original cigar factories has been turned into a lively shopping arcade. Named **Ybor Square**, it contains shops, restaurants and a "nostalgia market" of antique shops and stalls. Dating from 1887, the building has brick walls 60-cm (2-ft) thick and windows of hand-crafted glass, and its gracious courtyard is the scene of outdoor concerts and art festivals held throughout the year.

When Plant's massive **Tampa Bay Hotel** was built in 1891 Hillsborough County became a fashionable resort area, and visitors came from all over the world to stay in what was described as "the world's most elegant hotel". Today, the building serves as administrative headquarters of the University of Tampa, and its Moorish architecture, with 13 silver minarets, is a landmark. Colonel "Teddy" Roosevelt and his Roughriders used the hotel as their headquarters in 1889 and trained there for the Spanish–American War. A British war correspondent also stayed there. His name: Winston Churchill.

Busch Gardens

Tampa's best-known attraction—indeed, it is said to attract more visitors than any other Florida theme park, except Walt Disney World—is Busch Gardens, a family entertainment centre and one of America's top four zoos, where endangered species are featured in natural habitat exhibits. Situated on Busch Boulevard at 40th Street, 13 km (8 miles) north-east of downtown Tampa, the 120-hectare (300-acre) park has more than 3,300 animals displayed within eight distinctly themed African sections. There are shops, restaurants, games, thrill rides and live entertainment.

Map of Central West Florida.

The Dark Continent theme is maintained throughout Busch Gardens, and the atmosphere of turn-of-the-century Africa quickly comes to life. A bejewelled snake-charmer glides by in "Morocco". Delicate antelope scamper across the grassy "Serengeti Plain". An excursion in an air-conditioned monorail or steam train gives close-up views of Cape buffalo, impala, gazelles, reticulated giraffes and Grevy zebra. Elephants roam in a natural environment with huge rock formations, tropical greenery, waterfalls and a swimming hole.

Animals are well looked after in **Busch Gardens**. Behind the scenes is a catering set-up that would do credit to many a top-class restaurant, except that the kitchen has no ovens, hotplates or hobs. In their natural state, of course, animals do not eat cooked

Busch Gardens is Tampa's best-known attraction— a family entertainment centre and one of the top four zoos in the United States.

food—and at the Dark Continent the aim is to make things as natural as possible. Mind you, the alligators and crocodiles are fed on sausages. Chimpanzees love strawberry or raspberry jelly. Popcorn is popular with orangoutangs. And any primate loves to sit down and munch on a honey sandwich.

"All animals appreciate a change in their diet from time to time—a treat, if you like," says John Jernigan, the man who makes sure that the many

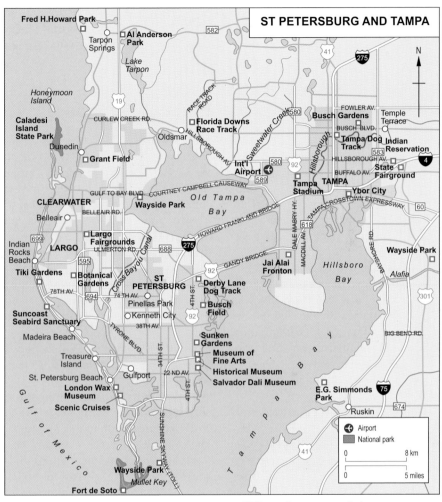

Town plan of Tampa.

"The advantage of the sausages—the skins are just the same as you'd find on sausages in the shops—is that we can add medication for an individual animal, and we can prevent the food from getting into the wrong hands, or mouths, like turtles or fish."

Once a fortnight, the crocs and 'gators get chicken, just for a change. The chimps get jelly for the same reason. "There's no special nutritional value in jelly," says John. "The chimps just like it—as long as it's red."

different creatures get enough of the right things to eat. "The sausages we give to the crocs and 'gators are specially prepared on the premises. We do no meat-cutting in the kitchen—bones can be a problem, but we add bone-meal and other vitamins.

239

Keeping the animals happy and healthy is the main preoccupation at Busch Gardens. That means providing 4.5 kg (10 lb) of horsemeat a day for each fully grown lion and tiger, as well as 410,000 kg (900,000 lb) of hay and 100,000 large sacks of grain a year for such free-roaming African mammals as elephants, giraffes and antelopes. Dietary information is exchanged with zoos throughout the world, and when a new animal joins the Dark Continent's population, stringent efforts are made either to match the menu it last enjoyed or gently wean it to a new eating pattern.

"All feeding is strictly controlled by vets and animal nutritionists," John emphasizes, "and everyone involved keeps an eye open for the slightest deviation in an animal's feeding habits. Keeping our animals happy and well-fed is keeping them alive.

"Let's face it, extermination is forever . . ."

Busch Gardens offers a generous range of entertainment. The **Marrakesh Theater** features *Sounds of the Sixties*, a musical revue complete with Beatles' tunes and rhythm and blues numbers. The theatre also features gospel music and contemporary country sounds. German folk songs and dance are on the menu at Timbuktu's spacious **Das Festhaus** beer hall, along with bratwurst, Black Forest gateau and other Bavarian fare. *Around the World on Ice* features an exotic journey through six countries, with elaborate staging and costumes, all performed on ice in the **Moroccan Palace Theater**. The recently opened **Animal Tales Theater** introduces live animals to young visitors through stories drawn from classic myths. The bold drums and brassy notes of the Mystic Sheiks Marching Band are likely to resound anywhere, any time.

Pinellas Suncoast

Most visitors to Busch Gardens, or indeed anywhere else in the Tampa area, are likely to be staying across Tampa Bay in St Petersburg and beyond—the area known as the **Pinellas Suncoast**. At slack times of the day, Tampa can be reached in 30 minutes, but to be on the safe side allow an hour, especially if you are staying on the Clearwater Beach side of Pinellas County. Tampa Bay is crossed by causeways and bridges, which get clogged up at rush hours.

The Pinellas side of Tampa Bay is quite different. Admittedly, **St Petersburg**—the locals call it St Pete—is a big city with its fair share of high-rise buildings, but the emphasis seems to be less commercial than it is in Tampa. The key phrase there is "seems to be". Tampa is collar-and-tie, denims-and-hardhat, sweat-of-the-brow big business. St Pete wears the shorts and sneakers of tourism, peers through sunglasses at a world of indulgence, sport, culture—and still makes megabucks, thanks to Pinellas County's 45 km (28 miles) of white, talcum-fine

The pier at St Petersburg stretches out into Tampa Bay and offers a mixed bag of entertainment.

beaches, and a string of islands which add the spice of variety.

Early Days

Pinellas County was founded in 1912, but long before then a diverse cast of characters played major roles in the area's history. There were Spanish explorers seeking gold and the fabled fountain of youth, a French surgeon, a Russian political exile, an enterprising group of Scottish merchants, and a daring young pilot from Washington, DC.

The Suncoast is made up of eight resort communities—Clearwater Beach, St Petersburg, St Petersburg Beach, Treasure Island, Madeira Beach, Indian Rocks Beach, Dunedin and Tarpon Springs—each with its own individuality. The area is now a popular resort area and its beaches attract more than three million visitors a year, but 150 years ago those same beaches were so isolated that pirates were able to hide out in the uncharted waters.

Ponce de Leon visited Mullet Key, on the county's southern tip, in 1513. Two other early Spanish explorers were Panfilo de Narvaez, in 1528, and Hernando de Soto, in 1539. They called the area *Punta Pinal*, meaning "point of pines". De Soto discovered five mineral springs near a large Tocobaga village in what is now Safety Harbor. He named the body of water, now called Tampa Bay, Espiritu Santo or "Springs of Sacred Spirit" because the Indians claimed the springs had healing qualities, a belief that persists.

A group of pirates advised Dr Odet Philippe to visit the area in the 1830s. Philippe, a surgeon in the French navy, had been captured by the pirates while exploring Florida's east coast. He treated a fever outbreak among the pirates and was rewarded with stolen treasure and a map describing Old Tampa Bay as "the most beautiful body of water in the world". Philippe established a plantation near Safety Harbor, today the site of a park named after him.

The Seminole Indian Wars started in 1835 and hampered further settlement, but Clearwater's roots were established as a result. In 1841, Fort Harrison was built on Clearwater Harbor. In less than a year, the war ended and the fort closed, but the area was opened to homesteaders.

In 1875 General John C. Williams, of Detroit, Michigan, bought 640 hectares (1,600 acres) in what is now downtown St Petersburg. After failing as a farmer, he dreamt of building a city complete with railway service.

In the northern part of the county Scottish merchants opened a general store and petitioned the government for a post office named Dunedin, a Gaelic word meaning "peaceful rest". They hoped the post office would increase trade. A wave of Scottish settlers moved to Dunedin and it became a major citrus-producing area. Today, the community's Scottish heritage is kept alive with the annual **Highland Games** and other festivals.

Before the turn of the century, a doctor and a Russian immigrant placed the Pinellas Suncoast in the spotlight as a holiday destination. Dr Van Bibber concluded, in a paper presented at a meeting of the American Medical Society in New Orleans, that Point Pinellas was the ideal location for a "health city".

Reaching paradise at that time, however, was another matter. The peninsula was almost an isolated island because overland travel was so difficult. But General Williams's idea of building a city with a rail service moved closer to reality when he made a land deal with Peter Demens, a Russian immigrant who brought his small-gauge Orange Belt Railroad to the Gulf Coast. The new railway and Dr Bibber's publicity produced a flood of new residents and visitors, and the city of Williams's dream.

Demens and Williams differed about a name for the new community. Legend has it that they drew lots and Demens won, naming the city after his home town in Russia—St Petersburg.

The American rail tycoon Henry Plant later purchased the Orange Belt and converted it to standard gauge. In

Peace and quiet as the sun goes down on a lonely stretch of beach at St Petersburg.

1896, Plant built the plush Belleview Hotel, near Clearwater, and the area became a playground for the rich. The hotel, now known as the Belleview Mido, is the world's largest occupied wooden structure.

Pinellas witnessed the birth of commercial aviation. Airline passenger services originated in St Petersburg in 1914 when a flying boat called the *Benoist* flew 34 km (21 miles) across the bay to Tampa. Tony Jannus was the pilot for the inaugural flight that carried one passenger—the mayor of St Petersburg.

Sport and Fishing

Naturally enough, they make great play of the climate on the Suncoast. The average temperature is 23°C (73°F) and the sun shines on average 361 days each year. The water temperature along the area's 206 km (128 miles) of shoreline is 24°C (75°F), so it comes as no surprise to learn that waterborne activities—swimming, boating, sailing, fishing—continue throughout the year. More than 60 marinas and yacht clubs provide pleasure,

sightseeing, dinner and deep-sea fishing cruises. Catamarans, windsurfing boards, parasailing and jet skis are available for hire along the beaches.

The Suncoast is known worldwide for its tarpon fishing. Noted fighters, tarpon grow to more than 44 kg (100 lb) and are pursued as trophies by fishing enthusiasts, using both artificial and live bait. Piers are choice spots for "table trophy" fishing, and local anglers are usually happy to share their knowledge with holiday-makers. There is no charge to fish from the pier at Fort DeSoto Park, near St Petersburg Beach. Another favoured spot, also free, is the pier on St Petersburg's downtown waterfront. There is a modest charge for fishing from Clearwater Beach's big Pier 60 and the Redington Long Pier. Charter and party boats are available for half- and full-day trips and several provide weekend trips. Charter boats usually accommodate six to ten fishermen.

Shore-based sports enthusiasts will find golf-courses and tennis courts galore, and at some resorts you can learn from world-class instructors. Just south of Tarpon Springs, **Innisbrook** is a conference, sports and leisure resort offering top-class facilities—and instruction—in both golf and tennis. The complex consists of 1,000 guest suites housed in 28 lodges set in 400 hectares (1,000 acres) of rare, rolling countryside—some hills reach a giddy 25 m (80 ft) above sea level. The suites feature separate bedrooms, living areas and fully equipped kitchens, and the lodges are placed around the resort's three golf-courses, one of which—the **Copperhead**—is regarded as Florida's finest and ranked one of the world's

top 100 courses. The Copperhead, a par 71 course with 27 holes, measures from 6,246 to 6,429 m (6,830 to 7,031 yds), depending on which combination of nines is played. A scuba-diver who recovers golf balls from alligator-infested pools on the courses at Innisbrook is said to earn more than $70,000 a year.

The **Innisbrook Golf Institute** offers comprehensive instruction for all levels of play—including juniors—throughout the year, and resort guests can attend three daily clinics which provide highly intensive training and practice sessions concentrating on a single aspect of golf. A practice tee and driving range are available for guest use and for private and group instruction, and a golf shop features a complete line of golf clothing and equipment as well as golf club and car rentals.

Tennis at Innisbrook has earned a five-star rating from *World Tennis* magazine. The **Innisbrook Tennis and Racquetball Center**, built at a cost of $1 million, has 18 courts, illuminated for night-time play, four indoor, air-conditioned racquetball courts, and is home of the famous Australian Tennis Institute, which offers year-round instructional clinics at all levels of play. Private and group lessons use high-tech equipment, such as remote-control ball machines and audiovisual instant replay cameras.

Innisbrook also has a **Recreation Centre** designed with parents as well as children in mind. It has a children's play area, a putting course, video-game room, fishing rod and bike rentals and a snack bar. There are daily activities for children aged four to eleven.

If you'd rather watch than play, the Suncoast offers horse-racing, greyhound racing, baseball, American football—even soccer and cricket. St Petersburg has a new multi-purpose high-tech stadium. Built at a cost of $110 million and opened early in 1990, the **Florida Suncoast Dome** has ingeniously movable stands that enable its seating capacity to vary from 11,000 to more than 50,000 people. With a cable-supported translucent roof—the first of its kind in the United States and the world's largest—the Dome is used for track and field events, basketball, tennis tournaments, concerts, exhibitions and conventions.

Wining and Dining

Night-life offers a choice of celebrity entertainment, ballet, opera, symphony concerts and Broadway shows. At nightclubs and lounges you can enjoy Country 'n' Western, jazz and Rock 'n' Roll. Dining can be as formal or as casual as you chose. More than 1,600 restaurants offer everything from gourmet cuisine and elegant, tableside service to casual beachside dining and the frankly sloppy, where you'll use up more napkins than dollar bills—and have the time of your life. With more than 300 varieties of fish waiting to be caught in those Gulf waters, seafood is an area specialty. Many waterfront restaurants are the favourite gathering spots for locals and provide the tropical equivalent of a pub atmosphere.

As a change from gazing out of a restaurant window at blue water dotted with exotic yachts and cruisers you can take to the water itself, admiring a lovely shoreline as you enjoy a sumptuous meal or a simple snack.

Starlite Princess, a three-decked 33-m (106-ft) sternwheeler, fitted out in luxurious riverboat style, offers three-hour dinner cruises along the Intracoastal Waterway from Hamlin's Landing, at Indian Rocks Beach. Diners are entertained with Mississippi riverboat tunes, jazz and contemporary music. **Hamlin's Landing** itself is worth a visit. Built satisfyingly in sturdy timber, it's a rambling structure in Victorian style with waterfront shops, restaurants and bars, as well as residential apartments.

From St Petersburg Beach the *Captain Anderson Dinner Boat* takes pleasure seekers on two-hour luncheon cruises and on dinner-dance cruises, lasting three hours, on Wednesday, Friday and Saturday nights. There's a live band and cash bar on board. Luncheon cruises along the Intracoastal Waterway, between Madeira Beach and Treasure Island, are the speciality aboard *Southern Belle*, a new 30-m (100-ft) paddle riverboat. Two vessels are based at Clearwater Beach. The *Admiral Dinner Boat* offers three-hour cruises with dinner and dancing, and *Captain Memo's Pirate Cruise* does day cruises and evening champagne trips. More adventurous voyagers might like to try a full day out aboard *SeaEscape*, an ocean-going ship that cruises into the Gulf of Mexico from the port of St Petersburg. Passengers get three meals, a variety of on-board activities—including gambling, music, dancing and swimming in the upper-deck pool. *EuropaSun,* based at Treasure Island, takes six-hour luncheon and dinner cruises out into the Gulf and also offers casino gambling.

Shopping

Shoppers will find plenty of places to spend their money. The area has close on 80 major shopping centres and malls, and a variety of quaint, waterfront villages offer antique shops, boutiques and craft workshops. The best of these are at **Johns Pass Village** in Madeira Beach, **Hamlin's Landing** at Indian Rocks Beach, and along the sponge docks at **Tarpon Springs**. Souvenir hunters will find an endless source of shells along the beaches.

Culture

Art and history are celebrated throughout the year at numerous festivals, shows and museums. The **Salvador Dali Museum**, in downtown St Petersburg, is home to the world's most comprehensive collection of the great Spanish master's works—93

*T*he Salvador Dali Museum in St Petersburg houses the worlds most comprehensive collection of the Spanish master's works.

original oil paintings, more than 100 watercolours and drawings, nearly 1,300 graphics, sculptures, *objets d'art* and photographs, and an extensive archival library. Right next door is **Great Explorations**, a new museum with six "hands-on" areas in which visitors can pit their wits, test their muscles, fire their imagination among a series of challenging exhibits which include mazes, computer puzzles, mathematical problems and a 30-m (100-ft) pitch-black Touch Tunnel that puts all your senses in doubt. The **Haas Museum**, also in St Pete, features restored homes and buildings—including an old barber shop, a smithy and a railroad depot—in a nostalgic setting. Another fascinating collection of restored homes and buildings can be found on 8.5 wooded hectares (21 acres) at **Largo**, a short drive from Clearwater Beach. Self-guided tours at the **Heritage Park and Museum** give an insight into Pinellas County's pioneer lifestyle, while the **Historical and Fine Arts Museum** at Safety Harbor has a variety of exhibits tracing the area's development from Indian through to Spanish settlements and to Philippe's arrival.

Tarpon Springs— Sponge Capital

The northern part of the Suncoast, Tarpon Springs is known as America's sponge capital, a title it gained in the early 1900s when sponge divers from the Greek island of Kalymnos settled in the area to reap the undersea harvest. Plastic has put an end to the traditional industry, but sponges are still garnered and sold in abundance at shops along the dockside. The Stars and Stripes and the blue and white flag of Greece snap side by side in the breeze above the old Sponge Exchange building, and the exotic rhythms of Greece drift from the waterfront tavernas. One establishment,

specializing in kebabs, proclaims itself "The Greek answer to McDonald's". Traditional Greek festivals—such as Epiphany when young men dive for a cross thrown into the sea—are celebrated throughout the year. The cross is from St Nicholas's Greek Orthodox Church on North Pinellas Avenue, which is a replica of St Sophia's in Istanbul.

Harry Klimis can tell you all about Tarpon Springs. In his lifetime he has

Tarpon Springs is America's sponge capital, and a city that is almost as Greek as ouzo.

seen the town's fortunes rise and fall . . . and rise again.

Harry runs a wholesale and retail business, Tarpon Sponge Inc., from a small shop that smells of the sea in the Sponge Exchange, now converted into a shopping and dining mall but still distinctly nautical. A courtyard in front of the Exchange displays a number of brightly painted boats, and an old storm-warning tower casts a trellised shadow on the pavement.

Harry's shop is full of sponges. The whole town is full of sponges. Small sponges, soft as silk, the size and shape of a lady's finger; fez-shaped sponges for growing plants in; sponges for the bath and sponges for the car—heaps of them on shop counters, trestle tables and the decks of boats moored at the town's quayside.

"There aren't so many," says Harry. "Not like in the old days. Then we used to sell them by the million to buyers all over the world. Now they mostly go to tourists. Not many people use sponges these days—Americans certainly don't. But the British appreciate a good sponge."

Fifty years ago Tarpon Springs was recognized as the largest sponge-trading centre in the world with annual sales worth more than $3 million. It all began at the turn of the century when property developer John Cheyney decided to make a modest investment in a sponge-harvesting venture and met John Corcoris, a Greek buyer for a New York sponge company.

Corcoris visited Tarpon Springs and was convinced that the Gulf of Mexico held rich and sizeable sponge beds. He joined Cheyney's company and encouraged his two brothers to move to Tarpon Springs from the island of Kalymnos in the southern Aegean Sea. Other Greek divers followed—men like Harry's father bringing equipment and plans for boats, as well as their customs, traditions and a different way of life. "They came full of hope," says Harry. "Sponge-diving in Greece had always been a tough way to earn a living. The divers used to go down on a line tied to a big rock, holding their breath for up to two minutes while they harvested the sponges with a knife. "Here at Tarpon Springs they used hard-hat diving suits, the work was much easier and they had a far higher standard of living."

Then it all fell to bits. In 1933 the Depression caught up with Tarpon Springs, boats were sold, men lost their jobs.

"I was just a kid—one of four sons, and my parents were desperate," Harry recalls. "We had relatives in Gary, Indiana, hundreds of miles north of here, and my father decided we should go up there until things got better. We had a 1928 Hudson convertible and it was loaded with sponges, food, clothing, bedding and the four kids. Mom's sewing machine was tied on the running board. Dad took a compass to help him find the way to Indiana."

Three years later, though, Tarpon Springs was booming again. Greek divers flooded into the town from Aegina, Halki, Symi, Kalymnos and other Aegean islands. The industry prospered until the 1940s when a marine bacteria, known as the "red tide", destroyed the sponge beds. Divers turned to fishing, shrimping and other occupations.

The sponge beds eventually recovered, but the industry never got back to its old level. Ironically, the sponges in the Gulf of Mexico off the northern Pinellas Suncoast are the best ever. "The beds have had a good rest," Harry explains, "and now they're producing abundant, top-quality sponges. And all we can do is sell them as souvenirs."

Festivals

Clearwater's **Jazz Holiday**, held in October, is noted as one of Florida's leading jazz festivals, and the city celebrates the arrival of spring with its two-week **Fun 'n' Sun Festival**. St Petersburg's **Festival of States**, the South's largest civic celebration, is another springtime rite featuring parades, art shows and athletic competitions. The **Johns Pass Seafood Festival**, held in November, is one of the largest in the state.

Fishermen's Tales

If you feel like it, you can hold your own seafood festival three times a day on the Suncoast. Eat at the **Friendly Fisherman** at St Johns Pass Village, Madeira Beach, for example, and you can watch holiday anglers unloading a catch that might well appear on tables in the restaurant later in the day. It is an unpretentious restaurant with great cooking smells and a view across the Intracoastal Waterway. It's crowded most evenings and a loudspeaker system tells diners on the boardwalk outside, watching the marine world go by, when their tables are ready.

Captain Wilson Hubbard, the colourful sea dog who owns the Friendly Fisherman, is a storyteller. He's also a television personality, a restaurateur, an entrepreneur and, above all, a fisherman. You'll find him at six o'clock most mornings by switching your TV set to Channel 13 where he presents a daily fishing report—and tells a few tales. You'll find him most evenings in the lounge bar beneath the Friendly Fisherman where he meets his cronies—and tells a few tales.

In between times, you could find him anywhere, but most likely in the vicinity of the higgledy-piggledy, Popeye world of **St Johns Pass Village**, with its boardwalk landings, little shops, restaurants and bars—one of them with an excellent jazz trio, by the way—and heaps of freshly caught fish from the Gulf of Mexico.

"We land 2,000–3,000 lb from each overnight trip, and most of the guys sell the fish to me," says Captain Hubbard. "I'm delighted to buy it from them for it means we have a regular supply of fresh fish for our restaurant."

Captain Hubbard operates a fleet of "party" boats, large seagoing craft with all mod-cons—snack bars and lounges—that take groups of anglers on fishing trips in the Gulf of Mexico, sometimes as far as 160 km (100 miles) offshore. For those overnight trips, which actually last close on 36 hours, there is comfortable bunk accommodation, and cooked meals are served.

Anglers with uncertain sea legs can fish freely from the very solid dockside, or even the nearby St Johns Pass Bridge. The Pass Port Marine tackle shop offers rod 'n' reel rentals, and there's a selection of live bait.

"Ashore or afloat, we like our customers to catch fish," says Captain Hubbard. "My crew will always help inexperienced fishers. They won't land the fish—that's your own personal triumph—but they'll show you all the right things to do.

"And you don't need to make a reservation to join one of our trips. You can just turn up at the dock. We have all kinds of people on board—why, we've even had ladies in tea gowns with us on occasions."

249

St Johns Pass Village, Madeira Beach, is a boardwalk community with bars, restaurants, shops and a fishing fraternity.

The son of itinerant fairground folk, young Wilson Hubbard first came to St Johns Pass Village in 1929 when his family visited relatives on their way to Miami. It was the time of America's big economic crash, and Wilson's parents decided to stay there until things got better. Things did get better, but the Hubbards stayed—mainly as a result of their son's enterprise.

"In 1930, at the age of 15, I bought a fishing rental business from a guy who was in trouble," says Captain Hubbard. "He wanted $150, and I paid him $20 down and the rest when he could catch me. I owned 40 cane rods and five rowboats, and I did pretty well, making around $40 a week, which was good money in those days. So my Dad came in to help me.

It was a long time before I got my business back."

It was after World War II, in fact, before Wilson Hubbard was able to take control of his fishing charter business again. He had served as a bomber pilot in the US Air Force, and when the war ended several big airlines offered him jobs flying airliners for $350 a week.

"Hell, I thought, I can make more than that running my fishing charters—and, you know, I did. My accountant tells me I'm worth about $2 million, but I'd like to know where it is 'cos we always seem to be broke."

Restaurants and Entertainment

Another fun place for a meal is **Crabbie Bill's** at Indian Rocks Beach. The menu, handwritten on pieces of paper plastered on the walls, offers steamed blue crabs in oil or garlic, stone crab claws, and Alaskan snow crabs. There's crab served mild, crab served spicy. There are crab cakes and crab sandwiches. But you don't have to have crab. Specials include oysters, steamed shrimps, mussels, clams and Maine lobster.

If you want to go out simply for a drink and a bit of fun there is a wide choice of places. At the **Joyland Country Night Club** on US Highway 19, between Clearwater and St Petersburg, for example, you can enjoy the best of Country 'n' Western music, with live top-name groups, high-boot dancing and reasonably priced beer and liquor. Wednesday night is Ladies' Night at Joyland, when drinks are half price and customers can have a free dancing lesson.

251

Time-Warp Restaurant

The 94th Aero Squadron is a most peculiar restaurant, locked in a time warp, circa 1917. In a quiet rustic area beside the St Petersburg/Clearwater International Airport, just off Highway 686, the "squadron" is headquartered in a convincing French farmhouse, complete with barbed wire, sandbags, leather jackets and flying helmets. In the sandbagged entrance, the Flight Commander's office door is slightly ajar and from within comes a murmur of conversation. First-time visitors have been known to knock and wait respectfully before realizing that it is all part of the act. Diners choose from a menu of "Mess Hall Favourites"—including Twin Tails (lobster), Veal Normandy, Steak Rickenbacker, Upside-Down Apple Walnut Pie—to the sounds of aircraft screaming out of the sun, chattering machine guns and the songs of World War I.

Rather quieter, oddly enough, is Biff-Burger at 49th Street/38th Avenue North, St Petersburg. This is a reconstructed drive-thru diner of the early 1950s Rock 'n' Roll heyday. The fare is uncompromisingly American: wholesome, generous, inexpensive. And the more you buy, the cheaper it is. The house specialty is Buffalo Wings, spicy pieces of chicken named after the city in New York State, you may be relieved to hear.

You get live Rock 'n' Roll music as you eat, and at weekends there's a splendid *concours d'élégance* of privately owned cars of the same glorious era. A parking lot full of chrome, fins, whitewall tyres. Drophead coupés, sleek sedans: the Buicks, the Chevvies, the Oldsmobiles. Many a car's hood (bonnet, in English, remember) is left proudly opened, revealing a gleaming engine so clinically clean you could eat your Buffalo Wings from it—though the owner wouldn't thank you if you did.

At the **Harp 'n' Thistle** pub, in Corey Avenue, St Petersburg Beach, you can knock back draught Guinness or Bass as you listen to live Irish folk music. This is the headquarters of the British-Floridian Society whose members put on pantomimes and hold cricket matches. In their time the Brits have been soundly trounced by teams from a nearby US airbase, though to be fair, it should be pointed out that the Americans have fielded RAF personnel on secondment.

Parks and Trails

Florida's natural beauty can be enjoyed in the area's public parks and nature trails. Honeymoon Island and Caladesi Island state parks, near Dunedin, provide 400 hectares (1,000 acres) of unspoiled space for picnics, nature walks and beach activities. The Dunedin Causeway connects the mainland with Honeymoon Island. Caladesi Island is accessible only by boat.

Studies of local history and ecology can be combined at Fort DeSoto Park, near St Petersburg Beach, and at Philippe Park at Safety Harbor on Tampa Bay. **Fort DeSoto Park**, located on five islands, is noted for its wide unspoiled beaches, camping and fishing facilities. It is also the site of a fort built in 1898 during the Spanish–American War. The islands were explored by Ponce de Leon in 1513. **Philippe Park** was the site of three distinct historical periods—a settlement of Timucan Indians, an encampment for the Spanish explorer Hernando de Soto, and later, a plantation installed by the French surgeon, Odet Philippe, who introduced grapefruit trees to Florida. A large Indian ceremonial mound is preserved in the park.

In the Central West region there are two forests, the **Withlacoochee State Forest** and, to the south-west, the **Ocala National Forest**. Between the two is some wonderful lakeland scenery. On the forest's north-eastern edge is the pleasant little town of **Inverness**, with a population of about 6,000, and, since a century-old general store was converted into the **Crown Hotel** in the early 1980s by a British investor, a noticeable British influence. Outside is a vintage London bus. Inside: a bar called the Fox and Hounds, a restaurant named after Churchill (it serves excellent food) and a display of the Crown Jewels in replica.

Inverness is handy for canoeing and fishing along the Withlacoochee River—like the St Johns it flows northward—and in the Withlacoochee State Forest. Twenty-four kilometres (15 miles) from the town, close to the Gulf Coast, is the **Crystal River State Archaeological Site**. Guided tours of this Indian mound complex are available. It is one of the state's longest continually occupied sites, pre-Columbian Indians having been there from 200 BC to AD 1400.

Homasassa Springs, about 120 km (75 miles) north of St Petersburg, is a State Wildlife Park with a floating underwater observatory. It is a tremendous experience to watch thousands of salt-water and freshwater fish congregate at the spring, which is the headwater of the Homasassa River. No one has been able to explain exactly what

attracts the fish to the 15-m (45-ft) deep spring which gives out 27 million litres (6 million gallons) of water an hour. As you stand watching the fish, several herbivorous manatees, huge and amiable, are likely to swim into view. The park is a haven for injured or orphaned manatees. A wide range of native Florida creatures can also be seen in the grounds.

The **Weeki Wachee Springs Complex**, 32 km (20 miles) south of Homasassa, on US 19, is a different kettle of fish. Here a mind-boggling entertainment with a cast of mermaids takes place in "The World's Only Underwater Spring Theatre". The air-conditioned theatre, 5 m (16 ft) below the water surface, accommodates 400 people in tiered seating. The mermaids, their long hair streaming, drift gracefully about the liquid stage, occasionally joined unofficially by a school of small fishes or a turtle trying to get into the limelight.

Whether you find the mermaids' performance enchanting or simply over the top depends on your inclinations (and possibly your age). It certainly takes a lot of nerve and months of training to do their job. Off duty, they are confronted by people who ask what they do for a living and think they're getting a sarcastic answer. One of the mermaids is married to a naval officer. The taxman wasn't amused when he saw the officer's tax return. Against "Wife's Occupation", he'd put, naturally, "Mermaid".

Weeki Wachee has more entertainment from free-flying vultures and eagles, and a boat trip along the Weeki Wachee River, through one of Florida's most interesting ecosystems,

The Weeki Wachee Springs Complex boasts the world's only underwater springs theatre with mermaids performing before an audience of up to 400 people.

wildlife watching along the way. Buccaneer Bay, part of the Weeki Wachee complex, is a place for family fun with flume rides, rope swings over the water, and a Fantasy Island for tots, with mini slides and animal rides. There's a white, sandy beach, and the water is a constant 23.4°C (74.2°F) year-round.

Central Florida's man-made attractions—Walt Disney World, Sea World and the rest—are only a couple of hours from the Suncoast by car, but the area has its own selection of places to visit. St Petersburg's **Sunken Gardens** is a tropical showplace with more than 5,000 flowers, plants and exotic birds and animals. The **London Wax Museum** at St Pete Beach presents lifelike renditions of the noteworthy and notorious from past and present. **Tiki Gardens** at Indian Shores offers a slice of Polynesia in its shops, gardens, restaurants and adventure trail.

Samples of marine life are on show at the **Clearwater Marine Science Center**, a research facility that is successfully conducting a "headstart" programme for baby turtles. Summertime visitors can take part in evening turtle walks and watch young turtles being released on the beaches.

At Indian Shores the **Suncoast Seabird Sanctuary**, run by Ralph Heath, is a refuge for injured and crippled birds. It is set on 0.6 hectare (1½ acres) of land, surrounded by high-rise apartment blocks near the beach, and it pulls in visitors from all over the world. The sanctuary has achieved worldwide status as one of America's most unusual conservation projects and is a Mecca for birdwatchers, researchers, wildlife artists and photographers. It has also become a very important place for the 5,000 or so injured birds who pass through each year.

The Suncoast Seabird Sanctuary at Indian Shores has achieved worldwide status as a conservation project.

More than 40 different species reside at the sanctuary, including the largest collection of brown pelicans in captivity. Other patients are hawks, owls, eagles, vultures, egrets, herons, ducks, crows, gulls and a wide range of songbirds and other shore birds.

Although visitors are free to roam among the cages, the residents are more than mere exhibits. Many of the birds have mated and produced healthy offspring which have been released to their natural habitat. Crippled adult birds act as foster parents to abandoned youngsters. In 1975 two permanently crippled pelicans produced one offspring—named Pax—the first to be hatched and raised in captivity. Pax was subsequently released, but five years later he came back on his own—injured by a fish hook.

Injured birds frequently find their own way to the sanctuary. "They seem to know this is a safe place, and we've had several walk right in here from the beach," says Ralph. "And we've had quite a few come back, besides Pax."

Birdman of Pinellas

The story of the Suncoast Seabird Sanctuary began in December 1971 when Ralph Heath, then aged 25, saw a cormorant struggling along the road with a broken wing. A zoology graduate, he recovered the bird from among the speeding traffic, took it home and treated the wing. A vet friend said it would be six weeks before the cormorant could be released again, so Ralph went down to a nearby fishing pier to see if he could arrange a regular supply of food for the patient.

Word spread about the new "Bird Doctor" and soon other casualties began to arrive. Someone turned up with an injured seagull. Another person called him out to a crippled pelican, and a box left anonymously on his doorstep contained a dove with a mangled wing.

Ralph's first casualty department was a rabbit hutch behind his home. Today, cages and compounds cover the site, a permanent building houses an operating theatre and intensive care unit, and the sanctuary treats an average of 20 new patients each day. About 60 per cent of the sanctuary's patients survive, and most of them are soon healthy enough to return to the wild. Some are too crippled to survive on their own and become permanent residents.

An astonished TV crew once filmed a pelican with a broken wing as it dragged itself a couple of kilometres (over a mile) down the beach to the sanctuary gate. A heron, formerly treated for disease, staggered in one day and collapsed in front of its old pen. All treated birds are ringed for identification and tracking.

"Fisherman are the biggest threat to pelicans," says Ralph. "Discarded fishing line and hooks cause more than 85 per cent of all injuries. We've removed as many as nine hooks from one pelican."

The sanctuary has published brochures and posters showing the proper way to handle injured birds and how to remove fishing lures and hooks. Ralph also conducts seminars, encouraging fishermen to be more cautious and considerate.

Pelicans from the Suncoast Seabird Sanctuary have been shipped to parks and zoos throughout the United States and to the Bahamas. In Britain some of them can be found at the Flamingo Gardens and Zoological Park at

Ralph Heath, who runs the Suncoast Seabird Sanctuary, has nursed thousands of sick and injured birds back to health.

Olney, in Buckinghamshire, where Ralph is a frequent visitor.

The sanctuary, open the year round during daylight hours, has been established as a non-profit organization since its beginnings. Operating expenses are offset by donations ranging from oil company grants to "What-you-like" offerings dropped in a box by the gate. Visitors may participate in an "adopt a bird" programme.

Local volunteers help with building cages, feeding and caring for birds, maintaining the grounds, leading tours and searching waterways for injured birds. The sanctuary has more than 12,000 supporters, mostly from Florida, but a growing number from other parts of the United States as well as Canada, Germany, France and Britain.

Appropriately, perhaps, the Birdman of Pinellas Suncoast has taken part in the bizarre Birdman Rally at Bognor Regis, Sussex, England, joining those doughty eccentrics in attempting unpowered flight from the resort's pier.

Sunshine Skyway

South of St Petersburg, Interstate 275 and US 19 merge for a spectacular 17-km (11-mile) crossing of Tampa Bay by way of the Sunshine Skyway, a bridge whose central section alone covers 6.4 km (4 miles) and soars 75 m (250 ft) above the surface of the Intracoastal Waterway. It was built high to allow big ships to pass to and from the Port of Tampa, but in May 1980 the bridge was struck by a freighter, causing a truck, a bus and several cars to plunge into the water with the loss of 35 lives.

Put thoughts of disaster behind you, though, as you enjoy the sensation of flying from Point Pinellas to Terra Ceia Point, where US 19 joins US 41——the Tamiami Trail. For 1,700 years, from about the time of Christ, the area was occupied by Indians who left behind a 6-m (20-ft) high burial mound and a temple site. Artefacts found in the area are on display at the **Madira Bickel Mound Historic Memorial**.

Ellenton, 8 km (5 miles) south of Terra Ceia, on US 301, is worth a stopover to see the **Gamble Plantation State Historic Park**. The restored mansion was built between 1845 and 1850 and is the oldest residence on the west coast. Built largely of "tabby", a kind of concrete composed of water, sand and oyster shells, it was the home of Major Robert Gamble, Jr, a Civil War veteran on the Confederate side who employed 300 slaves to work his 600-hectare (1,500-acre) sugar plantation. Some sugar cane is still grown on the estate. After the Civil War, Gamble gave sanctuary to the Confederacy's Secretary of State, Judah P. Benjamin.

The quickest way to Sarasota is to take I-75, but US 41 is the more interesting route, and if you have all the time in the world you can drive west to Anna Maria Key, the most northerly of a chain of islands that hug the coast down to Fort Myers.

Stop off first at **Bradenton**, where there are more opportunities to look in on the past. Here is the **Manatee County Courthouse**, the oldest surviving structure of its kind on the south Florida mainland. It was built in 1860 at a cost of $700 and is now the

An impressive collection of baroque art is on display at the John and Mabel Ringling Museum of Art.

centre-piece of the **Manatee Village Historical Park** which also features a 100-year-old church and a bizarre house, dating from 1912, built in a style described as "Cracker Gothic", reflecting the whimsy of pioneer architectural taste.

The **South Florida Museum** at Bradenton has two floors of vivid exhibits and tells the story of the state from prehistoric times to the Space Age. Life-size dioramas and a collection of artefacts give an insight into Indian life in early Florida. The Spanish Courtyard contains replicas of 16th-century Spanish buildings, including Hernando de Soto's home and chapel. The museum is home to Snooty, a 225-kg (500-lb) manatee who serves as the county's mascot. Manatees are to be found throughout the area.

Just outside Bradenton is the **De Soto National Memorial Park**, overlooking the mouth of the Manatee River and commemorating the Spanish explorer's landing in 1539. The park has a visitor centre, and there is a 1-km (0.6-mile) riverside nature trail. From December to April employees dress in period costume and re-enact the lives of the Spaniards and Indians.

Two roads lead to Anna Maria Key out of Bradenton. Manatee Drive—State Road 64—sets you on the way to the De Soto National Memorial Park and Holmes Beach. Three km (2 miles) to the south, SR 684 leads to Bradenton Beach by way of the fishing village of Cortez, where excursion boats leave for remote **Egmont Key** at the mouth of Tampa Bay. Virtually abandoned, the finger-shaped island of sand and sea oats has a fort dating from the

Spanish–American War and is the refuge of a population of threatened gopher tortoises. Chief Billy Bowlegs brought his 138 tribespeople to Egmont Key at the end of the Third Seminole War. They were later shipped to a reservation in Arkansas.

Anna Maria and **Longboat Keys** attract the shell hunters. Both are abundant in sand dollars and scallop-shaped shells of all sizes. There are several marinas with excursion boats and charter fishing vessels. Longboat is known for its quaint **Avenue of the Flowers**, an arcade of arts and craft boutiques and outdoor cafés.

The route south, from Anna Maria Key to Lido Beach, is called Gulf of

259

Circus Master

John Ringling moved to Sarasota in 1925 and began building an Italian-style manorial estate on 27.5 hectares (68 acres). He brought artisans and art from all over the world, and "Ca'd'zan", a 30-roomed mansion modelled on the Doges' Palace in Venice, was completed in only a year. Ca'd'zan means "House of John" in the Venetian patois. The house and grounds were bequeathed to the state of Florida and are open to the public. Adjoining the mansion is the John and Mabel Ringling Museum of Art with an impressive baroque collection, including works by Rubens, Rembrandt and other masters. The estate also contains the Museum of Circus and the Asolo State Theater, an 18th-century theatre which Ringling dismantled and brought from Asolo, Italy, and reconstructed in Sarasota in 1950.

Mexico Drive, and the crossing from the islands to the city of Sarasota is made by way of the Ringling Causeway, named after the world-famous circus master, John Ringling. **Sarasota** could just as easily—and relevantly—be called Circusville, for the city has been very much influenced by the "Greatest Show on Earth".

The influence of the sawdust ring has now spilled into the resort of Venice, 32 km (20 miles) south of Sarasota, where the Ringling Brothers and Barnum and Bailey Circus has its winter headquarters. During the winter, members of the public can sit in on dress rehearsals as next year's show

Ca'd'zan, home of John Ringling.

takes shape. Here also is the Clown College, where instruction is given in the peculiar skills required of circus performers and technicians.

Sarasota has other attractions. Right next to the Ringling Museum is **Bellm's Cars and Music of Yesterday**, an arcade of antique games with a collection of cars, bicycles, nickelodeons, jukeboxes and gramophone records. Also nearby, on the Tamiami Trail, is the **Lionel Train and Seashell Museum**, featuring operational toy trains and a collection of shells and coral from around the world. The **Marie Selby Botanical Gardens**, just off US 41 on Sarasota's downtown waterfront, specializes in plants from the tropics, and houses an outstanding collection of orchids.

Spanish Point at the Oaks, at Little Sarasota Bay, has prehistoric Indian mounds, restored cottages featuring hands-on museum exhibits, and a tour through a Victorian pioneer home. **Crescent Beach** on Siesta Key, at the southern end of Sarasota Bay, is said to be one of the world's best beaches, while nearby **Lido Key** has an elegant area of shops and restaurants surrounding St Armand's Harding Circle. At the other extreme is the **Myakka River State Park**, about 10 km (15 miles) inland from Sarasota, on State Highway 72. The park is a 12,000-hectare (30,000-acre) wildlife refuge with a wilderness preserve and a paved, 11-km (7-mile) drive for touring by car or bike. Bikes can be rented nearby. There are also guided boat tours and a 90-minute train ride which provide opportunities for birdwatching and spotting the other local wildlife.

History and a Feeling of the Deep South

A sense of history pervades this region of Florida. Called "The First Coast" because the earliest European settlements grew up in this area, it retains a charming old-world ambience. The dazzling white beaches are made from quartz from the Appalachian mountains, crushed into fragments as it was washed down the coast. Follow the Buccaneer Trail in the footsteps of smugglers, pirates and slave traders. Watch Florida's official state play in the open-air at St Augustine. And those who love big city life need look no further than Jacksonville.

Few transatlantic visitors to Florida have penetrated to the northern part of the state. Not too many American tourists have been there, either. Yet it is one of the more historic regions, with a generous share of natural attractions, and a feeling of the Deep South—Alabama and Georgia are just over its northern borders. Antebellum plantation homes can still be seen, with their slaves' quarters. The coastline is less developed than elsewhere in

*B*uilt to keep invaders out, this cannon is now redundant as the only modern invaders are welcome tourists.

Florida, but it has great expanses of beach. The dazzling white sand, typical of the north-west coast, is like fine sugar, and is in fact 99 per cent pure quartz crystal. The surfing is good in the winter when the waves are 2 to nearly 4 m (7 to 12 ft) high.

Major cities are few and far between. The state capital, Tallahassee, is just about in the centre of northern Florida, Jacksonville the biggest conurbation. Jacksonville Beach is on the east (Atlantic) coast, and Pensacola on the extreme west, in the so-called Panhandle, on the Gulf of Mexico, with Alabama a close neighbour. Gainesville, where the University of Florida is based, St Augustine, the oldest city in the United States, Ocala, famous for its racehorse breeding and

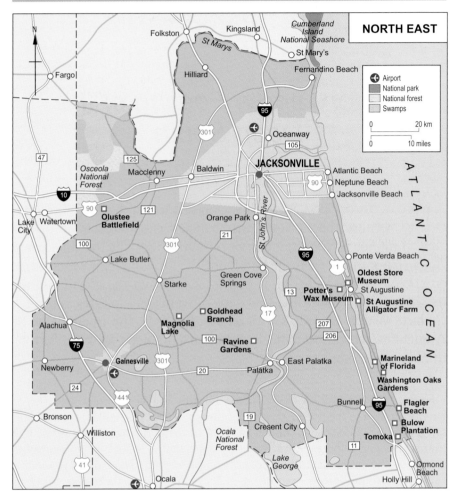

*M*ap of the North
East—"The First Coast".

training, and Panama City are the
other major centres in the region. Two
national forests and a state forest occupy vast tracts of land.

Interstate Highway 10 bisects the
state between east and west. US 19
links the Pinellas Suncoast with Tallahassee; I-75 leads north from Fort

Myers, joining I-10 between Jacksonville and Tallahassee, and I-95 runs
parallel to the Atlantic Ocean from the
Gold Coast to Jacksonville. SR A1A
does likewise, but on the oceanside of
the Intracoastal Waterway. From Orlando, I-95 is reached via I-4.

Those who can't stand the summer
heat of southern Florida may find
northern Florida's average temperatures more amenable—22°C (the
mid-70°sF) from September toNovem-
ber and, in the north-east, about 16°C

(63°F) from December to March. In the north-west the winter temperature is only about 13°C (55°F).

It was in north-eastern Florida that European settlers first established themselves in what was to develop into the United States of America. Spanish explorers, French settlers and English pirates arrived in the 16th century. The region is known as the First Coast. St Augustine, claimed to be the first permanent settlement in the country, was named in 1565, when Pedro Menendez of Spain sailed into the harbour. Ponce de Leon had discovered the same area some 50 years earlier.

The First Coast, so called because of its early European settlements, is gradually making itself known to North Americans and transatlantic visitors, though up until now coastal areas in other parts of Florida have had the lion's share of tourism. The choice of Atlanta, Georgia, as a site for the Olympic Games has no doubt helped promote the attractions of this long stretch of beach, as spectators from around the world add a relaxing beach holiday to the excitement of watching international athletics and sports events.

Certainly the area, which takes in ten counties, has great charm. The wide beaches, with firm sand, seem to go on forever and are uncrowded. There's an old-world ambience in some of the communities and a strong sense of history.

Ponce de Leon landed on Florida's north-east coast in 1513 in search of gold, and claimed the land for Spain. Hard on the heels of Spanish settlers were the French, and later came Sir Francis Drake.

Jacksonville

We begin our exploration of the north-east in Jacksonville, a major commercial and industrial centre which in sheer volume is said to be the largest city in the United States, covering an area of nearly 1,370 km² (850 square miles). In fact, it isn't all metropolitan—the city and Duval County boundaries are the same, and the population at the 1980 census was below 600,000, with a further 15,500 at Jacksonville Beach.

The wide St Johns River flows through the city north-east to join the ocean at Fort George. **Jacksonville Landing** has grown up in recent years on its north bank and it's the place to go to for concerts, up-market shopping, restaurants, festivals, fireworks, dancing, mime shows and other street entertainment. A new elevated light-rail system links Jacksonville Landing with hotels and convention centres.

On the opposite bank, stretching for about 2 km (over a mile) in the downtown area, is another development of the 1980s, the Riverwalk, with pedestrian boardwalks, shops, restaurants, hotels, entertainment pavilions and cultural amenities. Special events are often staged there at weekends during spring and autumn months. The extensive **Florida National Pavilion and Metropolitan Park** is also on the waterfront. It has a canopied pavilion, docking for boats, and open parkland. Free attractions, concerts and festivals are staged year-round. The park is the site of the annual **Jacksonville Jazz Festival** in October, a three-day event with performances by top musicians and displays of arts and crafts. The

festival, with free entry, includes the **Great American Jazz Piano Competition.**

*J*acksonville, a major commercial and industrial centre, straddles the St Johns River.

Other events at the Metropolitan Park include the **River Festival** in March, the Country Music Festival in

A number of museums and attractions are handy for the downtown area—even the 25-hectare (61-acre) Jacksonville Zoo, with its miniature railroad and elevated walkway. It has 700 inmates from many parts of the world, including a herd of white rhinos in the African Veldt section. Buggies and wheelchairs can be rented and elephant rides are available. Parking is free and there are picnic facilities. Among the downtown museums are the **Jacksonville Art Museum** and the Gummer Gallery of Art, both with free admission. The Art Museum, which has among its collections contemporary paintings, sculptures, Oriental porcelain and pre-Colombian artefacts, is closed throughout August. The Gummer Gallery displays some Old Masters, Oriental ivory and Meissen porcelain. It has ten galleries and is set in waterfront gardens.

Also centrally situated is the Museum of Science and History, on Gulf Life Drive. It incorporate a 20-m (65-ft) diameter state of the art planetarium, where Friday and Saturday night Cosmic Concerts, with special effects, are popular. The museum has displays on Florida history and wildlife, and ancient Egypt. There's a Victorian home, a dinosaur skeleton, and a number of exhibits with special appeal for children, including a marine aquarium and live marshland creatures.

The **Civic Auditorium** overlooks the St Johns River. Its 3,000-seat theatre features touring Broadway shows, light entertainment and music, including concerts by the Jacksonville Symphony Orchestra. Also overlooking the river, but farther east, is the **Fort Caroline National Memorial**, on the site of the

April and the **Spring Music Festival** in May. The River Festival includes a 15-km (9-mile) River Run, which 61usually attracts more than 6,000 local and national runners and is quite a sight.

first Protestant colony of what is now the United States. It was founded by French Huguenots in 1564, and the memorial is a replica of the original fort. There are a museum and a nature trail. Admission is free.

After all the sightseeing, visitors deserve a free tour of the **Anheuser-Busch Brewery**, seeing the automated machinery used in the beer-making processes and packaging methods used at this large enterprise. Over-21s can afterwards enjoy sampling beer and pretzels in the Hospitality Room.

Sport and Events

Major sporting and light musical events of many kinds take place at the **Veterans' Memorial Coliseum** in downtown Jacksonville. They include pop, rock and country music concerts, wrestling, gymnastics, basketball and ice-skating.

An important aspect of life in Jacksonville, of course, is sport. There are three easily accessible tracks which between them provide the greyhound-racing public with year-round excitement. **Jacksonville Kennel Club** holds its races from early May to early September. **Bayard Raceways** presents the sport from around 9 September to 23 October, and again from early

Getting afloat need not be costly. Tubing provides a fun way to cool off, and the clear waters of Northern Florida provide an ideal environment for it.

March to early May. **Orange Park Kennel Club** holds races from early January to early March and from late October to the end of December.

Space is no problem in a big city like Jacksonville. Among the parks and complexes downtown is the **Gator Bowl**, with seating for 82,000 people. One of the most exciting annual events for the local people, the football match between the Universities of Georgia and Florida, is held at the Gator Bowl in November. Professional baseball is also played there. In December the **Gator Bowl Classic** is a series of post-season matches between top college football teams from different parts of the nation. The event has taken place every year since 1946.

Golf, tennis, fishing—freshwater and offshore—and sailing all have their special tournaments and competitions during the year. In May the world's longest sailing-boat race is held on the St Johns River. Called the Mug Race, it is a course of about 80 km (42 nautical miles) from Palatka to Jacksonville.

The major event in late October is the **Greater Jacksonville Agriculture Affair**. It lasts eleven days, and as well as agricultural pursuits and displays there are performances by nationally known artists, parades, rides, fireworks and a range of entertainments.

Amelia Island

At the northernmost part of the coast is Amelia Island, the only location in the United States to have been governed under seven different flags since 1562—Spanish, British, French Patriots, the Green Cross of Florida (who were also patriots), Mexican, the

Confederacy and the United States. The island is about 48 km (30 miles) from Jacksonville. It was originally settled by the British in the mid-18th century when Spain ceded Florida to the British and named it after a daughter of King George II. Britain's rule over the island lasted until the end of the American Revolution.

Amelia Island is 22 km (13.5 miles) long and up to 3.2 km (2 miles) wide. The major city is **Fernandina Beach**. It's well worth taking a look at the buildings in the Center Street area— the Old Town—beautifully restored to 18th- and mid-19th-century architectural style. Nearly 50 blocks in the historic area have been restored. For an in-depth look at the place, take a tour with a registered guide. As well as specialty shops, boutiques, restaurants and ice-cream stores, **Center Street** has a winery, with the product made from Florida-grown grapes. Victorian houses line the side streets, and the interiors of some of these private homes can be visited by arrangement (tel: (904) 261-7378).

Fernandina Beach was an important shipping port in the 19th century. Today, Amelia Island is known for its shrimping industry, celebrated every May with the Isle of Eight Flags Shrimp Festival, at Fernandina Beach. The three-day event includes street art exhibitions, antique and craft shows and stalls, music and live entertainment, not forgetting seafood sampling, with shrimps served in a number of delicious ways. The unenlightened should be aware that the Florida shrimp is not the tiny mollusc known in Europe but a sizeable prawn that takes at least two bites to consume.

Fine golden sand, occasional dunes and sea oats waving and whispering in the breeze are typical of the wide beaches which stretch along the north-east coast. On Amelia Island the sand is white, and each grain is actually fine quartz, which originated as part of the Appalachian Mountains, crushed into fragments as it was washed down the coast, coming to a halt on the barrier island which juts out into the Atlantic Ocean.

In the northern tip of Amelia Island, 5 km (3 miles) from Fernandina Beach, is Fort Clinch State Park. The fort itself is among the most interesting of a number of First Coast fortifications. **Fort Clinch** is a pre-Civil War fort and although it was never completed, it was occupied by troops in the Civil War and was used for training US troops during the Spanish–American War. Construction of the fort, strategically located to protect shipping in the St Mary's River and to defend the port of Fernandina, began in 1847, but progress was slow and, in effect, the fort was overtaken by the technology of the time. The masonry walls became obsolete as more powerful armaments were developed.

Visitors, who enter the fort through a drawbridge gate, can climb to the battlements to see the giant cannon. They will get a superb view of the coastline, with the mouth of the St Mary's River in the foreground—and the state of Georgia on the opposite bank.

Soldiers dressed in the uniform of the Union Army escort visitors around the fort. The scene is set in 1864. On view are the enlisted men's barracks, officers' quarters, stockade, mess hall, ammunition magazines and a quartermaster's supply store containing uniforms, boots, musket balls and salt pork. Those who really want to absorb the atmosphere of the time can take a tour by candlelight. On the first weekend of every month it all comes to life, when the 1864 occupation of the fort is re-enacted.

The 445-hectare (1,100-acre) **Fort Clinch State Park** is one of the oldest state parks in Florida, having been acquired in 1935. Plant life grows in a variety of environments, including sand dunes, over-wash plains, hammock and salt marsh. Camping is available in the park. Hiking and surf and pier fishing are among the activities and there are nature trails to follow, and picnic areas.

Amelia Island's 400-year-old history is traced at the **Museum of History**, on South Third Street in Fernandina Beach, with information about each of the eight periods under different flags, and artefacts from the 16th century.

Popular with yachtsmen, powerboaters and people on charter fishing boats, the island has a large and unusually packed marina. In the southern half of Amelia Island is tiny Amelia City, and farther south is the large resort of **Amelia Island Plantation**, with 1,300 rooms, 125 suites, fine restaurants and 25 pools. It has 6.5 km (4 miles) of beach. Sporting facilities include golf (45 holes), horse-riding, racquetball and tennis (25 courts). Another prestigious hotel was opened on the island in 1991 by the Ritz-Carlton group. It has 449 rooms, 45 suites and conference space for up to 1,500. There are 13 tennis courts and an 18-hole golf-course.

Buccaneer Trail

Take SR A1A southward from the island and you are on the **Buccaneer Trail**. It follows the shoreline all the way down to Daytona Beach. Now known for its sport fishing and pleasure boating, the trail was once the haunt of smugglers, pirates and slave traders.

On the north bank of the St Johns River is **Fort George Island**—also reached by the Mayport Ferry—where you can take a guided tour of the nearby **Kingsley Plantation State Historic Site**. This is the oldest plantation still in existence in Florida and one of the few remaining examples of the plantation system. One of the slaves' cabins has been restored to its original state. The plantation dates back to 1792. Slave labour was used to sow and harvest such produce as cotton, corn, black-eyed peas, sugar cane and sweet potatoes. The remains of the slaves' quarters can be seen, forming a defence system around the plantation houses.

The plantation flourished under its owner, Zephaniah Kingsley, who believed in slavery, and felt it was the sure method of succeeding in agriculture in the South, but he also believed in treating slaves leniently. He was married to an African. The tour of the main house begins at the cookhouse, dated around 1794. Authentic antiques, some hand-made on the plantation, are displayed. Guided tours are available daily except Tuesdays and Wednesdays, leaving at set times during the day, but tours may be arranged at other times for groups (tel: (904) 251-3122). The grounds are open year-round between 8 a.m. and 5 p.m.

Close to Fort George is **Little Talbot Island State Park**, with its wide, 8-km (5-mile) beach and woodland. This is an ideal spot for setting up camp and using as a base for visiting Jacksonville and the sights of the area. The Fort George River, the ocean and creeks provide fishing opportunities. Hiking, surfing, swimming and nature study are other activities on the island, where otters, marsh rabbits, bobcats and a variety of shore birds may be observed.

Continuing south on Route A1A, the next place of interest to many tourists is **Mayport Naval Air Station**, the second biggest aircraft-carrier port on the United States east coast. (Norfolk, Virginia, is the largest.) Reached by car ferry, the base arranges tours for the public at certain times, and there is usually at least one ship in port that visitors can tour. Visitors must check in at the gatehouse on entering the base. For further information, tel: (904) 246-5226.

The **Kathryn Abbey Hanna Park**, south of Mayport, has facilities for tent camping and recreational vehicles. The 180-hectare (450-acre) ocean-front park has 2.4 km (1.5 miles) of beach. It also has nature trails, picnic areas and well-stocked freshwater fishing lakes.

Mayport itself has been a fishing village for more than 300 years. It is the base for a large commercial shrimp boat fleet. The ferry goes across the mouth of the St Johns River between Mayport and Fort George Island. The first trip is from Mayport at 6.20 a.m. and the service closes at 10 p.m. A charge is made for both vehicles and pedestrians.

271

The Beaches

Atlantic Beach, Neptune Beach and Jacksonville Beach are 19 km (12 miles) from downtown Jacksonville. If you're driving to the Beaches from Jacksonville, take Atlantic Boulevard (SR 10) or Beach Boulevard (US Highway 90). The J. Turner Butler Expressway, a toll road, is a slightly more southerly choice. There are miles and

*H*istory is alive and well in the old city of St Augustine. Here the Spanish influence is demonstrated with a musical parade.

miles of wide beaches, and various types of accommodation and eating-out places to suit everyone's budget and taste. Jacksonville Beach has a fishing pier nearly 330-m (1,000-ft) long at Sixth Avenue South. A fee is charged for admission.

Concerts and big-band music are presented at the Jacksonville **Beach Flag Pavilion** at North Second Street,

a 2,000-seat auditorium and exhibition hall with a display of state and foreign flags. Admission is free to the **Lighthouse Museum** at 1011 Third Street, Jacksonville Beach.

St Augustine

If you've been staying at the Beaches and are bound for St Augustine, go south on the coastal A1A. If you are in Jacksonville, take I-95 or US 1. The nation's first permanent European settlement, sitting astride Matanzas Bay, is 56 km (35 miles) from Jacksonville. There are more than 400 years of history to explore, and an assortment of up-to-date attractions.

St Augustine is a popular resort, with beaches, nightspots, good restaurants and sophisticated shopping. A good way to see the sights is to take the special train which goes through the streets. An 11-km (7-mile) narrated tour is offered by St Augustine **Sightseeing Trains**. Passengers may get off at any of the stops to visit an attraction, have a meal or do some shopping, and reboard another train to continue the tour. Scenic tours can also be taken by horse-drawn carriage, by boat or by open-air trolley, starting at the waterfront section facing Matanzas Bay.

Tourists can walk in the narrow streets restored to 16th-century Spanish style in the **George Street** area, up to the old City Gate—**San Agustin Antiguo**—featuring restored buildings and gardens. Guides are in Spanish colonial-style costumes, and costumed craftsmen demonstrate the pursuits of the early settlers. You can buy some of

*F*ort Matanzas is an outpost of the Castillo de San Marcos, 22½ km (14 miles) to the south of it. The massive structures were completed in 1695.

the products, from perfumed candles to wooden carvings.

One edifice nobody can miss is the **Castillo de San Marcos National Monument** at the entrance to Matanzas Bay. Its outpost, **Fort Matanzas**, is some miles away at Rattlesnake Island. Building of the moated Castillo de San Marcos began in 1672 and took 15 years to complete. The walls are 10-m (33-ft) high and 5-m (16-ft) thick at the base, built of coquina, a native shellstone. Guided tours are available.

Florida's official state play, *Cross and Sword*, is performed in the open air nightly, except Sundays, in high summer at the atmospheric **St Augustine Amphitheater**. It is a symphonic drama with 100 singers, dancers and actors, depicting the founding of the city by Spanish colonists. The season is from mid-June to late August. In spring, a citywide celebration takes place—the **Easter Festival** and *St Augustine Passion Play*—with performances and festivities from Palm Sunday weekend through Easter weekend.

October sees the three-day **Maritime Festival**, with dinghy races and fancy dress ball and plenty of seafood. In December the Grand Illumination takes place—torchlit processions through the Spanish Quarter, re-enacting battles and British customs, with fife and drum music and carol singing. Also in December is the **Holiday Regatta of Lights**, a boat parade in Matanzas Bay. Another annual date is the **Spanish Night Watch** weekend in June, with a re-enactment of the **Battle of Fort Mose**. Musicians entertain in 18th-century style and artisans of the period ply their trades. Soldiers in a Spanish camp talk of military life and the battles they have fought.

Historic St Augustine
Sample all the historic spots in St Augustine and you will soon feel a stranger to the 1990s. Open to visitors are the Oldest House, the Oldest Store Museum, the Oldest Wooden Schoolhouse and the Authentic Old Jail. The Oldest House—Gonzalez-Alvarez House—was built from coquina on the site of a wooden structure thought to date from the early 1600s. The British are believed to have added the upper part, which is timber. It contains numerous antiques. The Store Museum is crammed with 100,000 fascinating products from the turn of the present century. Some things are just to look at, some are on sale. The Schoolhouse was originally built as a home during the first Spanish occupation before the American Revolution, and utilized as a school later. It is constructed of red cedar and cypress joined by wooden pegs. The jail, built in 1891 to contain the felons of St Johns County, also had living quarters for the sheriff and his family. It remained in use until 1953, and is listed in the US National Register of Historic Places. A collection of weapons used in crimes is on display.

Zorayda Castle, in King Street, is a replica of one wing of the Alhambra, Spain's castle in Granada, reflecting the lifestyle of Moorish kings. It contains treasures from around the world. Craftsmen in wax can be seen at work in **Potters Wax Museum**, where there are more than 170 figures from history, a waxworks theatre and a museum shop. Curiosities from scores of different countries are on show at **Ripley's Believe It or Not exhibition** at Castle Wardenon, San Marco Avenue. Some of the exhibits are intriguing, like the oil painting on a pin head. Others, like the two-headed calf, are grotesque. Apparently Robert Ripley collected some 750 oddities from every continent.

A 60-m (200-ft) illuminated cross, made of stainless steel, is an impressive sight, especially at night, at the **Mission of Nombre de Dios**, on San Marco Avenue. This is believed to be the site of the nation's first Mass.

Mechanical musical instruments, antiques and collectables, mainly of the 19th century, are featured at the **Lightner Museum**, housed in the former Alcazar built in 1888.

Claimed to be Florida's oldest attraction of its kind, St Augustine **Alligator Farm** has been drawing the crowds since 1893. Crocodiles, monkeys, deer, ducks and giant tortoises can also be seen. Alligator and reptile shows are given, and an elevated walk leads over an alligator swamp.

Just north of St Augustine Beach is the **Anastasia State Recreation Area**, where the energetic visitor can camp by the sea, go swimming and surfing, or hire a bicycle, a surfboard or a paddle boat on Salt Run Lagoon. The less energetic can rent a beach chair and an umbrella. Sailboard lessons are available. Bird-spotters may see sandpipers,

Fountain of Youth
The site of the Fountain of Youth, in Magnolia Avenue, now a memorial park to which an admission charge is made, is believed to be where Ponce de Leon first landed in 1513 in his quest for something precious he had heard about: a source of water that gave perpetual youth to anyone drinking it. Visitors can buy the water by the bottle to see if it works. A coquina-built shelter surrounds the natural spring.

The interior of St Augustine's oldest house.

terns, herons, egrets and other species on the tidal marshes.

 A little to the south on SR A1A is **Marineland of Florida**, right on the oceanfront. This is the state's original marine life attraction, which opened in 1938. Porpoises, manatees, turtles, dolphins, sharks, electric eels and other creatures cavort in oceanariums with a continuing supply of sea water. Some of these natural entertainers give performances at regular intervals through the day. A collection of shells is displayed. Marineland is not just an attraction for the public to visit. It is a residential place on the map, a village having grown up around the complex. On site is a resort hotel, the **Quality Inn Marineland**, with 125 rooms, two restaurants, two pools and tennis facilities.

Two peaceful recreation areas are in the vicinity. The **Washington Oaks State Gardens**, 4.8 km (3 miles) south of Marineland, are bounded by the Atlantic Ocean and the Matanzas River.

On down the coast is Flagler Beach, where a state recreation area borders the ocean. In summer sea turtles lay their eggs in the sand. Walks guided by rangers are available.

Inland Touring

Now we turn inland, taking SR 205 for the cultural centre and university city of Gainesville, pausing on the way to look at **Palatka** on the east bank of the St Johns River. Off Twigg Street, Palatka, where the Ravine State Gardens were established in 1933, are three ravines, with walks leading among the flowers and vegetation. The 100,000 azaleas are at their peak in March and April. Palatka is also noted for its bass fishing. In May the world's longest river sailing boat race, the Mug Race, is held on the St Johns River from Palatka to Jacksonville, a distance of more than 80 km (42 nautical miles).

Like St Augustine, Gainesville has its step-back-in-time region. This is the restored Mediterranean/Italian Renaissance **Thomas Center**. The **Northeast Historic Center** has 290 buildings, designed by various architects between 1880 and 1920.

Ancient history, computers and robotics, and many items in between, are covered by the exhibits at the **Florida Museum of Natural History** in Museum Road, Gainesville. This is one of the top ten natural science museums in the USA. Guided tours are available on weekdays.

People can stroll around the landscaped grounds of the university. Two galleries can be visited free year-round, the **University Art Gallery** and the

Waves have carried away the sand, and the beach is strewn with boulders and pools where shore birds feed at low tide. Ornamental gardens along the riverside provide a pleasant walk.

Family campground sites with electric hook-ups for 30 RVs, and a primitive camping area for up to 100 young people, are available at the **Faver-Dykes State Park** along Pellicer Creek, an aquatic preserve and quiet retreat with fishing, nature walks and picnicking areas.

Faver-Dykes is 24 km (15 miles) south of St Augustine at the intersection of US 1 and I-95.

Teaching Gallery. One of Florida's few carillons is in the Century Tower in the grounds. At one end of the campus is the **Lake Alice Wildlife reserve.**

As well as being home to the state's largest university, Gainesville is a major agricultural centre. The **Morningside Nature Center** demonstrates farm life a century ago, with a 112-hectare (278-acre) **Living History Farm.** There are miles of trails and boardwalks, farmyard animals and a wood cabin. Archery artefacts dating from the Stone Age can be seen at the **Fred Bear Museum** in Gainesville. There are bow hunting trophies and items of natural history interest among the many exhibits. Guided tours lasting an hour are available. The museum is closed on Mondays and Tuesdays.

One of Florida's most dramatic sinkholes is on the north-western outskirts of Gainesville. Such holes are formed in dry seasons when underground water dries up. The ground above the limestone base, no longer supported by water, caves in. The **Devil's Millhopper** is 155 m (500 ft) wide and 36 m (118 ft) deep. Typical rainforest vegetation has grown in it, and there are steps down and tracks to follow. Researchers tracing Florida's natural history have found sharks' teeth, marine shells and the fossilized remains of extinct land animals in the sink. Heavy rain fills some sinkholes, which is how many of Florida's lakes originated.

Any certified cave-diver or scuba-diver wanting to practise their skills can do so at **Manatee Springs State Park**, some 64 km (40 miles) west of Gainesville, near Chiefland. Camping is permitted. Both hummingbirds and butterflies add to the colour at **Kapaha Botanical Gardens** at Gainesville. South of the city on US 441 is **Payne's Prairie State Preserve**, 7,200 hectares (18,000 acres) of grass to the inexperienced eye, though experts identify 20 distinct "biological communities" providing a habitat for many different creatures. The 18th-century artist and naturalist William Bartram noted sandhill cranes, eagles, hawks, a variety of waterfowl and wading birds, alligators and otters—all still inhabiting the area today. He was so highly regarded that a special walk takes place at Payne's Prairie every April, when an interpretation of the history of north-central Florida from the 16th century to the present day is given.

Crafts and pioneer artefacts are on show. Fishing, camping, horse-riding and swimming are among the activities in the Preserve. There's a boat ramp for canoes, sailing boats and boats with electric motors.

From Gainesville, I-75 leads north to Lake City, gateway to the Osceola National Forest. Thirty-two kilometres (20 miles) before you reach Lake City, turn left to the **O'Lena State Park**, developed in the 1930s by the Civilian Conservation Corps on the site of a former small town founded in the mid-1880s. The Corps' suspension bridge still spans the Santa Fe River, a tributary of the Suwannee River. The Santa Fe re-emerges in the park after going underground for more than 4.8 km (3 miles).

There's another state park a few miles farther on—**Ichetucknee Springs State Park**, 6.4 km (4 miles) northwest of Fort White. The Ichetucknee River is another tributary of the

The Stephen Foster Folk Culture Center is a memorial to the composer of "S'wanee River". Memorabilia and musical instruments are displayed and a carillon plays Foster's music.

Suwannee River. Many consider this one of the loveliest riverfront parks in Florida. The headspring, one of nine springs along the river which produce more than 1,000 million litres (230 million gallons) of water a day, was officially declared a National Natural Landmark in 1972. Nature trails offer a good chance of spotting turkey, deer and fox squirrels. Canoes can be hired.

Lake City is proud of its new **Florida Sports Hall of Fame**, featuring the triumphs of more than 100 state athletes. About midway to Jacksonville, on US 90, is the **Olustee Battlefield State Historic Site**, commemorating Florida's major Civil War battle. It took place in 1864 and lasted for five hours, resulting in casualties of 1,860 Union and 946 Confederate soldiers. A trail can be followed around the battlefield, and an interpretive centre is open daily, except Tuesdays and Wednesdays. A memorial service and a re-enactment take place every February. The event includes a craft festival, a 10-km (6-mile) run and a parade.

About 24 km (15 miles) north of Lake City is the **Stephen Foster State Folk Culture Center** at White Springs—this is border country between the north-east and north-west of the state. On the banks of the Suwannee River, it is a memorial to the composer of "Old Folks at Home" and other ballads, though nobody even pretends that Foster actually set eyes on the river. The name just sounded right for the lyric. A carillon rings out Foster tunes, and animated dioramas provide information.

Another interesting area, an easy drive west of Gainesville, is Cedar Keys, a real bit of Old Florida. It is more easily accessible from Gainesville than from the populated areas of the north-west Gulf Coast, but as it comes within the north-west of the state it is dealt with in the next chapter.

Wilderness, Sun and a Whole Lot of Fun

An interesting mix, this area of Florida combines the southern grandeur of cities like Tallahassee with the undeveloped Florida landscape, which remains the undisputed territory of birds and beasts. Cedar Key is a glimpse of old Florida—quiet, hospitable and full of character. The focus of this area is Panama City, packed with restaurants, nightspots, sports and beaches. A great water park will thrill you and a reptile park will keep you mesmerized. The resorts of the Emerald Coast are growing more popular year by year.

Tallahassee

State capital since 1824, Tallahassee is the most southern in flavour of all Florida's cities. The Capitol Building, 22 storeys high, houses hundreds of government offices. There are viewing galleries from which debates can be watched when the Florida legislature is in session, and the public can get a splendid view of Tallahassee from the top of the building.

*B*uilt among the hills and forests of Northern Florida, Tallahassee, the state capital, retains a small-town ambience.

The city of Tallahassee, at the foot of the Appalachian Mountain range which extends to Virginia and Pennsylvania in the north, is built on seven hills. Although primarily an administrative centre, Tallahassee is well worth exploring by the Old Town Trolley, a replica of a turn-of-the-century tram. It goes along the restored Adams Street Commons and through the historic downtown area. The **Museum of Florida History** holds the 3-m (9-ft) skeleton of a mastodon—an elephant-like woolly mammoth. It was hauled out of Wakulla Springs in the 1930s. The museum also contains war relics and gold treasure from a wrecked Spanish galleon raised from the deep. Tallahassee **Junior Museum** has nature trails, an 1880s farm complex and

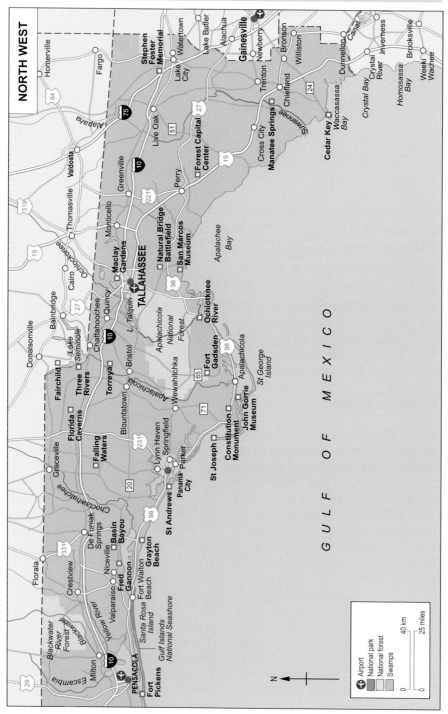

NORTH WEST

Homerville
Fargo
84
Alapaha
75
Valdosta
Thomasville
318
19
Donalsonville
Bainbridge
27
Cairo
Ochlockonee
Chattahoochee
Lake Seminole
Quincy
L. Talquin
TALLAHASSEE
10
Maclay Gardens
221
Monticello
Greenville
10
Live Oak
51
Perry
Forest Capital Center
27
Stephen Foster Memorial
Watertown
Lake City
Lake Butler
Alachua
Gainesville
Newberry
Bronson
Williston
24
Chiefland
Trenton
Cross City
Manatee Springs
Suwannee
Waccasassa Bay
Cedar Key
19
Dunnellon
Inverness
Brooksville
Weeki Wachee
Homosassa Bay
Crystal River
Crystal Bay

Natural Bridge Battlefield
San Marcos Museum
98
Apalachee Bay
Apalachicola National Forest
Ochlockonee River
Fort Gadsden
98
Apalachicola
St George Island
65
Wewahitchka
71
John Gorrie Museum
Constitution Monument
St Joseph
Parker
Springfield
Lynn Haven
231
Blountstown
Apalachicola
Torreya
Bristol
Three Rivers
Fairchild
Florida Caverns
20
Falling Waters
Graceville
Chipley
Choctawhatchee
Marianna
98
De Funiak Springs
Basin Bayou
Grayton Beach
St Andrews
Panama City
Niceville
Fort Walton Beach
Valparaiso
Fred Gannon
331
Crestview
Florala
Yellow River
Blackwater River Forest
Blackwater River
Milton
Escambia
29
PENSACOLA
Fort Pickens
10
Santa Rosa Island
Gulf Islands National Seashore

G U L F   O F   M E X I C O

N

✈ Airport
National park
National forest
Swamps

40 km
25 miles
0
0

other historic buildings, and animals, including the red wolf in its natural habitat. Perhaps at their most colourful in spring, with azaleas and camellias in bloom, the **Alfred B. McClay State Gardens** at Thomasville Road contain more than 200 plant species.

Tours and wine-tastings are offered daily at **Lafayette Vineyards and Winery**, east of Tallahassee. The winery, one of only six in the state, grows native Florida grapes.

West of the city is the **San Luis Archeological Site**, once the home of a 17th-century Spanish mission in a province of the Apalachee Indians. From February to May visitors can usually see archaeological excavations taking place. Free guided tours are available. North of Tallahassee, off US 27, 3.2 km (2 miles) north of Interstate 10, is **Lake Jackson Mounds State Archeological Site**, once the habitat of native Americans. Excavations indicate that the Indians were involved in a socioreligious complex flourishing around AD 1200. There are six earth temple mounds and one possible burial mound. Guided tours and interpretive programmes are given on request (tel: (904) 562-0042).

Parks and Museums

North-western Florida has about 30 state parks, recreation areas and historic sites, some of the more interesting being within a short drive of Tallahassee. In March each year a fierce

*M*ap of the region of North-west Florida.

Civil War battle of 1865 is re-enacted at the **Natural Bridge Battlefield State Historic Site**, 16 km (10 miles) southeast of the city. Confederate troops inflicted heavy casualties on the Union soldiers, making Tallahassee the only Confederate capital east of the Mississippi River that did not fall into Union hands. The full story of the battle makes exciting listening. The site, off SR 363, is extraordinarily peaceful, with picnic facilities.

A museum at the **San Marcos de Apalache State Historic Site** at St Marks (off SR 363) displays pottery and tools unearthed near the fort built at the confluence of the Wakulla and St Marks Rivers in the late 17th century.

In **Wakulla Springs State Park**, 22.5 km (14 miles) south of Tallahassee, observation cruises are available year-round, and when the water is clear tours by glass-bottom boats are operated. *Wakulla* is an Indian word for "mysterious waters", one of the mysteries being exactly how deep the spring is. No diver has ever reached the bottom. Every minute 1,818,000 litres (400,000 gallons) of water are pumped from the earth. The area is primitive—an ideal location for some of the Tarzan movies which were shot there in the 1930s. The springs and the Wakulla River provide a habitat for an abundance of waterfowl and other wildlife, and there are some magnificent tree specimens in the huge area of upland hardwoods. Visitors can stay at a comfortable 27-room Lodge and Conference Centre in the park. For reservations phone (904) 224-5950. The fee charged for entrance to the park is waived for people staying at the Lodge or eating in its restaurant.

Tallahassee sits at the eastern edge of the vast **Apalachicola Forest**—more than 200,000 hectares (500,000 acres) covering parts of four counties. There are many lakes and recreation areas with campsites. Some of the roads are no more than dirt tracks.

If you are interested in novelties, take US 319 for a look at **Carabelle**, on the Gulf Coast, about 64 km (40 miles) south-west of Tallahassee. The fishing and oyster-catching village and former lumber port of fewer than

2,000 people is a novelty in itself, because it has the smallest police station in the world. Hardly a special attraction? You'd be surprised. More than once vandals and villains have tossed the police station into the fields. The station is a converted glass-sided telephone booth, complete with a phone that only receives calls. The booth, installed in 1963, has featured on TV and radio shows in the United States. Soon people began to go to Carabelle to see this curiosity and take photographs of it. One of the Carabelle town councillors pandered to their interest by having the words: "World's Smallest Police Station" inscribed on the side. He also started making miniature wooden replicas of the police station, which sell for a few dollars each.

There are plenty of campsites to choose from, many, like this one in Northern Florida, in waterside locations.

Cedar Keys

You can drive eastwards for more than 249 km (150 miles) to Cedar Key and appreciate how much of Florida is still the territory of the birds and beasts, in which man has not yet made inroads to any effect. This great sweep of the Gulf of Mexico shoreline has remained in a primitive state for centuries, with shallow bays, marshland, inaccessible wetland and forest and countless rivers and creeks. At the southern end of north-west Florida are the Cedar Keys, a group of about 100 barrier islands appreciated by many different species of migratory and shore birds, and therefore by birdwatchers as well.

It should be mentioned that this area is more easily reached from Gainesville in north-east Florida, but then you would miss the wild and lonely drive from the Carabelle area.

Cedar Key (resident population about 1,000) is on Way Key, reached by a 4.8-km (3-mile) causeway. Or you can arrive by boat or private plane—there's a 740-m (2,400-ft) airstrip just outside the town. This really is Old Florida. People say it must be similar to Key West before Hemingway hit it in the 1930s. You can wander through the town in the middle of the road, moving to the sidewalk just now and again when a truck trundles slowly into view. There's a fishing pier where men and women angle for speckled trout, whiting, flounder and Spanish mackerel. Most of the people make their living from the sea, harvesting crabs, oysters, scallops and clams according to season, or deep-sea fishing for grouper, pompano and cobia. A few sponge divers go out, their wares stacked up in the local stores. Artists and writers have settled in the town, and visitors can see, and buy, the work of outstanding artists and craftsmen in galleries, shops and studios. Art and craft festivals are held in April and December. Even Cedar Key's roads are busier then, and in mid-October when the annual seafood festival is held.

The little town has no cinema, no hamburger stands, no shopping centre, a beach not much bigger than a handkerchief and two small museums which make for fascinating browsing. It has small self-catering complexes for visitors, and the first condominiums have gone up along the coast—not high-rise blocks, but mainly three-storey buildings with sloping roofs and wooden balconies.

Only about three blocks long, but full of character, is the historic core, where one of the properties is the Island Hotel. Cedar Key has a number of good places to eat, like the **Brown Pelican**, and **Seabreeze** on the Dock. But for a leisurely gourmet meal, where the chef is an original thinker as well as a superb cook, go to the **Island Hotel**, the only property in Cedar Key which is on the National Register of Historic Places. The ten bedrooms are all different, but all have ceiling fans and cascades of mosquito netting.

The hotel is built of hand-hewn cypress boards, crushed oyster shells and lime rock combined from the material used for facing the timber. The atmosphere is of the Old South. Healthy eating is the order of the day. The menu offers no red meat. Several vegetarian dishes are available, and seafood can be replaced by tofu in entrées. Appetizers may include seafood stuffed mushroom caps or artichoke and crab fingers. For the entrée, shrimps and scallops can be chosen poached, sautéed, baked or Cajun, with different accompaniments. Or how about delectable soft-shelled blue crab, sautéed and finished with sherry?

Island hopping, stopping to swim from beaches along the way, is one of the pastimes in Cedar Keys. Boats can be hired. Some of the islands are privately owned and the public can go only as far as the high-water mark. **Seahorse Key**, named because of its shape, is the one to avoid. It has a cemetery and a lighthouse, but special permission is required to visit them. It also has a wildlife refuge maintained by the University of Florida Marine Laboratory. No one is allowed there, partly because of the nesting birds and partly because of the large population of cottonmouths—a deadly species of snake.

Tourism to Cedar Key is growing. Accommodation, still modestly priced, should be booked in advance. The town faces the eternal dilemma. The economy needs the boost that tourism brings, but too much tourism could ruin the product. The area has a history of biting the hand that feeds it. After the Civil War, the islands grew rich from the manufacture of pencils, the cedars and cypresses providing the raw material. It takes a lot of pencils to use up all that timber, but there came a time when the Keys were almost denuded. The sea was then over-fished for a decade, so that source of income dried up for a while. In 1910 a new industry was set up—making brushes and brooms from palm fibre. That went well until there were hardly any palm trees left. Now second homes are going up, the palms are growing again, tourists arrive in manageable numbers and (with fingers crossed) the future looks good.

Back to Carabelle, and westward along the coast to **Apalachicola**, where the river of the same name meets the sea. The name is Indian for "friendly people". Apalachicola, almost completely surrounded by water, produces nearly 90 per cent of Florida's oyster harvest. On Sixth Street is the **John Gorrie State Museum**, and if ever a man deserved a memorial such as this it was John Gorrie. In the first half of the 19th century he was postmaster, city treasurer, town councillor and bank director in Apalachicola. These posts must have occupied much of his time, but his main job was physician, and his concern for his yellow fever patients in the 1840s led him to invent an ice-making machine, the forerunner of modern refrigeration and air-conditioning. A replica of the machine is in the museum.

Within the boundaries of the Apalachicola National Forest, about 32 km (20 miles) north of Apalachicola, off SR 65, is **Fort Gadsden State Historic Site**, a British base for the recruitment of Indians and runaway black slaves to fight US forces during the War of 1812. An attack on the fort lasted for five shots—the fifth landed in the fort's magazine. Only 30 of the 300 people inside survived.

Follow US 98 west to Port St Joe, to the historic site where Florida's first constitution was written in 1838. The Constitution Convention Hall no longer exists, and the former boom town established as a trading port in

1835 has virtually disappeared. Port St Joe grew rapidly to a population of 12,000, then a devastating outbreak of yellow fever killed most of the people and a severe hurricane put the final nail in the town's coffin. The **Constitution Convention State Museum**, built on the site of the old hall, commemorates the work of the 86 delegates who drafted Florida's first constitution and applied for admission to the Union.

Cabins, camping, a boat ramp and miles of natural beach are among the attributes of St Joseph Peninsula, reached by SR 30. More than 200 bird species have been seen there. Fishing and hiking are popular activities, and guided walks and campfire programmes are organized from time to time.

Panama City

Forty-eight kilometres (30 miles) or so up the coast and you're in the commercial port of Panama City, with Panama City Beach, the amusement and entertainment centre of north-west Florida, across the bay. This is the place for restaurants, nightspots, sports and beaches. The sand really is fine and glistening white—there are 43 km (27 miles) of it—and the sea really is emerald green. Of Florida's top ten attractions, two are in Panama City Beach. They are Gulf World, an underwater extravaganza in a tropical garden, and the double-bill Miracle Strip Amusement Park/Shipwreck Island.

Gulf World is on the long City Pier. Visitors walk through exotic gardens and see shows with sea lions, porpoises and parrots in the cast. Sharks and sea turtles can be seen in a walk-through tank. There are also scuba-diving shows. Penguins have their own special habitat at Gulf World.

The **Miracle Strip Amusement Park and Shipwreck Island** are on the Miracle Strip, the vibrant stretch of attractions open all hours—miniature golf, arcades, open-air cafés, souvenir shops and malls. Miniature golf comes in all sorts of guises, designed to bring more adventure into the game. Panama City Beach has six major courses, all well-lit for nocturnal sessions. One has an adjacent maze as big as a football pitch. A course may feature jungle adventures, pirate ships or treasure hunts. Waterfalls, dripping caves and lush vegetation are encountered. The park has a huge roller-coaster and dozens of other rides, including a log flume and Ferris wheel. It has arcade games, carnival pastimes, competitions and live entertainment. A 12-m (40-ft) sea dragon rocks passengers up to 21.5 m (70 ft) in the air.

Shipwreck Island's 2.4 hectares (6 acres) form a great water park. The rides and adventurous pursuits are amid rushing water. If you don't get drenched you're not getting your money's worth. You can get beneath the waterfalls of Skull Island, grab a rope and leap into water, slither down the 56 kph (35 mph) Speed Slide, take the White Water Tube Ride, jump the waves in the "Ocean Motion" attraction (a re-creation of the Gulf of Mexico), or go at a slower pace down the 490-m (1,600-ft) Lazy River. These two parks, near the County Pier, are open in the summer season from April to September.

Panama City Beach is where the action is in summer in the state's westernmost region of the Panhandle. Golf courses, amusement parks, souvenir centres, sports and entertainments draw the crowds.

The **Snake-a-Torium** is open all year, though hours of opening vary according to season. Guided tours of this zoo and reptile park are available. The occupants include rattlesnakes, coral snakes, cottonmouth mocassins and giant pythons. Visitors can watch venom being extracted from the snakes.

How man has struggled to live, work and play under water is told in the **Museum of Man and the Sea**, on US 98 near the intersection of SR 79. Artefacts ranging from 19th-century air-supply hand-pumps to the US Navy's Sea Lab I deep-diving saturation capsule are on show. The museum is owned by the Institute of Diving and managed by the Panama City Marine Institute.

Divers in the Panama City Beach area have opportunities to suit all levels of ability—shallow reef and wreck-diving in sheltered areas close to shore and deep-reef and wreck-diving offshore. (A two-hour drive away there's cave-diving at **Florida Caverns State Park**.) They explore a number of shipwrecks. One of them is the 143-m (465-ft) British tanker *Empire Mica*, torpedoed by a German U-boat on her maiden voyage in 1942. Another is the 50-m (160-ft) *Tarpon*, built in the late 1880s and one of the oldest wrecks on the coast. The *Tarpon* served as a shuttle between Mobile, in Alabama, and Carabelle until she sank in heavy seas in 1937.

Small children can play Indian games and explore a full-size tepee at **Bay County's Junior Museum**, feed poultry at a pioneer village and follow nature trails through environments common to the Florida Panhandle—a

288

hardwood swamp, a pine island and a hardwood hammock.

Waterfront sites on Grand Lagoon are popular with RV travellers and camping enthusiasts at **St Andrews State Park**, at the eastern tip of Panama City Beach. The park encompasses more than 400 hectares (1,000 acres). It has full camping facilities, rest rooms, showers, a store, picnic areas with tables and grills, a playground and two fishing piers. Well-marked nature trails cross the dunes and woodland. Boats can be rented in summer, and a ferry boat leaves for Shell Island from a public boat ramp at Grand Lagoon.

Shell Island, a barrier island so named because of the variety and abundance of shells washed ashore, is an uninhabited natural preserve which is expected to achieve state park status

The Snowbirds

Panama City and Panama City Beach are increasingly popular with the "Snowbirds" who drift south to avoid the harsh winters in their home states of the northern USA. Northern Florida's winters are mild, but not usually hot as they are in southern Florida. However, they are very pleasant most of the time. Cold snaps occur occasionally, but rarely last for more than 48 hours because of warm Gulf Stream breezes. The snowbirds find the north-west Gulf Coast ideal, which gives the region the advantage of being a year-round resort. Special events are arranged for the snowbirds, including bridge and golf tournaments with local residents. There's heat in the sun by February, and from March or April to early October the summer season is in full swing.

One of Florida's most fascinating state parks is underground in Florida Caverns State Park. A popular cave-diving venue, it has caves with curious crystalline formations.

before long. Several companies run boat trips there, some stopping for their passengers to feed dolphins.

Sport

Golf, as everywhere in Florida, is a passion in the Panama City area, and there are plenty of courses, some geared to the expert and some to the average player. The newest is the

Hombre, in Panama City Beach, which hosts the PGA Ben Hogan Classic in March. The most challenging championship-level course in the entire state, according to the publication *Golf Digest*, is called **Lagoon Legend**, at Marriott's Bay Point Yacht and Country Club. One green is completely surrounded by water and the course, open to the public, is said to suit the position player rather than the hard hitter. Special golf packages are available (tel: (904) 235-6966). Public courses which shouldn't overtax the average player include Signal Hill and the Holiday Golf and Tennis Club and Driving Range.

Many of the large hotels have lighted tennis courts, and there are condominium resorts like Sunbird, the Summerhouse, Sunnyside Beach and Tennis Resort, which all have tennis courts. Panama City Beach municipal authority's recreation department runs public courts.

Deep-sea fishing boat trips are available from several marinas from March to November, for trips lasting from 4 to 12 hours. The boats have a capacity for up to 70, but for comfort and space the operators limit groups to only 25 or 30. Charter boats, taking up to 20 passengers, also offering 4- to 12-hour trips, go after all the species sought by the deep-sea boats, cruising to the Gulf Stream for marlin and other game fish, and also troll for Spanish mackerel and bluefish inshore. These will operate overnight fishing trips if requested. Boats taking two or four passengers with a guide fish the backwaters of St Andrew's Bay for trout and Spanish mackerel, or troll inshore waters of the Gulf. Saltwater licences are not needed for fishing from a deep-sea charter or guide boat, or from a licensed fishing pier.

Sailing boats, windsurfers, surfboards and jet skis can be rented by the hour from outlets along the beach, and vessels of various dimensions, from canoes to yachts sleeping 10 people, can be rented or chartered from a wide choice of marinas. Parasailing, snorkelling and scuba-diving are popular pursuits.

More than a million dollars is won each week at the **Ebro Greyhound Track**, open every night except Sundays from late March to late September. For the rest of the year Satellite Wagering greyhound racing can be enjoyed by way of closed-circuit television from other tracks. Bets are placed through a system called Simulcast Wagering, and punters can have dinner while watching the races on TV. In the season they can watch the racing while dining in the Greyhound Room. Reservations are necessary (tel. (904) 234-3943).

Eating Out and Entertainment

There's a tremendous choice of fast-food outlets—sandwich shops, oyster bars, waffle houses, pizza places, coffee shops, burger bars, cafés offering omelettes or pancakes. Many of them serve breakfast. For an excellent meal to relax over, there's a wide selection of restaurants with the accent on seafood. **Capt. Anderson's Restaurant**, open daily except Sundays from 4 p.m., has won the Florida Golden Spoon award nine times in the past ten years, and is ranked among America's top 100 restaurants. Renowned for oysters on the half-shell are the two Billys—**Billy!** and **Billy!!**—both open

Shrimp boats at anchor after bringing home the catch. Some of the world's most succulent shrimps come out of the north-west region of the Gulf of Mexico.

from 11 a.m. to 9 p.m., serving lobster, crawfish, clams, crab, shrimp and a variety of fish, as well as oysters. A number of restaurants in the region do not stay open late by European standards.

Panama City Beach Indian Summer Seafood Festival is held in the second weekend of October, with a parade, music, entertainment, fireworks, arts and crafts and non-stop seafood.

Night-life can be a dinner cruise, a gospel music cruise, all-night dancing, a disco, a show, adult entertainment at one of the beach nightclubs, with patio bars and beach service, or maybe an evening's greyhound racing. The **Ocean Opry Nightspot** is known for the world-class stage shows which come with the barbecue dinner and the wholesome family comedy. The best of Nashville and Broadway is always offered, and the musical emphasis is on

country style, featuring swing, rock 'n' roll and gospel.

Some three dozen lounges, many of which offer disco music, show bands, cabarets, rock 'n' roll and dancing are another option for the evenings. Some, like **Pineapple Willie's**, on Beach Boulevard, provide all those goodies and the top 40 in the charts. There's dancing, a show band and the charts at **Good Time Charlie's** on Front Beach Road. These two lounges are among those that open year-round. Some restaurants, clubs and lounges open only in the summer season.

Miniature golf is a night and day option. Addicts play until the small hours.

Accommodation

Resort hotels, motels and condominiums in Panama City Beach have between them 16,000 units of accommodation. There are also bed and breakfast inns, beach properties specializing in family-style holiday homes, RV resorts, well-serviced campgrounds and docking facilities for those cruising the Intracoastal Waterway.

Emerald Coast

The area between Panama City and Pensacola is the **Emerald Coast**. Beach communities between the two cities, such as Seaside and Destin, are largely undiscovered, though beginning to attract tourists in increasing numbers. There are 18 beach communities in a 42-km (26-mile) stretch west of Panama City Beach, with a range of visitor accommodation and excellent seafood restaurants. A considerable amount of development has been going on in the coastal area of the Panhandle. **Fort Walton Beach**, at the western end of Choctawhatchee Bay, has established itself as a resort city over the past few years. Someone is sure to tell you that as recently as 1940 the black bears outnumbered the people. Today your chances of seeing a black bear in the wild in Fort Walton Beach is almost nil. The human population has grown to almost 20,000.

In the middle of the town is the **Indian Temple Mound Museum**, a

National Historic Landmark depicting more than 10,000 years of South-east Indians' life in the area. Through a series of exhibits, the Mound portrays the technological, spiritual and artistic achievements of seven pre-Columbian cultures.

At **The Gulfarium**, across the bridge on Okaloosa Island, trained porpoises, sea lions (and scuba-divers) present shows, and penguins, otters and seals can be seen. Okaloosa Island also has a 270-m (1200-ft) fishing pier.

The shoreline around Fort Walton Beach, its eastern neighbour, Destin, where fishing tournaments worth thousands of dollars in prize money are held, and around Niceville and Valparaiso, across Choctawhatchee Bay, is known as Florida's sandbox, with high sand dunes and waving sea oats. Eglin Field, the US Air Force base, said to be the world's largest military installation, is at Valparaiso. Just inside the east gate is the **US Air Force Armament Museum**, containing aircraft, guns, bombs, missiles and rockets dating from World War I to modern times. Exhibits include the enormous F105 Thunderchief and supersonic F104 Star Fighter.

For a contrast, call in at the **Historical Society Museum** in Valparaiso to see Indian stone tools dating back over 8,000 years.

The whisper of sea oats in the breeze is a familiar sound along the beaches of Northern Florida.

Pensacola

The westernmost city in Florida, close to the Alabama border, is Pensacola, variously known as Florida's First Place City, the Cradle of Naval Aviation, and the City of Five Flags—the last because Pensacola has been under French, British, Spanish, Confederacy and United States rule.

Pensacola Bay was settled even before St Augustine was founded. It is believed the natural deep-water harbour

Blue Angel Base

Pensacola Naval Air Station is an important training site for American Navy pilots. The Blue Angels, famous for their formation flying and daredevil displays, are based there. The history of Naval aviation from before World War I to the Space Age can be traced at the newly expanded National Museum of Naval Aviation. Replicas are displayed of the flying boat which made the first transatlantic air crossing and the Skylab Command Module which circled the earth for 28 days. Visitors can sample the cockpit simulator of a fighter jet aircraft or sit at the controls of a helicopter trainer.

was discovered by explorers about 1519. Spain claimed the spot along the uncharted Gulf Coast, but abandoned it in the mid-16th century when a hurricane devastated the colony.

Beaches at Navarre, Perdido Key and Pensacola Beach have the dazzling white sand which is almost pure quartz. Camping is available among the live oaks of Santa Rosa Island.

Causeways connect Pensacola with the **Gulf Islands National Seashore**, a 389-km^2 (150 square mile) strip of barrier islands and natural harbours. Forts which once formed a triangle to protect Pensacola Bay were built on the islands and the mainland. **Fort Pickens**, a pre-Civil War bastion on Santa Rosa Island, and **Fort Barrancas**, within the Naval Air Station's site on the mainland, can be visited by the public. The Apache Indian chief and medicine man, Geronimo, was held prisoner for a time in Fort Pickens.

Two areas of Pensacola are listed on the national register of historic places. One is the **North Hill Preservation District**, which developed as an upper-class neighbourhood between 1870 and 1930. It contains more than 500 homes originally occupied by prominent businessmen, politicians and professional people. The other is the **Seville Historic District**, where a variety of achitectural styles, including Creole and Victorian, dating from the 1780s, to the late 1800s, can be seen. Two hundred years of history, covering the French, Spanish and English ruling periods, are revealed through a number of museums at the **Historic Pensacola Village** at East Zaragoza Street. It is open every day except Sunday.

At Gulf Breeze, near Pensacola, is a zoo with more than 500 residents, the most famous being a huge 272-kg (600-lb) gorilla called Colossus. He has a female companion, Muke. There are extensive botanical gardens, and visitors can observe free-roaming creatures from the Safari Line train.

With a population of about 60,000, Pensacola has two galleries where the work of local and regional artists is displayed—the **Museum of Art**, and **Quayside**. It also has operatic, dance and classical music companies and the beautifully restored **Saenger Theater**. The **T.T. Wentworth Junior Florida State Museum** has, among its many exhibits, a Coca-Cola bottle collection.

A greyhound track is open every evening except Sundays all year. Matinee meetings are held on Friday, Saturday and Sunday. There are three major state recreation areas around Pensacola—Big Lagoon, Grayton Beach and Perdido Key. **Big Lagoon**, an important bird and animal habitat, has an observation tower with a view of the Gulf Islands National Seashore across the Intracoastal Waterway. Camping is available at Big Lagoon and Grayton Beach.

Eating Out and Entertainment

Pensacola has an amazing variety of restaurants and lounges. Chinese, Tex-Mex, Swiss, Italian, Irish, Deep South and cowboy style are just a few. Charbroiled catfish fillet is one of the specialties at **Cock of the Walk**, overlooking Escambia Bay. The **Angus**, serving prime rib, steaks and seafood on Scenic Highway, has a children's menu. Irish entertainment at **McGuire's Pub** on Gregory Street is said to be the best south of Boston. McGuire's is famous for its steaks, and has featured in *Florida Trend Magazine*'s top 100 restaurants. **Perry's Seafood House and Gazebo Bar** on Barrancas Avenue, a family restaurant in a pre-Civil War house, serves 60 fresh seafood items. You can choose from fried, broiled, blackened or grilled. **Shoney's**, on North Davis

Highway, opens at 6 a.m. for breakfast, closes at midnight on weekdays and at 3 a.m. on Fridays and Saturdays. **Umbrellas**, at the Pensacola Hilton, has a 6.4-m (21-ft) salad bar and you can concoct your own sundae.

Palm Court, at Cordova Mall, North Ninth Avenue, is a food emporium with 14 different eateries and four cinema screens. **Trader Jon's**, an historical aviation museum-cum-pub, with live entertainment, stays open until 3 a.m. and offers a $100,000 reward if you catch Trader with matching socks. Reggae dancing on the beach is popular at **Flounder's Chowder** and **Ale House** on Quietwater Beach Road at Pensacola Beach—another place that stays open until the small hours. At the **Melting Pot**, at East Garden Street, you get the Swiss Alpine experience, with melted cheese and melted chocolate specialities.

Five shows a week, on Thursdays, Fridays and Saturdays, featuring nationally known comedians, are presented at **Coconuts Comedy Club** at the Holiday Inn, University Mall, Plantation Road. **Sam's** is a two-screen video dance club on Mobile Highway, where a live disc jockey serves up the Top 40. Not to be confused with **Sammy's**, on East Gregory Street. Here they have continuous adult entertainment and the happy "hour" lasts from noon until 8 p.m.

Other Attractions

From Pensacola you can travel 306 km (190 miles) along Interstate 10 back to Tallahassee, seeing the sights along the way. Near **Milton**, about 24 km (15 miles) north of Pensacola—and also north of Interstate 10—is **Adventures Unlimited**, where, from Tomahawk Landing, you can splash along scenic rivers by canoe, kayak or inner tube. Hiking, nature walks and bike trails are other options. Cabins and campsites, tours and facilities for the handicapped are available. The property is open all year, closing at 5 p.m. in autumn and winter, 6 p.m. in spring and 7 p.m. in summer.

One of Florida's most notable geological features is about 160 km (100 miles) from Milton, just north of Chipley, off SR 77A. This is **Falling Waters State Recreation Area**, a 21-m (67-ft) waterfall. There's a 33-m (100-ft) deep, 6-m (20-ft) wide cylindrical pit into which the stream drops. It is not known where the water goes from there. Unique geological formations can be seen in the park, which has camping, nature trails and picnic areas.

More geology a few miles farther on at **Florida Caverns State Park**, just north of Marianna. Guided tours are given of the connected caves, which have limestone stalagmites, stalactites, columns, draperies and other weird formations composed of calcite. The calcite is dissolved from the limestone when the surface water, containing carbonic acid, percolates through the rock into the caves. Camping, fishing, canoeing, nature study, horse-riding and picnic sites are available in the park's 518 hectares (1,280 acres).

Marianna also has two properties allowing visitors to glimpse early 1900s life. The **1840 House Ltd.** and **The Gallery** are at West Lafayette Street. Antiques from various periods, Victorian architecture and original furnishings can be seen.

Something for Everyone

Florida offers an immense variety of activities to suit every kind of holiday-maker. Nature has provided the basic necessities—warm sun, lovely beaches, miles of rivers for paddling down and acres of unspoilt countryside. Man has added his own attractions—theme parks, water parks, zoos, beautiful towns with a host of museums and galleries, restaurants and nightlife. Whether you are looking for a holiday where the days and nights are a whirl of activity, or if you prefer to look around at a more sedate pace enjoying the natural beauty all around, you have come to the right place.

Things to Do

Visit Florida once and you're bound to want to return to see a whole lot more, because there's enough to sustain the interested tourist for a long time. The state's tourism success has been based on the concept of the family destination: the toddler plays contentedly on the sandy beaches and paddles in the warm, shallow water; the older brother or sister windsurfs or water-

*P*laying baseball in the park at Lake Wales in Central Florida.

skis and enjoys the discos, the amusement centres, the tennis, and the hamburger bars. The children are not going to return to school and tell their friends they had to go to boring old Florida.

For the teens and twenties, and the middle aged onwards, there are wonderful things to do. Try deep-sea fishing. Go canoeing in wilderness areas. Meet manatees (sea cows). See Tiffany glass in a gallery. Sample Key lime pie. Discover Dali's genius. Spend a day on a cruise ship with a casino. Marvel at Edison's inventiveness. Become an obsessive shell collector. Take a hot-air balloon trip. Browse around a flea market. See racehorses in training. Tour a hospital for injured seabirds. And don't miss the factory outlets where you can find shelves full of textiles, ceramics, household goods, sportswear and countless other items offered direct to the public at bargain prices.

When your feet ache, make for a beach or lakeside, cool off and take it easy for an hour or two.

These are just a few ideas. Florida is full of opportunities for spending your free time, whether you want organized entertainment or to enjoy what nature has provided.

Wildlife

Florida is very conscious and protective of its wildlife. There are parks and refuges where many species of animal and bird can be seen. Hire a canoe for a wilderness river trip and you're almost certain to see alligators, the occasional turtle snoozing on the trunk of a fallen tree, and perhaps a group of white-tail deer and their young.

In the heat of the day, alligators are usually too lethargic to be a problem. Nevertheless they should be treated with respect, and should never be fed. A semi-tame 'gator is a dangerous one. There are alligator farms open to the public, but a good way of seeing wild ones in their natural habitat is from the safety of your car. One place to do this is in the J.N. "Ding" Darling National Wildlife Refuge on the Lee Island Coast.

An alligator poses sleepily in the sunshine at Silver Springs.

300

You can park your car and follow the boardwalk among the trees and mangroves and see more wildlife. You're sure to spot an anhinga hanging out to dry on a bush. These lovely birds cannot fly until their wings have dried off, so between fishing sorties they are forced to spread out their wings in the sunshine, like broken umbrellas.

As everywhere in the world, it is best to watch for wildlife early and late in the day, when more species are hunting for food.

Florida is rich in state and national parks where indigenous birds, animals and flora can be seen. One of the best known is Merritt Island National Wildlife Refuge, a 64-km (40-mile) long haven for some 300 bird species—right next door to the Kennedy Space Center at Cape Canaveral.

The Countryside

While the climate and the relaxed lifestyle of Florida appeal to those who move there for their retirement, the lack of hills is probably an added attraction for them. The flatness would probably be more noticeable if it were not for the billboards that dominate the edges of the highways, especially at the approach to cities and major tourism spots.

People may complain about the proliferation of billboards, but these do provide a point of focus in areas where the scenery is, to be candid, featureless.

Regattas draw the crowds in many parts of the state.

Events and Festivals

Most non-North Americans visiting Florida for the first time are families going to experience the organized attractions and to enjoy the climate. Others have a particular sporting or cultural interest that introduces them to the Sunshine State. At any given time there's a special event or festival going on somewhere.

International speedway races are held at Daytona Beach. Hot-air balloon events, art and craft fairs, jazz and folk festivals, golf and tennis tournaments and regattas draw the crowds in various parts of the state. You may come across a kite festival, a carillon festival, a seafood celebration or a bluegrass festival. Church Street Station, which is a fun place for shopping, eating and entertainment in Orlando, celebrates special dates like Halloween with a street party, and the New Year's Eve Bash is an event not to miss if you're in town at the time. At Disney World's Pleasure Island you can celebrate it every night of the year.

At Tarpon Springs, where Greek immigrant families perpetuate the sponge industry, there's an annual fiesta in November at the Sponge Exchange. Greeks in national dress serve ethnic food, display their arts and crafts and entertain with singing and dancing. Epiphany (6 January) is celebrated with pageantry and symbolism, young men diving for the cross from the local cathedral.

For a week in early February, Tampa's peace is disturbed by a shipload of pirates parading through the streets and contributing much fun and activity. This is the Gasparella Pirate Invasion Festival, dating back to 1904 and commemorating a fierce and entirely fictitious pirate called José Gaspar.

Fifty kilometres (30 miles) or so east of Tampa is Plant City, whose population of about 30,000 soars to 250,000 when the Strawberry Fair is held in February. Strawberry teas with strawberry shortcake and other delicacies are served, a local beauty is crowned Strawberry Queen and leads the Grand Parade. Another pretty girl is destined, slightly less flatteringly, to become Miss Speckled Perch, reigning alongside the chosen Seminole Indian Princess at the annual Okeechobee Speckled Perch Festival in March. A fishing contest, fish fry and bluegrass music are features of the event.

Also celebrating one of Florida's food specialities is the Swamp Cabbage Festival at Labelle, close to the north-west tip of the Everglades. This pays tribute to the cabbage palm, the state tree of Florida. It provides a heart which is very good to eat. Clog dancing, demonstrations of arts and crafts, a parade and sampling of the delicacy take place during a February weekend.

The English composer Frederick Delius, who died in 1934, has a festival dedicated to him in Jacksonville, in north-eastern Florida. He grew oranges beside the St Johns River for a couple of years, though not with outstanding success. Much of his music was inspired by the songs of the Black labourers.

Top Olympic riders compete in the Jacksonville Classic in spring.

People tend not to regard Florida as a cowboy state. In fact it is one of the leading beef-producing states in the

USA, and rodeos are held in a number of locations. The All-Florida Championship Event in March draws top riders from all over the country, demonstrating their bareback riding and calf-roping skills. This rodeo, the oldest in the state, has been held for more than 60 years. It takes place in Arcadia, some 80 km (50 miles) north of Fort Myers.

The Scots have spread themselves about the world, retaining much of their heritage. In Dunedin, just north of Clearwater, they have their Highland Games in spring—tug o' war, tossing the sheaf, dancing and bagpiping.

In Key West, where Ernest Hemingway wrote some of his most famous novels, there is an annual Hemingway look-alike contest, part of a week-long festival commemorating the writer, whose former home is open daily to the public.

Boat shows, surfing championships, fishing tournaments and all sorts of

As a leading beef producer, Florida is unexpectedly a cowboy state, and rodeos take place in a number of locations.

fairs, festivals, re-enactments and special events are organized throughout the year. Some are small, parochial celebrations. Others are major fund-raising extravaganzas, and the visiting tourist is always welcome.

Florida has well over a dozen public holidays in the year. Apart from obvious ones like Christmas Day, Independence Day and Thanksgiving Day, they have the day off for a succession of birthdays. These include Martin Luther King Junior's (15 January), Abraham Lincoln's (12 February) and Confederate President Jefferson Davis's (3 June). Shrove Tuesday is a recognized state holiday in some, mainly north-western, counties.

Florida has its flamboyantly scenic regions but they're not usually visible from the turnpikes and expressways, which tend to be wide, straight and terminally dull. Like motorways and autobahns, they provide a fast means of travelling between two places, but it is not possible to expect splendour all the way.

Ribbon development is a feature that goes on for kilometres outside some cities, and this, too, can be tedious. But you're never far from somewhere really pleasant and relaxing, like a place to swim or sunbathe. Even in the centre of the state, the nearest tidal water is only 100 km (60 miles) away.

Sport

Much space is devoted across the state to golf-courses, hiking trails, jogging tracks, tennis courts, harness racing tracks, greyhound racing and speedway racing, among many other outdoor activities. Windsurfing, water-skiing, sailing, scuba-diving, snorkelling and all the watersports are well catered for. At St Petersburg is the multi-purpose Florida Suncoast Dome, a stadium seating up to 50,000 people. Baseball, American football, basketball, concerts, exhibitions and conventions are held in the magnificent $110-million stadium, which opened in 1990.

There are three sports on which you can bet—horse-racing, greyhound racing and the fast and exciting game of jai alai. Jai alai is the ball and basket game which originated in the Basque regions of Spain and France. Its major centres are Miami and Fort Lauderdale, but active leagues are to be found throughout the state. Amateur soccer is popular in south-east Florida, where there are many schoolboy teams, and it is possible to find the odd cricket match being played from time to time.

Language Guide

It doesn't take long on a first visit by English speakers to realize the truth in that old saying about Britain and the United States being two nations divided by a common language. The two peoples do use English in different ways, and it is more noticeable in the South than in any other region of the US. "Admire" is a word used in a delightfully old-fashioned way in some rural areas—for instance, "I'd admire to buy you a drink." Or, "I'd admire to have you visit my home."

Restaurants and food shops are the places where British visitors are likely to notice the main differences in nomenclature. Jelly, for example, is jam. It is usually served with peanut butter and biscuits. American biscuits are like British scones. What the British call biscuits are cookies to a citizen of the USA.

Zucchini is courgette. Ask for eggplant and you will get aubergine. There is no equivalent to grits, or hominy grits, a dish as evocative of the Deep South as the chip butty is of northern England. Grits are white, mushy and coarse, and the ingredient is husked maize, usually served at breakfast.

Here is a short glossary of other useful words:

British	American

Food

British	American
Chips	French fries
Grill	Broil
Pancakes	Crepes
Runner beans	String beans
Salad cream	Mayonnaise
Swede	Rutabaga
Tomato sauce	Ketchup

Driving

British	American
Car bonnet	Hood
Car boot	Trunk
Car park	Parking lot
Car park, multi-storey	Parking garage
Dual carriageway	Divided highway
Give way	Yield
Lay-by	Rest area
Lorry	Truck
Pavement	Sidewalk
Petrol	Gasoline ("gas")
Windscreen	Windshield

Clothing

British	American
Plimsolls, trainers	Sneakers
Pullover, cardigan	Sweater
Trousers	Pants
Waistcoat	Vest

Miscellaneous

British	American
Autumn	Fall
Biro	Ballpoint
Chemist	Drugstore
Cheque	Check
Cloakroom	Washroom
Cotton wool	Cotton balls
Directory enquiries	Directory assistance
Face flannel	Washcloth
Football	Soccer
Hair slide	Barette
Head porter	Superintendent of service
Perspex	Lucite
Queue	Line
Restaurant bill	Check
Rubber	Eraser
Spectacles	Eyeglasses
Toilet	Rest room
Torch	Flashlight
Transfer charge call	Collect call

A Selection of Places that are Good at the Price

Hotels

The following selection of accommodation and restaurants throughout Florida provides a wide variety of locations, prices and facilities within towns and cities, listed in alphabetical order.

Key
Price per room.
||| Over $100;
|| $50 to $100;
| Less than $50.

Boca Raton

Boca Raton Resort and Club |||
501 East Camino Real,
Boca Raton FL 33432-6127
Tel: (407) 395-3000
Posh and big (988 rooms, 39 suites). Ten lounges, seven restaurants. Four pools, two golf courses, 29 tennis courts.

Boca Raton Marriott ||
Cracker Center
5150 Town Center Circle,
Boca Raton FL 33486
Tel: (407) 392-4600
Downtown location with golf, tennis, fishing nearby; 256 rooms, 16 suites.

Radisson Suites Hotel ||
7920 Glades Road, Boca Raton
FL 33434, Tel: (407) 483-3600
Self-catering and restaurant facilities; 200 suites, pool, three lounges.

Sheraton of Boca Raton ||
2000 NW 19th Street,
Boca Raton FL 33431
Tel: (407) 368-5252
188 rooms, five suites. Restaurant, lounge, pool, two tennis courts.

Clearwater

Belleview Mido Hotel ||||
25 Belleview Boulevard,
Clearwater FL 34625
Tel: (813) 442-6171
Top accommodation. Claimed to be the world's largest occupied wooden structure. Classic hotel built by railroad baron Henry Plant.

Clearwater Beach Hotel ||
500 Mandalay Avenue,
Clearwater Beach FL 34630
Tel: (813) 4412425
Elegant, 160-room property right on the beach. The main building is in classic Deep South style.

Sheraton Sand Key Resort ||
1160 Gulf Boulevard, Clearwater
Beach FL 34630
Tel: (813) 595-1611
Nearly 400 rooms; tennis, pool, and a 3-hectare (7-acre) beach of fine white sand.

Flaming Motel Apartments |
450 North Gulf Boulevard,
Clearwater Beach FL 34630
Tel: (813) 441-8019
Twelve efficiencies, 24 one-bedroom suites on private beach.

Cocoa Beach

Holiday Inn |||
1300 North Atlantic Avenue,
Cocoa Beach FL 32931
Tel: (305) 783-2271
Oceanfront hotel with 500 rooms, observation deck, restaurant and lounge.

Best Western Executive Motel ||
4001 North Atlantic Avenue,
Cocoa Beach FL 32931
Tel: (305) 784-1260
Olympic-size pool and Atlantic Ocean swimming. Children's playground, barbecue grills.

Polaris Beach Resort Inn ||
5600 North Atlantic Avenue,
Cocoa Beach FL 32931
Tel: (305) 783-7621
Twenty minutes' drive from Kennedy Space Center and handy for Port Canaveral; 120 rooms and fully-equipped efficiencies.

Econolodge Motel |
5500 North Atlantic Avenue,
Cocoa Beach FL 32931
Tel: (305) 784-2550
Self-catering rooms; handy for pier and beach.

Sea Missile Motel |
4292 North Atlantic Avenue,
Cocoa Beach FL 32931
Tel: (305) 783-6880
Self-catering rooms and apartments two blocks from the sea and within walking distance of shops and restaurants. Pool.

Silver Sands Motel |
225 North Atlantic Avenue,
Cocoa Beach FL 32931
Tel: (305) 783-2415

Daytona Beach

Acapulco Inn ||||
2505 South Atlantic Avenue,
Daytona Beach Shores FL 32818
Tel: (904) 761-2210
Deluxe resort with 130 rooms, each equipped with refrigerators and kitchenettes. Oceanfront restaurant.

Daytona Beach Hilton ||||
2637 South Atlantic Avenue,
Daytona Beach Shores FL 32118
Tel: (904) 767-8200
Distinguished 215-room hotel which has consistently been given four-diamond status by the American Automobile Association. Excellent amenities include rooftop restaurant. Complimentary beach bicycles.

Daytona Beach Marriott |||
100 North Atlantic Avenue,
Daytona Beach FL 32118
Tel: (904) 254-8200
$47 million hotel built in 1989. Directly opposite the Ocean Center and right on the beach. Swimming pool, three restaurants, beach bar.

Best Western Mayan Inn ||
103 South Ocean Avenue,
Daytona Beach FL 32118
Tel: (904) 252-0584
Oceanfront location, convenient for Boardwalk and Ocean Center. Rooms, efficiencies and suites.

Clarendon Plaza ||
600 North Atlantic Avenue,
Daytona Beach, FL 32118
Tel (904) 255-4471
Oceanfront resort within walking distance of Oceanfront Center and shops; 323 rooms, including suites and efficiencies.

Coral Beach Motel ||
711, South Atlantic Avenue,
Ormond Beach FL 32174
Tel: (904) 677-4712
High-rise resort opened 1990, featuring oceanfront rooms and two-bedroom apartments with efficiencies. Restaurants and shopping nearby.

Buccaneer Motel |
2301 North Atlantic Avenue,
Daytona Beach FL 32118
Tel: (904) 253-9678
Small motel with barbecue and picnic area within walking distance of shops.

Cove Motel |
1306 North Atlantic Avenue,
Daytona Beach FL 32118
Tel: (904) 252-3678
Convenient, quiet location. Owner-operated, with 40 oceanfront rooms, suites and efficiencies.

El Caribe Motel |
2125 South Atlantic Avenue,
Daytona Beach FL 32118
Tel: (904) 252-1558
Family-owned and operated oceanfront motel with 120 rooms, including suites and efficiencies. Free continental breakfast.

Fort Lauderdale

Palm-Aire Spa Resort and Country Club |||
2501 Palm-Aire Drive North,
Pompano Beach FL 33069
Tel: (305) 968-2705
191 rooms, 21 suites, three restaurants and two lounges; five golf courses, 37 all-weather tennis courts, three pools, world-class spa and private beach.

Pier 66 Resort and Marina |||
2301 SE 17th Street, Fort
Lauderdale FL 33316
Tel: (305) 525-6666
Popular venue for viewing millionaires' yachts; 380 rooms, four restaurants and lounges, two pools and tennis courts.

Sheraton Bonaventure Resort and Spa |||
250 Racquet Club Road, Fort
Lauderdale FL 33326
Tel: (305) 389-3300
504 rooms, four restaurants, two lounges. Two 18-hole golf courses, 23 tennis courts; racquetball, squash, bowling, roller skating. World-class spa.

Bahia Mar Resort and Yachting Center ||
801 Seabreeze Boulevard, Fort
Lauderdale FL 33316
Tel: (305) 764-2233
Facilities at this 298-room resort hotel include a yachting school, boat and yacht charters, scuba-diving and a dive shop.

Holiday Inn Fort Lauderdale Beach Galleria ||
999 N. Atlantic Boulevard, Fort
Lauderdale FL 33304
Tel: (305) 563-5061
236 rooms, four suites. Restaurant, lounge, pool. Most watersport rentals available.

Inverary Resort ||
3601 Inverary Road, Fort
Lauderdale FL 33319
Tel: (305) 485-0500
194 rooms, four suites, two restaurants, lounge. Three pools, 36-hole championship golf course, 30 tennis courts, croquet.

Days Inn Boca Deerfield |
1250 West Hillsboro Boulevard,
Deerfield Beach FL 33442
Tel: (305) 427-2200
Expressway location; 277 rooms, restaurant, pool.

Holiday Inn Fort Lauderdale Airport ||
2275 State Road 84, Fort
Lauderdale FL 33312
Tel: (305) 584-4000
300 rooms, six suites, restaurant, three lounges, two pools and tennis courts.

Rolling Hills Circle ||
Fort Lauderdale 33328
Tel: (305) 475-0400
Lounge, pool, two restaurants; 27-hole championship golf course, four tennis courts.

Fort Myers

Sonesta Sanibel Harbor Resort and Spa ||
17260 Harbor Point Drive, Fort
Myers, FL 33908
Tel: (813) 466-4000
240 rooms. 47 suites, 100 holiday condominiums. Four restaurants and pools, raquetball, tennis centre, health and fitness spa.

Days Inn South |
11435 Cleveland Avenue, Fort
Myers FL 33907
Tel: (813) 936 1311
122 clean and comfortable rooms 8 km (5 miles) from Southwest Florida Regional Airport.

Islamorada

Cheeca Lodge |||
PO Box 527, Islamorada FL
33036 MM 82
Tel: (305) 664-4651
Oceanfront resort with 200 rooms. Beach, 155-m (500-ft) fishing pier, golf, tennis, pool and salt water lagoon. Boat rentals.

Chesapeake of Whale Harbor |||
PO Box 909, Islamorada
FL 33036 MM 83.5
Tel: (305) 664-4662
Upscale motel units and self-catering villas in an oceanside, sandy beachfront setting with 2.5 hectares (6 acres) of landscaped grounds.

Holiday Isle Resort |||
84001 Overseas Highway,
Islamorada FL 33036 MM 84
Tel: (305) 664-2321
Oceanside complex of rooms, efficiencies and suites (70 in all). Continuous free entertainment, rooftop and oceanside restaurants, white sand beach.

HOTELS

Breezy Palms Resort
PO Box 767, Islamorada
Fl 33036 MM 80
Tel: (305) 664-2361
Motel rooms, efficiencies, one- and two-bedroom apartments, Pool, barbecues, white sandy beach.

Harbor Lights Motel
84951 Overseas Highway,
Islamorada FL 33036 MM 85
Tel: (305) 664-2321
Next to Whale Harbor Marina; 33 self-catering units. Freshwater pool and sandy beach. Use of Holiday Isle facilities (see above).

La Siesta Resort
PO Box 573H, Islamorada
FL 33036 MM 80.5
Tel: (305) 664-2132
Newlyrefurbished one-, two- and three-bedroom self-catering apartments in 2.5-hectare (6-acre) setting with 154 m (500 ft) of beach. Barbecue grills, games, lighted pier for night fishing.

Golden Key Motel
PO Box 710, Islamorada
FL 33036 MM 81.5
Tel: (305) 664-0418
Family operated motel with rooms and efficiencies on secluded bayside beach. Barbecue grills.

The Islander Resort
PO Box 766, Islamorada
FL 33036 MM 81.5
Tel: (305) 664-2031
More than 100 rooms on oceanside, Large beach, fishing pier.

Sands of Islamorada
80051 Overseas Highway,
Islamorada FL 33036 MM 80
Tel: (305) 664-2791
Small motel in serene oceanfront setting. Freshwater pool, pier, barbecues.

Jacksonville

Holiday Inn Oceanfront
1617 N. First Street, Jacksonville
FL 3225
Tel: (904) 241-4321
150 rooms, nine suites. Pool, lighted tennis courts. Country club. Free in-room movies.

Omni Jacksonville Hotel
245 Water Street, Jacksonville
Tel: (904) 355-6664
Downtown location; 354 rooms, four suites. Restaurant, lounge, pool.

Park Suites Jacksonville
9300 Baymeadows Road,
Jacksonville FL 32256
Tel: (904) 731-3555
210 suites, two restaurants, lounge, pool; free in-room movies and complimentary full buffet breakfast.

Ramada Resort
1201 N. first Street, Jacksonville
Beach FL 32250
Tel: (904) 241-5333
Oceanfront location; 140 rooms, seven suites, restaurant and lounge. Fishing, volleyball, free in-room movies.

The Keys

Sugar Loaf Lodge
PO Box 148S, Sugarloaf Key
FL 33044. MM 17
Tel: (305) 745-3211
Complete resort and marina on 48.5 hectares (120 acres). Pool, tennis, fising, mini-golf. Restaurant and grocery store.

Old Wooden Bridge Fising Camp
PO Box 810, Big Pine Key
FL 33043 MM 31.5
Tel: (305) 872-2241
Modern cottages off the beaten track. Paradise for anglers.

Parmer's Place
PO Box 445H, Big Pine Key
FL 33043
Actually on Little Torch Key at MM 28.5, just 1 km (½ mile) from US1. Quiet and small complex of waterfront cottages and apartments with good fishing, diving, boating.

Key Largo

Holiday Inn Key Largo
99701 Overseas Highway, Key
Largo FL 33037 MM 100
Tel: (305) 451-2121
Home of Humphrey Bogart's African Queen; 132 rooms, some non-smoking. Tennis, diving, fishing, boat rentals and entertainments lounge.

Marina Del Mar
PO Box 1050, Key Largo
FL 33037. MM 100
Tel: (305) 451-4107
Tastefully appointed hotel with 76 waterfront rooms and suites overlooking John Pennekamp Park and the ocean. Large pool, sundeck, tennis, marina, dive centre. Adjacent

54-room resort has similar amenities overlooking Florida Bay.

Sheraton Key Largo
97000 Overseas Highway, Key
Largo FL 33037. MM 97
Tel: (305) 852-5553
Two hundred-room resort overlooking Florida Bay. Two restaurants, two pools, tennis, nature trail, marina and private beach.

Anchorage Resort
PO Box 272-A, Key Largo
FL 33037. MM 107.5
Tel: (305) 451-0500
Twenty eight rooms with balconies overlooking Florida Bay. Tennis, fishing pier, boat rentals.

Best Western Suites
201 Ocean Drive, Key Largo
FL 33037. MM 100
Tel: (305) 451-5081
Forty spacious suites, each on two floors with kitchens and two bathrooms. Dive packages. Small pool, launderette, free continental breakfast.

Howard Johnson Resort
PO Box 1024, Key Largo,
FL 33037. MM 102
Tel: (305) 451-0500
One hundred spacious rooms, each with two double beds. Sandy beach, pool. Dive packages.

Gilbert's Resort and Marina
107900 Overseas Highway, Key
Largo FL 33037. MM 107.5
Tel: (305) 451-1133
Most of the 36 rooms overlook Florida Bay. Pool, jet ski and boat rentals; dive shop.

Rock Reef Resort
97850 Overseas Highway, Key
Largo FL 33037. MM 98
Tel: (305) 852-2401
Twenty one cottages in a tropical garden setting overlooking the bay. Tidal pool, sandy beach and picnic facilities.

Seafarer Motel
PO Box 185, Key Largo
FL 33037. MM 97.8
Tel: (305) 852-5349
Fourteen units—apartments, efficiencies and rooms—on the bayside. Private sandy beach, barbecue grills, launderette.

309

Key West

Holiday Inn La Concha Resort ‖‖‖
430 Duval Street, Key West
FL 33040
Tel: (305) 296-2991
Listed in thee US National Register of Historic Places, with 160 guest rooms decorated in 1920s style. Within walking distance of everything to see and do in Old Town.

Marriott's Casa Marina ‖‖‖
1500 Reynolds Street,
Key West FL 33040
Tel: (305) 296-1919
The end of the line for railroad baron Henry Flagler and the last work in grandeur and resort amenities for anyone else. Overlooking the ocean, but well away from the action end of Old Town.

Pier House ‖‖‖
1 Duval Street,
Key West FL 33040
Tel: (305) 296-4600
Just around the corner from Old Town shops, bars, restaurants, Mallory Square.

Best Western Hibiscus Motel ‖‖
1313 Simonton Street,
Key West FL 33040
Tel: (305) 296-6711
Two queen-size beds and refrigerators in each of 61 spacious rooms. Pool. Continental breakfast included.

Days Inn Key West ‖‖
3552 North Roosevelt Boulevard
Key West FL 33040
Tel: (305) 294-3742
Reached soon after arriving on the island by car; 134 rooms, including 18 suites wih full kitchen facilities. Pool.

Southernmost Motel ‖‖
1319 Duval Street,
Key West FL 33040
Tel: (305) 296-6577
One block from beach and Southernmost Point; 127 rooms, pool. Shops, restaurants, nightlife within walking distance.

Red Rooster Inn ‖
709 Truman Avenue,
Key West FL 33040
Tel: (305) 296-6558
Eighteen comfortable rooms in traditional Key West building, handy for downtown.

Santa Maria Motel ‖
1401 Simonton Street,
Key West FL 33040
Tel: (305) 296-5678
Attractively furnished rooms, efficiencies and apartments, with balconies overlooking pool. Close to City Beach.

Southern Cross Hotel ‖
326 Duval Street, Key West
33040
Tel: (305) 294-3200
The oldest hotel in Key West; 22 rooms in the heart of Old Town.

Guest Houses

Key West is one of the few places in Florida with an extensive choice of bed and breakfast accommodation. standards range from "good" to "luxury".

Authors ‖
725 White Street, Key West
FL 33040
Tel: (305) 294-7381.

Blue Parrot Inn ‖
916 Elizabeth Street,
Key West FL 33040
Tel: (305) 296-0033
Old-fashioned guest house (1864, but renovated 1989) with eight rooms. Continental breakfast at poolside.

Curry Mansion Inn ‖
511 Caroline Street,
Key West FL 33040
Tel: (305) 294-5349
Very upscale accommodation in delightful mansion, formerly home of Florida's first millionaire. Continental breakfast. Complimentary cocktail party daily.

Popular House ‖
415 William Street,
Key West FL 33040
Tel: (305) 296-7274
Casual atmosphere in gingerbread house within walking distance of downtown and Key West Bight.

Whispers ‖
409 William Street,
Key West 33040
Tel: (305) 294-5969
Homely historic building in charming Old Town street. Very full breakfast. Marriages performed!

Kissimmee

Comfort Suites ‖‖
4018 Vine Street,
Kissimmee FL 32741
Tel: (407) 870-2000
Mediterranean-style, all-suites motel fifteen minutes by car from WDW, ten minutes from Fort Liberty and WaterMania.

Econolodge Hawaiian Resort ‖‖
7514 W Irlo Bronson Memorial
Highway, Kissimmee FL 32741
Tel: (407) 396-2000
Good facilities in a South Pacific setting, ten minutes by car from WDW.

Hilton Inn Gateway ‖‖
7470 W. Highway,
Kissimmee FL 32741
Tel (407) 396-4400
One mile (1.6 km) from Walt Disney World Magic Kingdom and EPCOT, and 4.8 km (3 miles) from Disney-MGM Studios Theme Park. Two pools, miniature golf, cosy piano bar.

Larsons Lodge ‖‖
2009 W. Vine Street,
Kissimmee FL 34741
Tel: (407) 846-2713
Self-catering "efficiencies" in 200 rooms, just ten minutes by car from WDW.

Lake Buena Vista

Buena Vista Palace ‖‖‖
PO Box 22026, Lake Buena Vista
FL 32830-2206
Tel: (407) 827-2727
Just around the corner from Walt Disney World Village, the hotel has 841 rooms and 45 suites, with nine restaurants and lounges and full recreational amenities, including health club. Free shuttle to WDW attractions.

Vistana Resort ‖‖‖
PO Box 22051, Lake Buena Vista
FL 32830
Tel: (407) 239-3100
More than 500 spacious two-bedroom, two-bathroom villas on a 20- hectare (50-acre) site on SR 535, less than 8 km (5 miles) from the Magic Kingdom and the Epcot Center.

Howard Johnson Park
Square Inn
8501 Palm Parkway,
Lake Buena Vista FL 32830
Tel: (407) 239-6900
As homely an atmosphere as you will find in a place with 300 guest rooms—each with two double beds. Five minutes from WDW Village.

Grosvenor Resort
1850 Hotel Plaza Boulevard
Lake Buena Vista FL 32830
Tel: (407) 828-4444
An elegant hotel just a five-minute walk from WDW Village. Free shuttle to Disney attractions.

The Lee Island Coast
South Seas Plantation
Resort and Yacht Harbor
PO Box 194, Captiva Island
FL 33924,
Tel: (813) 472-5111
Tranquil atmosphere; 106 rooms, 550 suites. Extensive sporting and marina facilities, including water-skiing and 27-holes golf. Numerous pools. German, French, Italian and Spanish spoken.

Sundial Beach and
Tennis Resort
1451 Middle Gulf Drive,
Sanibel Island, FL 33957
Tel: (813) 472-4151
Waterfront location; 240 suites, four restaurants; 13 tennis courts, 18-hole championship golf-course, all watersports. Five pools.

Sanibel Island Hilton
937 Gulf Drive, Sanibel Island
FL 33957
Tel: (813) 472-3181
48 rooms, 52 suites. Restaurant, pool, tennis, barbecue grills. Good waterfront position.

'Tween Waters Inn
PO Box 249, Captiva Island
FL 33924
Tel: (813) 472-5161
Good food, casual atmosphere. Accommodation includes rooms, self catering rooms and apartments and cottages with or without kitchens. Boat trips and rentals, fishing.

Madeira Beach
Holiday Inn
15208 Gulf Boulevard,
Madeira Beach FL 33708
Tel: (813) 392-2275

Close to John's Pass Village, with 147 rooms, restaurant and lounge. Private beach.

Surfs Inn
14010 Gulf Boulevard,
Madeira Beach FL 33708
Tel: (813) 393-4609
Eight motel rooms and 17 efficiency apartments all facing the Gulf of Mexico.

Marathon
Banana Bay Resort
4590 Overseas Highway,
Marathon FL 33050 MM 49.5
Tel: (305) 743-3500
Sixty rooms in secluded tropical grounds; rear overlooks bayside charter fishing harbour. Pool, tennis, charter fishing, diving. Excellent restaurant.

Faro Blanco Marine Resort
1996 Overseas Highway,
Marathon FL 33050 MM 48
Tel: (305) 743-9018.
Something for everyone: garden cottages, luxury apartments, floating state rooms. Four restaurants, three lounges and lots of sporting opportunities.

Hawk's Cay Resort
Duck Key FL 33050 MM 61
Tel (305) 743-7000
West Indies-style resort on 24-hectare (60-acre) island. Four restaurants, two lounges; charter fishing, diving, sailing, tennis. Championship golf course nearby. Free buffet breakfast.

Lagoon Resort
7200 Aviation Boulevard
Marathon FL 33051
MM 50.5
Tel: (305) 743-5463
Bayside waterfront cottages with kitchen facilities. Pool, beach, fishing and diving charters. Picnic and barbecue area; coin-op laundry.

Ocean Beach Club
PO Box 9, Key Colony Beach
FL 33051 MM 53.5
Tel: (305) 289-0525
Spacious suites and rooms (38 in all); white sandy beach on oceanside. Freshwater pool, fishing pier.

SeaScape Ocean Resort
1499 76th Street, Marathon
FL 33050 MM 51
Tel: (305) 743-6455

One- and two-bedroom efficiencies and rooms in 1.6 hectares (4-acres) with private beach. Sunset cruises, reef trips and diving equipment available.

Grassy Key Resort
PO Box 357 FL 33050 MM 58.5
Tel: (305) 743-0533
Quiet motel with standard rooms and efficiencies on oceanfront. Private sandy beach, snorkeling, fishing.

Gulf View Motel
PO Box 543, Grassy Key
FL 33050 MM 50
Tel: (305) 289-1414
Small motel overlooking Gulf of Mexico. Freshwater pool, barbecue grills, fishing boat rentals, laundry.

Tropical Cottages
243 61st Street, Marathon
Fl 33050 MM 50
Tel: (305) 743-6048
Ten cottages with kitchenettes. Close to beaches, restaurants.

Miami
Doral Resort and
Country Club
4400 NW 87th Avenue, Miami
FL 33178-2192
Tel: (305) 592-2000
650 rooms, 38 suites; 99 holes of golf, 19 tennis courts, watersports. Equestrian centre.

Fontainebleau Hilton Resort
and Spa
4441 Collins Avenue, Miami
Beach FL 33140
Tel: (305) 538-2000
1,206 rooms, 62 suites, seven restaurants, five lounges. Children's programme; health spa, golf, tennis, two pools. Oceanside location.

Grand Bay Hotel
2669 South Bayshore Drive,
Coconut Grove, Miami FL 33133
Tel: (305) 858-9600
Overlooks Biscayne Bay, with 132 rooms and 49 suites.

Hyatt Regency Miami
400 SE Second Avenue,
Miami FL 33131
Tel: (305) 358-1234
Modern, downtown atrium hotel on Miami riverfront; 615 rooms, 55 suites. Two restaurants and lounges, nightclub, pool.

Miami Marriott Dadeland ‖
9090 South Dadeland Boulevard
Miami FL 33156
Tel: (305) 663-1035
Expressway location in downtown Miami. Pool, lounge, restaurant. Beaches within 5 km (3 miles).

Sonesta Beach Hotel ‖
350 Ocean Drive, Key Biscayne
FL 33149
Tel: (305) 361-2021
Oceanfront location, with 192 rooms, four suites. Tennis courts, pool, three restaurants. Children's programme. Courtesy van to Miami.

Broadmoor on the Beach Hotel ‖
7450 Ocean Terrace,
Miami Beach FL 33141
Tel: (305) 865-6500
100 rooms, three suites, restaurant, lounge, pool. French, German, Spanish spoken.

Everglades Hotel ‖
244 Biscayne Boulevard,
Miami FL 33132
Tel: (305) 379-5461
294 rooms, 82 suites; lounge, restaurant, pool. Bank facilities on premises; downtown location facing Bayside Marketplace and cruise ships.

Plaza Venetia ‖
555 NE 15th Street,
Miami FL 33132
Tel: (305) 374-2900
Downtown location with yacht basin and marina; 40 rooms, two restaurants and lounges, two pools, racquetball, tennis.

Orlando

International Drive area (roughly midway between downtown and Walt disney World, with all major attractions and the airport comfortably within a 30-minute drive).

Hyatt Regency Grand Cypress ‖‖‖
1 Grand Cypress,
Orlando FL 32819
Tel: (407) 239-1234
The place to stay for golfers, with 45 holes on courses designed by Jack Nicklaus. Swimming and tennis for everyone else.

Parc Corniche ‖‖‖
Condominium Resort
6300 Parc Corniche, Orlando
FL 32021
Tel: (407) 239-7100
Self-catering facilities in 292 one- and two-bedroom suites. Surrounded by Orlando International golf course. Swimming and tennis also available. Sea World nearby.

The Peabody ‖‖‖
9801 International Drive,
Orlando FL 32810
Tel: (407) 352-4000
Restful, Deep South ambience, and the famous Peabody Ducks in the lobby fountain. Very close to Sea World.

Stouffer Orlando Resort ‖‖‖
6677 Sea Harbor Drive,
Orlando FL 32821
Tel: (407) 351-5555
Lives up to the upmarket Stouffer image found throughout the United States. Close to Sea World.

The Courtyard ‖‖
8600 Austrian Court,
Orlando FL 32819
Tel: (407) 351-2244
In-room tea and coffee service (rare in the United States). Five minutes drive to Universal Studios; Mercado Village and King Henry's feast on the doorstep.

Holiday Inn ‖‖
International Drive Resort,
6515 International Drive,
Orlando FL 32819
Tel: (407) 351-3500
Resort facilities with 650 guest rooms in six buildings. Handy for Wet 'n' Wild.

Orlando Heritage Inn ‖‖
9861 International Drive,
Orlando FL 32819
Tel: (407) 352-0008
Very attractive antebellum-style of building with over 150 guest rooms decorated in 1800s' decor (but with 1990s' facilities). Sea World and Wet 'n' Wild a few minutes away.

Days Inn Lakeside ‖
7335 Sand Lake Road,
Orlando FL 32819
Tel: (407) 351-1900
Comfortable motel with 720 rooms, three pools and lakeside recreation area.

Gateway Inn ‖
7050 Kirkmamn Road,
Orlando FL 32819
Tel: (407) 351-2000
Ideal for families watching the budget; 350 rooms in eight buildings. Laundry facilities. Wet 'n' Wild close by. Airport ten minutes.

Inns of America ‖
8222 Jamaica Court,
Orlando FL 32819
Tel: (407) 345-1172
Value for money motel with 121 rooms. Complimentary buffet breakfast. Close to Wet 'n' Wild, with shops and restaurants nearby.

Palm Beach

The Breakers ‖‖‖
1 South County Road,
Palm Beach FL 33480
Tel: (407) 655-6611
488 rooms, 40 suites, four restaurants, two lounges, two pools. Two championship golf courses and 19 tennis courts, as well as croquet, volleyball and shuffleboard courts.

PGA National Resort ‖‖‖
400 Avenue of the Champions
Palm Beach Gardens, FL 33418
Tel: (407) 627-2000
Five championship golf-courses, plus five croquet courts and 19 tennis courts. The hotel has 335 rooms, including 57 suites.

Ritz-Carlton Palm Beach ‖‖‖
100 South Ocean Boulevard,
Manalapan FL 33462
Tel: (407) 687-9505
Opened in the summer of 1991; 270 rooms, 60 suites, four restaurants, two lounges. Seven tennis courts on beach; pool.

Brazilian Court ‖‖
301 Australian Avenue,
Palm Beach FL 33480
Tel: (407) 655-7740
Afternoon tea is served in two landscaped courtyards around which the 134-room hotel is built. Two restaurants, pool. Downtown location, two blocks from Worth Avenue shopping.

Howard Johnson Palm Beach ‖‖
2870 South Ocean Boulevard,
Palm Beach FL 33480
Tel: (407) 582-2581
99 rooms, pool with bar. Beach across the street, watersports and playground nearby.

Radisson Suite Hotel ‖‖
4350 PGA Boulevard,
Palm Beach Gardens FL 33410
Tel: (407) 622-1000
160 suites, two restaurants and lounges. Two tennis courts, pool.

Panama City Beach

Edgewater Beach Resort ‖‖‖
11212 Front Beach Road,
Panama City Beach FL 32407
Tel: (904) 235-4044
Centrally situated condominium resort within walking distance of Miracle Strip attractions. Waterside golf and tennis villas, 600 m (2,000 ft) of beach; lagoon. Twelve tennis courts, nine-hole golf-course.

Marriott's Bay Point Yacht ‖‖‖
and Country Club
100 Delwood Beach Road,
Panama City Beach FL 32411
Tel: (904) 234-3307
Extensive property with championship golf-course and 12-court tennis centre. Seven restaurants and lounges.

Holiday House Motel ‖‖
15405 West Highway 98,
Panama City Beach FL 32413
Tel: (904) 234-6644
102-room beachside property near Gulf World attraction. Restaurant and lounge.

Pinnacle Port ‖‖
23223 West Highway 98,
Panama City Beach FL 32407
Tel: (904) 234-8813
One-, two- and three-bedroom suites with Gulf views. Two pools, tennis, 1 km (½ mile) of beach.

Sea Witch Motel ‖‖
21905 Front Beach Road,
Panama City Beach FL 32413
Tel: (904) 234-5722
Apartment-type units with fully equipped kitchens; 90 new units added recently are designed for families with children. Sun deck and general lounging area. Pool and children's pool.

La Brisa Inn ‖
9424 Front Beach Road,
Panama City Beach FL 32407
Tel: (904) 235-1122
Rooms with kitchenettes and king-size bed or two double beds. Complimentary coffee and doughnuts each morning.

Surf High Inn ‖
10611 Front Beach Road,
Panama City Beach FL 32407
Tel: (904) 234-2129
Rooms and one- and two-bedroom cabanas. Beachside pool.

Tripps Motel ‖
14929 West Highway 98A,
Panama City Beach FL 32407
Tel: (904) 234-2763
40 rooms, most with kitchenettes, all with balconies. Centrally located on the Miracle Strip.

St Augustine

Colonyh's Ponce de Leon ‖‖‖
Conference and Golf Resort
4000 US Highway 1 North,
St Augustine FL 32085-0098
Tel: (904) 824-2821
225 rooms, seven suites, restaurant, lounge, two pools. PGA Championship golf course, six tennis courts. Historic sightseeing tours.

Days Inn Downtown ‖
2800 Ponce de Leon Boulevard,
St Augustine FL 32084
Tel: (904) 829-6581
124 rooms, restaurant, pool, game room.

St Petersburg

Don CeSar Resort ‖‖‖
3400 Gulf Boulevard,
St Petersburg Beach,
Florida 233706
Tel: (813) 360-1881
Looks good enough to eat—all pink and sugary, and a favourite hideaway for F. Scott Fitzgerald; 227 splendid rooms.

Tradewinds ‖‖‖
5500 Gulf Boulevard,
St Petersburg Beach,
Florida 33706
Tel: (813) 367-6461
A network of canals connects the lobby with other parts of the resort which also features white gazebos and bridges. One-, two- and three-bedroom suites are included in its 381 rooms.

Beach Park Motor Inn ‖
300 Beach Drive,
St Petersburg FL 33701
Tel: (813) 898-6325
Eleven motel rooms, three apartments, eight efficiencies within walking distance of Spa Beach, Bayfront Center and The Pier.

Tampa

Harbor Island Hotel ‖‖‖
725 South Harbour Island
Boulevard, Tampa FL 33602
Tel: (813) 229-5000.
Downtown waterfront resort with 300 elegantly appointed rooms and suites. Tennis, pool, health club.

Hyatt Regency Westshore ‖‖‖
6200 Courtney Campbell
Causeway, Tampa FL 33607
Tel: (813) 874-1234
Ideal for an active holiday: golf, tennis, fishing, sailing, swimming even a 14-hectare (35-acre) nature preserve; 448 rooms with kitchenettes.

The Residence Inn ‖‖‖
3075 Rocky Point Drive,
Tampa FL 33607
Tel: (813) 887-5576
Upscale self-catering in 176 deluxe suites which include sitting rooms and work areas. Complimentary continental breakfast.

Embassy Suites Hotel ‖‖
4400 West Cypress Street,
Tampa FL 33607
Tel: (813) 873-8675
Close to airport (free transport available), with 259 two room suites. Free breakfast and free cocktails for two hours every evening.

Holiday Inn Sabal Park ‖
10315 East Buffalo Avenue,
Tampa FL 33610
Tel: (813) 623-6363
East of the city, yet handy for Seminole Cultural Center, Busch Gardens and I-4/I-75 intersection; 265 rooms. Tennis, pool.

Hall of Fame Inn ‖
222 North Westshore Boulevard,
Tampa FL 33607
Tel: (813) 877-1600
Bargain-rate golf and tennis resort with pool and 185 rooms.

Restaurants

Everywhere you turn, there's somewhere to eat, almost all open seven days a week. Here is given a selection of full-service restaurants, buffet restaurants and food courts (multiple outlets sharing a table area). There is no space to list even a fraction of the vast number of restaurants and all-you-can-eat buffets well within our lowest price range. Each entry is marked with a symbol indicating the price range, per person, for a dinner comprising starter or salad, main course and dessert. (Drinks, gratuities and 6% sales tax are not included.)

Key

⫿⫿⫿ $30 and over;
⫿⫿ $15–30;
⫿ up to $15.

Miami and Miami Beach

A Mano ⫿⫿⫿
1440 Ocean Drive, Miami Beach. Tel. (305) 531-6266
In the heart of the fashionable Art Deco district. Latin and Pacific flavours influence the "New World cuisine".

Brasserie LeCoze ⫿⫿⫿
2901 Florida Avenue, Coconut Grove. Tel. (305) 444-9697
Classic French brasserie design and imaginative French/Mediterranean cooking.

Café Abbracci ⫿⫿⫿
318 Aragon Avenue, Coral Gables. Tel. (305) 441-0700
Northern Italian. Grilled veal, swordfish or tuna with inventive salads.

Café Med ⫿⫿
3015 Grand Avenue, Coconut Grove. Tel. (305) 443-1770
Hearty, healthy Italian.

Café Tu Tu Tango ⫿
3105 Grand Avenue, 2nd floor, Coconut Grove.
Tel. (305) 529-2222
Innovative cosmopolitan cuisine—Italian, Oriental, Californian—with oddball entertainment.

Islas Canarias ⫿
285 NW 27th Avenue, Miami. Tel. (305) 649-0440
Popular traditional Cuban cooking in Little Havana area.

Joe's Stone Crab ⫿
227 Biscayne Street, Miami Beach. Tel. (305) 673-0365
An institution since 1913, open from October to May. Chilled crab claws and a full menu.

Los Ranchos ⫿⫿
Bayside Marketplace, Miami. Tel. (305) 375-0666
Nicaraguan-style steakhouse. Steaks and beef, spiced or not, with Latin accompaniments.

Malaga ⫿
740 SW 8th Street, Miami. Tel. (305) 858-4224
On "Calle Ocho", traditional Cuban and Spanish dishes, especially seafood.

Mayfair Grill ⫿⫿⫿
3000 Florida Avenue, Coconut Grove. Tel. (305) 441-0000
Brasserie setting for modern American cooking, colourful and inventive. Famous desserts.

Rascal House ⫿
17190 Collins Avenue, Miami Beach. Tel. (305) 947-4581
New York-style delicatessen known for its big sandwiches and authentic raucous atmosphere.

Sakura ⫿
8225 SW 124th Street, Miami. Tel. (305) 238-8462
Sushi, tempura, teriyaki dishes. One of many small Japanese restaurants all over Miami.

WPA ⫿⫿
685 Washington Avenue, Miami Beach. Tel. (305) 534-1684
Relaxed bistro-style modern American cooking with Italian and Tex-Mex variations.

Yuca ⫿⫿⫿
177 Giralda Avenue, Coral Gables. Tel. (305) 444-4448
Upscale, advanced Cuban cuisine in an elegant setting. Traditional ingredients in new forms.

Gold Coast

Café Arugula ⫿⫿⫿
3110 N. Federal Hwy, Lighthouse Point.
Tel. (305) 785-7732
The best and brightest ingredients combined in New American-Mediterranean cuisine.

Café l'Europe ⫿⫿⫿
150 Worth Avenue, Palm Beach. Tel. (407) 655-4020
The elegance and price to be expected on this famous street. Traditional French and middle-European dishes.

Ruth's Chris Steak House ⫿⫿
661 US Highway 1, North Palm Beach. Tel. (407) 863-0660
Specializing in steaks, as well as seafood.

Studio One ⫿⫿
2447 E. Sunrise Boulevard, Fort Lauderdale. Tel. (305) 565-2052
French and Caribbean-influenced, traditional and creative cuisine side by side on the menu.

Testa's ⫿⫿
221 Royal Poinciana Way, Palm Beach. Tel. (407) 832-0992
Old-established Italian and seafood eating place in garden courtyard.

TooJay's Gourmet Deli ⫿
313 Poinciana Place, Royal Poinciana Center, Palm Beach. Tel. (407) 659-7232
Delicatessen favourites, generous sandwiches in a relaxed atmosphere.

Space Coast and St Augustine

Capt. Jack's on the Ocean ⫿
2929 South A1A, Beverly Beach. Tel. (904) 439-1000
Informal bar-restaurant with fresh seafood and steaks, south of St Augustine.

Gypsy Cab Company ⫿⫿
828 Anastasia Boulevard, St Augustine. Tel. (904) 824-8244
Relaxed setting, creative cooking—soups, pastas, salads and seafood. Famous for their desserts.

Live Oak Inn ⫿⫿
448 South Beach Street, Daytona Beach. Tel. (904) 252-4667
Elegant older house overlooking marina. American menu with healthy slant. Closed Mondays.

The Pier Restaurant
Cocoa Beach Pier, 401 Meade
Avenue, Cocoa Beach.
Tel. (407) 783-7549
*Elegant dining on the old wooden
pier. Fresh fish and American stan-
dard menu.*

Raintree
102 San Marco Avenue, St
Augustine. Tel. (904) 824-7211
*International cuisine in elegant sur-
roundings.*

St Regis
509 Seabreeze Boulevard,
Daytona Beach.
Tel. (904) 252-8743
*An old home converted to a bed-and-
breakfast inn and restaurant. American home cooking.*

Orlando and Central Florida
Walt Disney World (including Vil-
lage/Plaza)
Akershus Restaurant
Norway Pavilion, EPCOT,
(reservations at EPCOT Earth
Station)
*Norwegian buffet of cold and hot
dishes, from herring and salmon to
goats' cheese and desserts.*

Baskervilles
Grosvenor Resort, Walt Disney
World Village/Plaza. Tel. (407)
828-4444 ext. 6117
*A la carte and buffet service. Roast
prime rib of beef, seafood dinner
buffets.*

Biergarten Restaurant
Germany Pavilion, EPCOT
(Reservations at EPCOT Earth
Station)
*Veal, smoked pork, bratwurst and
other German specialities, with tra-
ditional entertainment by musicians,
dancers and yodellers.*

Bistro de Paris
France Pavilion, EPCOT
(reservations at EPCOT Earth
Station)
*Traditional French ambience. Fine,
colourful and inventive cuisine, the
menu devised by master chefs.*

Cape May Café
Beach Club Resort.
Tel. (407) 934-3358
*New England-style clambake every
night. Seafood buffets.*

Cap'n Jack's Oyster Bar
Disney Village Marketplace.
Tel. (407) 828-3900
*Crab, lobster, clams and oysters,
plus vegetarian and non-seafood
alternatives.*

Crystal Palace
Main Street and Central Plaza,
Magic Kingdom.
Tel. (407) 824-6517
*Cafeteria service of American cui-
sine—roasts, fish, salads, desserts.*

50s Prime Time Café
Disney-MGM Studios Theme
Park. Tel. (407) 560-7729
*Sit by a 50s TV playing 50s sitcoms
and eat 50s favourites—meatloaf,
grilled chicken.*

Fireworks Factory
Pleasure Island.
Tel. (407) 934-8989
*Operated by The Levy Restaurants
of Chicago. Barbecues, smoked
chicken, citrus chicken. Vegetarian
and low-calorie dishes available.*

Fisherman's Deck
Aboard Empress Lilly riverboat,
Disney Village Marketplace.
Tel. (407) 828-3900
*Seafood specialities—shrimp, scal-
lop, fresh fish—but non-seafood and
vegetarian alternatives too.*

Harry's Safari Bar and Grill
Dolphin (Sheraton).
Tel. (407) 934-4000 ext. 6155
*Safari decor, grilled seafood and
steaks.*

Le Cellier
Canada Pavilion, EPCOT
(no reservations)
*Cafeteria service of international
and Canadian dishes.*

Liberty Tree Tavern
Liberty Square, Magic Kingdom.
Tel. (407) 824-6461
*In the style of an 18th-century inn.
Cooking is American with a New
England touch. Oysters, chowders,
pasta and chicken dishes.*

Marrakesh
Morocco Pavilion, EPCOT
(reservations at EPCOT Earth
Station)
*Moroccan specialities—couscous,
kebabs, tadjine to the accompani-
ment of musicians and belly dancer.*

Old Port Royale
Caribbean Beach Resort.
Tel. (407) 934-2830
*Food court with six counter-service
outlets: roasts, barbecues, Italian.*

Palio
Swan (Westin).
Tel. (407) 934-1281
*Mostly northern Italian specialities
in an elegant setting. Strolling mu-
sicians.*

San Angel Inn
Mexico Pavilion, EPCOT
(reservations at EPCOT Earth
Station)
*Beside the River of Time ride, serv-
ing Mexican dishes both familiar
and unusual.*

Yacht Club Galley
Yacht Club Resort.
Tel. (407) 934-3355
*Informal café serving grills, New
England-style seafood and salads.*
Elsewhere in the Orlando Area

Bonanza
3615 West Highway 192,
Kissimmee. Tel. (407) 932-4464
Lavish buffet with entree order.

Capriccio
Peabody Hotel, 9801 Interna-
tional Drive, Orlando.
Tel. (407) 352-4000
Genuine Italian country cooking.

Charlie's Lobster House
Mercado Mall, 8445
International Drive, Orlando.
Tel. (407) 352-6929
*Everything in shells or scales, any
way you like.*

Chatham's Place
7575 Phillips Boulevard,
Orlando. Tel. (407) 345-2992
*Informally elegant dining, French-in-
fluenced and innovative cuisine.*

Chris's House of Beef
801 John Young Parkway,
Orlando. Tel. (407) 295-1931
*Traditional steakhouse in a cattle-
raising area. Roasts, steaks and
some non-beef alternatives.*

Dux
Peabody Hotel, 9801
International Drive, Orlando.
Tel. (407) 352-4000
*Fine elegant restaurant with inno-
vative and colourful cuisine, includ-
ing some daring combinations.*

Hard Rock Café
Universal Studios Florida, 5800 Kirkman Road, Orlando. Tel. (407) 351-7625
Burgers and sandwiches, fries and shakes. Entry from street as well as from Studios.

Jordan's Grove
1300 S. Maitland Avenue, Maitland. Tel. (407) 628-0020
Inventive modern American cuisine in the setting of a gracious old house.

Lili Marlene's
Church Street Station, Orlando. Tel. (407) 422-2434
Part of the downtown entertainment complex, in an elaborate 1890s revival setting. Standard American menu.

Ming Court
9188 International Drive, Orlando. Tel. (407) 351-9988
Cantonese and other regional Chinese cooking in elaborate setting.

Siam Orchid
7575 Republic Drive, Orlando. Tel. (407) 351-3935
The taste of Thai—chili, coriander, lemon grass, garlic, coconut milk—adapted to American palates unless you tell them to give it to you straight.

Western Steer
6315 International Drive, Orlando. Tel. (407) 363-0677
All-you-can-eat buffet with steak or seafood.

The Keys

A & B Lobster House
700 Front Street, Key West. Tel. (305) 294-2536
Oysters, clams, steamed shrimp, barbecues and a view of the harbour.

Balamonte's
1223 White Street, Key West. Tel. (305) 296-2200
Informal Italian and seafood restaurant, from antipasto to Key lime pie.

Danny's Fish Market
627 Duval Street, Key West. Tel. (305) 296-3777
Informal café-bar serving fresh fish—steamed shrimp is the speciality.

Half Shell Raw Bar
Lands End Village, Key West. Tel. (305) 294-7496
Relaxed café-bar by the marina. Oysters and clams, crabs, chowder and conch fritters.

Louie's Backyard
700 Waddell Avenue, Key West. Tel. (305) 294-1061
By the sea. Imaginative modern American cuisine using local seafood, Caribbean and even Thai flavours.

Quay Restaurant
MM102.5, Key Largo. Tel. (305) 451-0943
Open air or indoor tables on the waterfront. Seafood, steaks and pastas.

Ship's Pub Galley
MM61, Duck Key. Tel. (305) 743-7000
Terrace at the dockside; steaks, seafood and salads.

Whale Harbor Inn
MM84, Islamorada. Tel. (305) 664-4959
Next to the fishing boat dock. A la carte plus seafood dinner buffet.

Gulf Coast—Naples to Fort Myers

Cande's
1707 Cape Coral Parkway, Cape Coral, Fort Myers. Tel. (813) 542-0085
Informal steak and seafood restaurant and bar.

Chef's Garden
1300 3rd Street S., Naples. Tel. (305) 262-5500
Elegant restaurant serving international and original cuisine.

Farino's/Gilda's Casa Italiana
4000 Tamiami Trail N., Naples. Tel. (813) 262-2883
Seafood, pastas, grills.

Tootie McGregor's
Fort Myers Country Club, McGregor Boulevard, Fort Myers. Tel. (813) 939-7300
Elegant and relaxed club setting. Comprehensive menu, good seafood.

The Mucky Duck
5500 Estero Boulevard, Fort Myers Beach. Tel. (813) 463-5519
Informal setting for chowders, all kinds of seafood—grilled, steamed and deep-fried.

Gulf Coast—Tampa Bay Area

L'Auberge du Bon Vivant
7003 Gulf of Mexico Drive, Longboat Key, Sarasota. Tel. (813) 383-2421
Classic French and international dishes in a country inn setting.

Boathouse
Hyatt Sarasota, 1000 Boulevard of the Arts, Sarasota. Tel. (813) 366-9000
Seafood, salads and sandwiches in an informal setting over the water.

Charlie's Crab
St Armand's Circle, Sarasota. Tel. (813) 388-3964
All kinds of seafood and home-made pasta, with meat and vegetarian alternatives.

Columbia
800 2nd Avenue NE, St Petersburg. Also at 2117 7th Avenue, Ybor City, and at Sarasota Clearwater Beach. Tel. (813) 822-8000
At the end of the Pier, the Spanish way with seafood and rice, meats and salads.

Eugen's
100 N. Indian Rocks Road, Belleair Bluffs. Tel. (813) 585-6399
Seafood, lamb, German and Hungarian dishes.

Leverock's
551 Gulf Boulevard, Clearwater Beach. Tel. (813) 446-5884
Next to the beach, one of a local group of reliable seafood restaurants.

Michael's on East
1212 S. East Avenue, Midtown Plaza, Sarasota. Tel. (813) 366-0077
Healthy accents to the lively menu of salads, pastas, meats and fish.

Pippindales
Clearwater Beach Hilton, 715 S. Gulf Boulevard, Clearwater Beach. Tel. (813) 447-9566
Excellent value American buffets.

Summerhouse
6101 Midnight Pass Road, Siesta Key, Sarasota. Tel. (813) 349-1100
Woodland setting for fish, lobster and crab, steaks and chicken.

Index

INDEX